Globalization, Modernity and Social Change

SOCIOLOGY FOR A CHANGING WORLD

Series Editors: **Graham Allan and Mary Maynard**
Consultant Editor: Janet Finch

This series, published in conjunction with the British Sociological Association, evaluates and reflects major developments in contemporary sociology. The books will focus on key changes in social and economic life in recent years and on the ways in which the discipline of sociology has analysed those changes. The books will reflect the state of the art in contemporary British sociology, while at the same time drawing upon comparative material to set debates in an international perspective.

Published

Graham Allan and Graham Crow
FAMILIES, HOUSEHOLDS AND SOCIETY

Rosamund Billington, Annette Fitzsimmons, Lenore Greensides and Sheelagh Strawbridge
CULTURE AND SOCIETY

Lois Bryson
WELFARE AND THE STATE WHO BENEFITS?

Frances Heidensohn
CRIME AND SOCIETY

Stephen J. Hunt
RELIGION IN WESTERN SOCIETY

Mike Savage and Alan Warde
URBAN SOCIOLOGY, CAPITALISM AND MODERNITY

John Solomos and Les Back
RACISM AND SOCIETY

Philip Sutton
NATURE, ENVIRONMENT AND SOCIETY

Andrew Webster
SCIENCE, TECHNOLOGY AND SOCIETY

Jörg Dürrschmidt and Graham Taylor
GLOBALIZATION, MODERNITY AND SOCIAL CHANGE

Forthcoming

Kevin Brehony and Rosemary Deem
RETHINKING SOCIOLOGIES OF EDUCATION

Series Standing Order

If you would like to receive future titles in this series as they are published, you can make use of our standing order facility. To place a standing order please contact your bookseller or, in case of difficulty, write to us at the address below with your name and address and the name of the series. Please state with which title you wish to begin your standing order. (If you live outside the United Kingdom we may not have the rights for your area, in which case we will forward your order to the publisher concerned.)

Customer Services Department, Macmillan Distribution Ltd, Houndmills, Basingstoke, Hampshire RG21 6XS, England

---

Globalization, Modernity and Social Change

Hotspots of Transition

Jörg Dürrschmidt and Graham Taylor

First published 2007 by
PALGRAVE MACMILLAN
Houndmills, Basingstoke, Hampshire RG21 6XS and
175 Fifth Avenue, New York, N.Y. 10010
Companies and representatives throughout the world

PALGRAVE MACMILLAN is the global academic imprint of the Palgrave Macmillan division of St. Martin's Press, LLC and of Palgrave Macmillan Ltd. Macmillan® is a registered trademark in the United States, United Kingdom and other countries. Palgrave is a registered trademark in the European Union and other countries.

ISBN-13: 978–0–333–97157–4 hardback
ISBN-10: 0–333–97157–4 hardback
ISBN-13: 978–0–333–97158–1 paperback
ISBN-10: 0–333–97158–2 paperback

This book is printed on paper suitable for recycling and made from fully managed and sustained forest sources. Logging, pulping and manufacturing processes are expected to conform to the environmental regulations of the country of origin.

A catalogue record for this book is available from the British Library.

A catalog record for this book is available from the Library of Congress.

10   9   8   7   6   5   4   3   2   1
16   15   14   13   12   11   10   09   08   07

Printed in China

Contents

Preface

The origins of this book can be traced back to 1999 when we presented a postgraduate course on 'Advanced Sociological Analysis' at the University of the West of England, Bristol. As the title of the course suggests, the project was from the beginning a continuous work in progress. The title of the course was rather sober; neither fancy and highfaluting like 'analyzing global society' nor staid and worn out like 'developments in modern society'. The globalization paradigm was already beyond its fashionable peak but the questions that it had raised made a straightforward return to the analysis of modern society a practical and intellectual impossibility. The discourse of globalization had fundamentally questioned the basic assumptions of modernization theory, particularly the notion that the nation state constituted the principal territorial organization of belonging. The natural reaction at a time like this was to say: 'Hey! Let's hold on for a second! Pause for a while and take stock!' and ask the question 'Where are we going and where do we stand?', an intellectual position perhaps influenced also by the fast-approaching turn of the millennium.

Thus, we found ourselves sitting with a cluster of extremely interested and keen MSc students, debating the continuities and discontinuities of contemporary society. However, there was at that time no textbook that could provide us with a map to guide us in our journey into the unknown territory between the continuities and the discontinuities of globalizing modernity. The dominant titles were keen to push either the modernization or the globalization paradigms. As young academics, we felt unqualified to provide the comprehensive counterpart of a society locked in the in-between. Our response to this dilemma was not to develop an authoritative horizontal view across the entire landscape of shifting social realities and fluid sociological terminologies, but rather to focus on a few 'hotspots' in which continuity and change could be observed most intensely. We felt that these analytically inclined 'deep drillings' could provide a rich insight into the shifting landscape of contemporary society. Thus, the book that we felt was missing was something of an in-between in itself: a hybrid between a course textbook and a research monograph that combined an attempt to not only summarize and order insights into contemporary society, but also develop and advance an alternative analytical agenda wherever we felt we had the expertise. We are very grateful to *Palgrave* for encouraging us to pursue such a hybrid at a time when publishing relies on the rather clear-cut labelling of themes and discourses.

Between the germinal phase of 'globalization, modernity and social change – hotspots of transition' and its publication lie changes in job and geographic relocation. Most importantly, there was the challenge to continue what originated from a very close day-to-day working relationship based on regular face-to-face discussions to one based on time–space distanciation and a working relationship mediated by information and communication technology. The re-embedding of the project in two different academic contexts (the UK and Germany) was not just an obstacle, but also, and in hindsight, a great help in writing the book. Looking from the post-empire and neo-liberal UK onto the landscape of globalizing modernity or modern globalization triggers different thoughts than viewing it from a Germany self-absorbed in its reunification process and its role in Europe. Thus, though we shared a basic cluster of ideas and concepts, regional varieties of perception and perspective have contributed to a reflexive stand towards certain ideas. Moreover, the re-embedding in two different academic settings with, inter alia, different academic terms and semesters, helped to keep the project going. When one was worn out following a teaching semester, the other could take over the role of main contributor. Of course, distance only works where there is also occasional proximity. London and Berlin, the global city and the former metropolis, located conveniently close to our bases in Kassel and Bristol, became the meeting points whenever there was need for a 'crisis meeting' and more often than not we both went off from these encounters full of renewed vigour and enthusiasm. Thus the book, not just in its intention, but also in the lived reality of its realization is a reflection of the continuous 'liminality' that opens up somewhere between proximity and distance and which provides the dominant organizational lexicon for contemporary society.

The fact that we have both remained committed to the project over time and across distance demonstrates the desire and commitment that we have developed towards the ideas developed in this book. However, writing a joint-authored book between proximity and distance is often a lonely business and there are many people who have encouraged us and given us a push in the right direction at various times during the writing process. First, thanks to Emily Salz, Sarah Lodge and Sheree Keep at *Palgrave* who have shown incredible patience and understanding for the rythmicity of academic writing. Thanks also to our partners, Andrea and Hilary, who have been of great support, both emotionally and intellectually, throughout this project. We have learned a lot from many people during the six years in which the book has been taking shape. Jörg Dürrschmidt has benefited greatly from the few, but as always very inspiring, conversations with Martin Albrow at the LSE and from regular discussions with

Paul Kennedy and Robert Grimm at Manchester Metropolitan University. He would also like to acknowledge the impact that Heinz Bude at Kassel University has had on this project, both as a very critical mind as far as globalization theory is concerned and as someone who has the skill to ask the right questions at the right time. Last, but not least, thanks to the anonymous reviewers of this project who provided critical but extremely constructive and helpful comments and remarks on an earlier draft of this book. They certainly helped to get this project into shape. Needless to say, the usual disclaimers apply.

Abbreviations

ABM	Arbeitsbeschaffungsmassnahme
ACD	Automated call distribution
BPO	Business process outsourcing
BPR	Business process re-engineering
BSE	Bovine Spongiform Encephalopathy
CND	Campaign for Nuclear Disarmament
CPR	Customer process re-engineering
CSR	Customer service representative
CTI	Computer telephony integration
EPZs	Export processing zones.
ETUC	European Trade Union Confederation
EU	European Union
EWC	European Works Council
GJM	Global justice movement
GDR	German Democratic Republic
GM	Genetically modified
HRM	Human resource management
ICT	Information and communications technology
IGO	Intergovernmental organization
IMF	International Monetary Fund
KWS	Keynesian Welfare State
NAFTA	North American Free Trade Agreement
NATO	North Atlantic Treaty Organization
NGO	Non-governmental organization
NIDL	New international division of labour
NSM	New social movement
SMU	Social movement unionism
TNC	Transnational corporation
UNI	Union Network International
UNICE	Union des Industries de la Communauté européene
WSF	World social forum
WTO	World Trade Organization

1
Introduction: Theorizing 'Undefined Society'

By settling for one or other interpretation, ambiguity is often reduced.

(Mary Douglas, 1996: 40)

The anthropological perspective informs us that quite regularly our experience does not confirm exactly to the classifications by which we order our environment. Anomalies are routinely absorbed into our cultural milieux by being ignored or condemned. A stable categorical system and legitimizing rituals of learning allow this to happen rather efficiently. In this sense, our cultural and social milieux work like a filter or alphabet through which we focus on things which are in accordance with our categorical system and filter out those which are not (Douglas, *ibid*: 37–41). The above claim is made with reference to the small routines of everyday life. However, it is a different story when a whole society or culture is experiencing a state of *ambiguity* and where social and cultural reality are open to two or more competing interpretations. We could imagine this as something of a meta-anomaly, which develops when the cognitive and symbolic frame of reference of a society that normally deals with discrepant experiences is itself dissolved and put into question. Often, and this still in line with the anthropologically informed argument pursued so far, such conceptual ambiguity reflects a state of disorder or transition in society or culture itself. Such a comparatively unstructured state of the in-between, where neither the old nor the new frames of reference work properly, has been described as *liminality* (Turner, 1969).

We experience this sense of liminality in our everyday experience of a world that is increasingly difficult for us to comprehend. How is it possible for human beings to catch influenza from birds? We have been forced to come to terms with this enigma owing to the global spread of 'HN51' or 'bird flu' and its potential to introduce a global pandemic of deadly proportions. This phenomenon highlights the prevalence of ecological fear in contemporary Western society, which can be interpreted as anxiety

1

about a social order that is 'out of order' or, to put it more gently, a social order in transition (Douglas, 1991: 230). Behind the prominence of ecological issues, there lies the uneasy awareness of 'a profound change in our cultural and social perceptions of the reality in which we live', including the end of linear and monocausal explanations (Melucci, 1996b: 58–59). We see this uneasiness in our perception of other areas of social life. Also linked to increasing ecological concerns are phenomena such as *Reclaim the Streets* that involve a challenge to the spatial and discursive domination of everyday culture by the motor car. But how do we define phenomena such as *Reclaim the Streets*? Is it an organization or an event, is it politics or fun, is it a political or a cultural form of expression? A clue to the answer to this question can be found in the spaces created by this form of action: an inner-city dual carriageway transformed into a Carib-bean beach complete with sand, sound system and carefree partygoers is neither a dual carriageway nor a beach but a liminal space that defines the in-betweennesss of this form of 'political' action. We also face this experience of liminality every time we visit the supermarket or shopping mall. The intensification of global capitalism has heightened the import-ance of shopping and consumption and increasingly transformed us into 'desiring machines' (Deleuze & Guattari, 2004) with unlimited appetites for the symbolic markers of identity and success. The resulting symbolic universe, however, transforms consumption into a totally idealist practice (Baudrillard, 1998) which makes the satisfaction of desire impossible. The result is a form of 'abstract happiness' in which what we desire is the 'idea' of consuming. In this context, while the 'dream' of a 'dream holiday' may generate feelings of ecstasy and longing, the arrival at our destina-tion is likely to be accompanied by feelings of ambiguity, disappointment and unease as the rationalized and homogenized experience the holiday becomes palpable.

The introduction of information and communications technology (ICT) into the workplace has also created liminal spaces within the global economy. The Indian call centre worker serving clients in the USA or Europe inhabits a world of 'real virtuality' (Castells, 2000a) plugged in or connected into the global communications network, but disconnected from workplace colleagues and neighbourhood community in a timeless, spaceless world that nevertheless remains 'placed'. While these workers are relatively privileged in the context of Indian labour markets, they nonetheless experience work as a liminal space marked by alienation and cultural dissonance. This example highlights the way space itself has become increasingly liminal, particularly in the form of the 'global city'. Canary Wharf in the London Docklands highlights these tenden-cies. Canary Wharf exists at the confluence of a complex set of inclu-sions and exclusions, continuities and changes. Canary Wharf contains the headquarters of multinational financial and media organizations and luxury and executive housing and hotel accommodation and as such constitutes an important hub in a shifting global network of money, media images and people. However, Canary Wharf is surrounded by the relics and detritus of the British Empire: the docks that established London as the imperial metropolis in the nineteenth century and the East End and, in particular, the borough of Tower Hamlets, that houses colonial migrants in varying degrees of relative and real poverty alongside the pretentious affluence of Canary Wharf. Our everyday experience of the global city reflects the liminality of its form: complex patterns of inclusion and exclusion; belonging and not-belonging; rootedness and uprootedness; and engagement and non-engagement. How can we explain these feelings and experiences of liminality? The examples highlighted above suggest that the explanation lies somewhere in the complex relationship between the spatial restructuring associated with globalization and the temporal re-ordering associated with the developmental narrative of modernity.

The drift between a society in transition and a conceptual unitary frame-work, which is in the process of dissolving, lies at the heart of the debate in contemporary sociology: a debate focused on the dynamics and direction of social change according to the logics of globalization and/or modernity. The sociological projects that have developed from these positions have generated comprehensive models of social change that attempt to isolate the logic underpinning the multiplicity of transitions in the contemporary world. However, therein lies a problem. Does a society at the beginning of a process of epochal change warrant or require an overall definition? If the anthropological observation outlined above is correct, that it is difficult for any society to live in a state of categorical ambiguity, then it must be even more difficult for contemporary society, with its thorough embed-dedness in rationalized systems of knowledge, to live with this ambiguity. Consequently, there have been several attempts to remain within the overall conceptual framework of modernity whilst stretching the concept to its limits in order to explain novelty associated with epochal change. Anthony Giddens (1990, 1991), for example, has developed the concepts of 'high' or 'late' modernity to highlight the development and intensific-ation of institutional reflexivity across time and space. Zygmunt Bauman (2000) has developed the concept of 'liquid' modernity in order to under-line the rapid changes resulting from the 'melting powers' of contemporary modernity. But most emphatically, it is the theory of 'reflexive' or 'second modernity' developed by Ulrich Beck that explores the contemporary process of transition *from within* the context of modernity itself (Beck, 1992). Second modernity is a 'radicalized' modernity insofar as it becomes reflexive towards itself or, to be more precise, towards the unwanted side-effects of its own development (Beck et al., 1994). However, if the changes

envisaged within Western modernity are indeed so radical that 'the transition to a reflexive second modernity not only changes the social structure
but also revolutionizes the very coordinates, categories and conception of
change itself' (Beck et al., 2003: 2), then why not leave the conceptual
framework of modernity altogether? If the meta-change towards 'second
modernity' involves 'everything that defines first modern society' (Beck
et al., *ibid*: 8), then it would seem somewhat problematic to analyse this
fundamental transition within the conceptual legacy of modernity.

Consequently, there have been various attempts to analyse contemporary society within the narrative of globalization. Expressed in the
form of its lowest common denominator, globalization implies a historical process by which the economic, political and cultural geographies of
society are redrawn beyond the territoriality of the nation state. Axford
(2000) differentiates between a 'weak' and a 'strong' version of the globalization model. The weak version is premised on the notion that globalization
involves an increasing connectedness between places and people across
distance and within the economic, political and cultural sub-spheres of
society. This approach focuses on the historicity and novelty of the interdependencies generated by the world market and new technology. In many
ways, this approach constitutes a further elaboration of modernization
theory as globalization is often presented as a narrative plot that more or
less continues the linear story of modernity. The most prominent examples
here are Paul Hirst and Grahame Thompson (1999) who in *Globalization
in Question* focus on the issue of continuity and discontinuity within the
economic sphere; Goran Therborn (1995) who presents the global arena
as stage for competing *Routes to/through Modernity*; and Ulf Hannerz (1998)
who presents *The Global Ecumene as a Landscape of Modernity*, effectively
constructing a continuity between modernity and the intensified cultural
interconnectivity of contemporary society.

The 'strong' version of globalization theory takes as its starting point
the claim that the world has become a single place with its own systemic
properties (Axford, *op cit*: 239; Robertson, 1992: 135). The analytical
consequences of shifting the focus from 'globalization' to 'globality' have
been developed most systematically by Martin Albrow (1996) in his
conceptual model of the *Global Age*. Albrow argues that we have to leave
the conceptual framework of modernity behind if we are to grasp the new
configurations that underpin a new epoch of human society. The new
material reference for both individual action and institutional structuring
within this new configuration is 'globality' or the spatiality and finitude of
the planet. In contrast to the 'weak' version of globalization theory, which
presents global interconnectedness as a product of modernization, Albrow
presents these as the necessary products of globality. Globality is a frame
of reference in which the modern project is increasingly relativized and

contextualized, and hence the global shift is a process of transformation rather than the culmination of social change as manifested in a new institutional configuration beyond the nation state (Albrow, *ibid*: 100). The agenda for modern society is set by 'planetary globality' rather than the narrative and technological plot of modernity.

Contrasting the positions of Beck and Albrow as the most radical formulations of social change within the respective narratives of modernization and globalization, we are left with two contradictory but overlapping positions. While both positions are underpinned by the claim that an understanding of contemporary society has to go beyond the established categories of nation state sociology, one position continues within the time-oriented narrative project of modernity, while the contrary position seeks to frame contemporary social change through the spatial frame of 'globality'. We argue that both accounts fail to recognize sufficiently the essential ambiguity of contemporary social change and transition. The idea of a 'second modernity', no matter how radicalized, is a foregone conclusion in that it conceals the state of liminality we are experiencing through the construction of a conceptual continuity between first and second modernity. On the other hand, 'globality' opens up a new perspective that is sensitive to novelty and discontinuity, but in so doing serves to sideline important instances of continuity within radical processes of transition. It is not our intention to take sides in the global age/reflexive modernity debate. Instead, we observe that the debate reveals a constellation of blurred vision (*Unschärferelation*) between two theoretical approaches that are both premised on a 'totalizing viewpoint' (Lyon, 2000: 229–231).

So, where do we go from here? We are attracted to the observation of Melucci (1996a: 486), which suggests that it is awkward to pose new questions using old language as an alternative to the development of a new of paradigm. However, it has become increasingly obvious that a new paradigm, such as that provided by 'globalization', is unable to grapple with the complexity of contemporary patterns of continuity and change in a satisfactory way. In this context, maybe it is a good idea to avoid the temptation of imposing an overall definition on a process of transition that is only just beginning. Instead of slipping from one pair of old shoes that are worn out into a new pair that are a bit too tight, perhaps it is quite adequate to walk on bare feet for a while. Hence, Melucci argues that:

> rather than denying this quandary or hiding behind words, it is preferable . . . to clearly state that we do not know what society we are talking about. We definitely do know, empirically, but our theories do not provide adequate tools to enable us to forge an overall interpretation. (Melucci, *op cit*: 486)

To take up this idea of an 'undefined society' (Melucci, *ibid*: 485) is not an alibi to refrain from conceptual work or to ignore the work done by others, especially the approaches mentioned so far. However, it does mean to take a step back from approaches that attempt to develop an overall definition of society and to recognize the complexity of social change that overall definitions tend to simplify or obscure. This reservation applies to both the theory of 'second modernity' and the uncritical use of the concept of globalization. Indeed, Roland Robertson, one of the founders of the globalization discourse, has called for caution against the uncritical use of the term; arguing for 'analytical strategies of *complexification*. . . . before we engage in the task of simplification' (Robertson & Khondker, 1998: 27). Complementary to the claim for complexity is the request for empirically grounded analysis. We agree with Gøsta Esping-Andersen (2000: 60, 72), who advocates 'intentional and purposeful empiricism' for a sociology that effectively 'hovers between the known and the unknown'. Rather than subsuming change within the certainties provided by an old or new framework, we need to grasp the processes of transition that are at work in the concrete configurations of social, political and cultural practice. In this way, we can rediscover the complexity of overlapping, and perhaps contradictory, changes that are occurring in contemporary society.

What we develop in this book is an analysis based on a patchwork of 'thick descriptions' of transition, rather than an overall definition of contemporary society. This might imply an untheoretical approach insofar as we do not attempt to come up with a term that can challenge the formulae of epochal change implied by 'reflexive modernization' or the 'global age'. If we were pushed to define our own standpoint it would have to be that contemporary society can be defined as an 'age of transition' (cf. Wallerstein, 2000). However, our approach is certainly not theory-less; we make critical use of the concepts developed in the theories of reflexive modernization, transformation theory and theory of globalization. We believe that there are hotspots of transition where the complexity of change can be observed most vividly: the world or global city, East-Central European borderlands, the workplace, consumption, politics and the environment. The picture is by no means complete, but we believe to have picked those hotspots, which, based on empirical evidence, appear as important gravitational centres of change and which have become the focus of intense, cross-disciplinary, debate. In each case, we highlight the complex processes of continuity and disjuncture underpinning the rapid transformations in these hotpots of transition. Our aim is to highlight the complexity of social change and to highlight the ways in which processes of social change produce an aggregate of societal complexification. Indeed, what the approaches explored in this book share is a focus on the ways in which contemporary patterns of social changes are underpinned by the operation of complex, non-linear, dynamic processes that possess emergent or vitalist properties (Urry, 2005). As Urry (*ibid*: 235–236) notes, the principal contemporary commentators of modernity and globalization at times articulate this complexity. The analysis of 'second modernity' is thus characterized as a driverless out-of-control juggernaut (Giddens, 1990) producing irreversible processes and unintended 'boomerang effects' (Beck & Willms, 2003) on a global scale. The non-linear nature of social change has been highlighted by commentators that focus on the intensification or relativization of temporal and spatial ordering. Hence, Harvey (1989) has described the process of 'time–space compression' by which temporal and spatial frames of reference have been radically rescaled by the effects of ICT and transportation technologies. Bauman (*op cit*) describes the contemporary state of modernity as 'liquid' as people, images, information and money flow with increasing intensity around the globe. The complex and dynamic nature of contemporary social change is also stressed by Castells (*op cit*) who highlights the 'self-organizing' and 'non-hierarchical' dynamics of the globalized 'network society'. Finally, Appadurai (1990) describes the landscape of the global cultural economy as a 'fluid, irregular shape' with 'fundamental disjunctures' between economy, politics and culture. Our aim is thus to highlight the ways in which these processes of complexification underpin the dynamic patterns of social change in the 'hotspots of transition', which we will now briefly introduce.

In Chapter 2, we focus on the dynamic and changing forms of urbanism underpinning the global expansion of urbanization. The process of urbanization and the development of the modern metropolis were central to modern development and the cultural and aesthetic sensibilities of modernism. The expansion of the city underpinned the consolidation of state power, the growth and expansion of modern industry and the corresponding growth in mass consumption. The modern city in modern times became the ultimate centre of innovation and creativity and a melting pot of ethnic and cultural milieux. In the context of globalization and the crisis of 'first' modernity, the city has returned as a key focus of sociological enquiry. The processes of urbanization and industrialization that occurred in the Global North in the nineteenth and twentieth centuries are now repeated in the developing countries of Asia and the Global South, but now on a far more intensive and expansive scale and often with rather different outcomes than those envisaged by the basic assumptions of modernization theory. In the Global North, the process of de-industrialization has resulted in the decline of many industrial cities while other cities have become increasingly detached from their national hinterlands and integrated into a new form of 'networked capitalism'. The development of the 'global city' raises two fundamental questions that will be explored in this chapter. First, what are the main spatial configurations of globalized urbanism and how is this different in developed and developing societies? Second, can these changes in the spatial and social organization of the city be grasped as a process of transition from modern metropolis to global city or are more complex theoretical tools required?

In Chapter 3, we focus on borders and border regions in order to highlight important changes in the geography of power and identity. The modern nation state comprised a unitary system of power with fixed territorial borders and a monopoly of legitimate violence (Weber, 1948). While there is a long-standing debate as to whether nationally defined communities were 'real' or 'illusory' (cf. Anderson, 1983; Smith, 1983), these communities undoubtedly contributed to the relatively stable and 'centred' identities of the modern era. The process of globalization has undermined these modern configurations of power and identity. In this context, a new geography of power and identity is emerging as territorially defined cultures, and spatially bounded communities become increasingly eroded and challenged by a socio-cultural logic of the 'in-between'. While this would apply to almost any border setting, the East-Central European region is of particular interest insofar as it has become the site of an intense and multi-layered transformation from post-socialism towards open society. This makes this particular region a kind of laboratory for researching the impact of the intersecting, and partly conflicting, dynamics of globalization, catching-up modernization and revitalized regionalism. These borderlands constitute a form of 'pilot-region' for the analysis of hybrid identities, cosmopolitan citizenship and multi-level governance. These developments raise a number of issues that form the analytical and conceptual focus of this chapter. First, what is the structural logic behind the inherent ambivalence of borders? Second, to the extent that state borders are becoming more porous, what are the main historical and geographical factors contributing to this ambiguity? Third, how are these historical and geographical specificities manifesting themselves in the new borderlands of Central-East Europe? Finally, can this setting serve as a seedbed of transnational cosmopolitan citizenship?

In Chapter 4, we explore the workplace in transition and the temporal and spatial reordering of labour in the global age. The modern workplace occupied a nodal position in the socio-economic and socio-cultural configuration of modern society. The labour market was the principal mechanism for the distribution of material and symbolic rewards and provided the basis for a stable set of inequalities and cleavages around the categories of class, gender and ethnicity. The workplace was also an important source of meaning, motivation and identity and an important component in the generation of workplace collective identity and neighbourhood community. This rested on a stable international division of labour in which workers in the developing world produced the raw materials required by workers in the dynamic industrial economies of the developed world. During recent decades, a process of intense post-industrial restructuring has resulted in the flexibilization not just of the work process, but also of labour itself, with workers and managers increasingly becoming entrepreneurs of their own labour. At all levels a state of persistent precariousness has replaced once stable professional careers, and unemployment increasingly appears as personal failure in a process of self-management. These tendencies have been accentuated by the development and application of ICT. Firms and capital have become even more footloose and industrial processes and indeed whole industries have been reconfigured on a global scale. This suggests an orderly transition between a modern, industrial, 'Fordist' and spatially embedded workplace towards a postmodern, post-industrial, post-Fordist and 'networked' workplace. The reality, however, is more complex and, through an exploration of the global call centre industry, we highlight the main contours of a liminal workplace in transition. This process of transition raises a number of questions. First, how does the introduction of ICT affect the organizational design and labour process within networked TNCs and who are the winners and losers in this process? Second, to what extent have patterns of collective resistance been overcome in the contemporary workplace and to what extent have corporate attempts to re-engineer workplace identity and subjectivity been successful? Third, how do these changes influence gender relations within the workplace and to what extent does the increasing importance of emotional labour in the global service economy result in the feminization of the workplace?

In Chapter 5, we explore changes in the discourse and practice of consumption with a particular focus on the complex and ambiguous relationship between money and identity. The ambiguous nature of money was explored in the work of both Marx and Simmel who both emphasized, in somewhat different terms, the way in which money constitutes both ultimate freedom and ultimate domination and control. This tendency was intensified by the development of Fordism and a system of mass consumption underpinned by assembly line mass production and the development of marketing and advertising. The current phase of neo-liberal restructuring and the development of a globalized post-Fordist economy are widely regarded as having intensified consumer culture. The development of ICT, for example, has resulted in an intensification in the circulation of consumer images and signs to such a degree that social reality has imploded into a new form of hyper-reality (Baudrillard, 1983a). The flexible and increasingly precarious nature of post-Fordist work has resulted in a situation in which consumption is *the* source of identity and meaning in the postmodern world (Bauman, 1992). However, there are also a number of accounts of postmodern consumption that highlight the deeply alienating nature of the new 'means of consumption' (Ritzer, 2005) and the way in which these are underpinned by intense processes of monitoring, manipulation and control (Davis, 1998; Harvey, 1989; Jameson, 1991). The world of consumption has not, therefore, been transformed as part of a straightforward shift from modernity to postmodernity. This raises a series of important questions. First, what are the origins of intensified or 'hyperconsumption' and how is this transforming the spatial and organizational form of contemporary consumption? Second, how are these changes affecting individual identity and autonomy in the context of the hyper-real spaces of contemporary consumption? Finally, how are these ambiguous and contradictory tendencies interwoven into the spatial fabric of the global city and how does this impact on culture and identity in these new socio-cultural spaces?

In Chapter 6, we explore the new individualities and solidarities that are developing based on the new forms of politics beyond and below the nation state. The modern age was an age of meta-ideologies: total ideologies (*weltanschauungen*) that defined past, present and future in terms of a linear trajectory towards a pre-defined utopia. In geo-political terms, the principle cleavage was between liberal democratic capitalism and authoritarian state socialism: manifested in a geo-political alignment around the USA and USSR, respectively. In this context, and in the context of the above geo-political cleavage, the dominant tendency in liberal societies was towards various forms of 'class compromise' and the development of the social democratic welfare state. The specific form of the welfare state varied markedly in different national contexts (Esping-Andersen, 1990), but overriding these differences was a commitment to social justice and egalitarian collectivism manifested in an extensive system of state planning, state ownership and social insurance. During the 1970s, commentators began to spot a range of contradictions and systemic failures within the welfare state that were undermining popular support for welfarism (Habermas, 1976; Offe, 1984, 1985a) and, during the 1980s, these internal contradictions were intensified by two powerful and related external dynamics: the fall of the Berlin Wall in 1989 and the emergence of networked global capitalism. In this context, the nation state increasingly lacks both the capacity and the legitimacy to deliver welfare and this has resulted in an extensive programme of neo-liberal restructuring including the privatization and liberalization of industries and services and the promotion of individualist and entrepreneurial values. In a wider context of de-industrialization, this has resulted in the decline of the labour movement as a political actor, the increasing importance of new social movements (NSMs) and symbolic forms of political action and the crisis and recomposition of social democracy. While these developments could be presented as a straightforward transition from a collectivist form of modern politics to an individualist form of postmodern politics, we would argue that this is simplistic and masks a complex pattern of continuity and change around the generation of both new individualities and new solidarities. In order to explore this complexity, we will focus on the following questions. First, how are global configurations of power being transformed by networked neo-liberal globalism and does this mark the end or the transformation of social democracy? Second, does the politics of NSMs go beyond individualistic forms of symbolic politics and if so what are the social and political implications of the resulting cleavages and solidarities? Third, to what extent are global forms of resistance emerging to challenge neo-liberal globalism, what forms does this resistance take and how successful has it been in challenging the neo-liberal agenda?

In Chapter 7, we explore life in risk society through an analysis of the relationship between nature, the environment and individual milieu. The dominant ideologies of modern societies were premised on anthropocentric or human-centred assumptions. Throughout the twentieth century, humanity clung to this 'arrogance of humanism' (Ehrenfeld, 1978) and the resulting naive view that the negative effects of growth and development could be controlled and neutralized by the 'technological fix' of further scientific development. However, the emergence of complex 'planetary risks' such as nuclear fallout and global warming, and the increasing perception that contemporary westernized lifestyles are not ecologically sustainable, has increasingly undermined the 'environmental' perspective of 'first modernity' (Beck, 1995). The ecology movement has played a key role in questioning and relativizing the assumptions underpinning the rational-scientific paradigm and the long-term unsustainability of current patterns of growth and development. Environmental problems highlight planetary interconnectedness and have provided the impetus for new types of social movement and forms of civic consciousness beyond the nation state. However, it has also become apparent that the environmental discourse can reproduce an important fallacy of modern society: the projection of fundamental crisis within society onto nature. If anything, global environmental problems point us towards a turning point in contemporary society where crucial foundations of modernity – such as the Cartesian World View, North/South exploitation, gender inequality and trust in science – are put into question. The relationships between nature, environment and individual life world are becoming increasingly complex and this raises a number of important questions. First, what is the precise relationship between perceptions of nature and existential uncertainty and how is this reflected in contemporary perceptions of risk? Second, how does the development of 'risk society' change the spatial and temporal ordering of modern society? Third, how are increasing perceptions of ecological risk linked to wider processes of social transformation and the dynamic of reflexive modernization? Finally, how are perceptions of nature and environmental risk 'embodied' in the everyday life of milieu?

In the final and concluding chapter, we address the problem of the 'social' in a globalized and de-territorialized world. We explore how the processes of social, spatial and technological restructuring explored in this book render the traditional sociological focus on to face-to-face interaction increasingly problematic. Throughout this book, we highlight the corrosive effects of powerful disembedding mechanisms and the ways in which these are responsible for processes of de-traditionalization and individualization and an intensification of alienation and anomie. However, we reject the post-structuralist proposition that contemporary patterns of social change approximate to 'disembedding without re-embedding' or the 'end of the social'. We highlight the way in which the hotspots explored in this book are also sites of at least partial re-embedding and the way that the development and application of ICT provides the basis for new forms of social engagement, intimacy and trust. We explore the extent to which these new social forms can be conceptualized adequately through the sociological category of 'community'. We argue that in the context of time–space distanciation, the concept of 'community' is ineluctably 'place-bound' and we explore the analytical potential of the alternative conceptualizations of 'neo-communities' (Lash & Urry, 1994), 'pure relationship' (Giddens, 1991) and 'sociosphere' (Albrow, *op cit*). We argue that in a 'network society' (Castells, *op cit*) 'abstract systems' (Giddens, 1990) do not lead in an unproblematic way the 'colonisation of the life-world' (Habermas, 1987) but have an enabling and empowering function with regard to maintaining life worlds across time and space. This, however, is a complex process and generates ambiguity. We thus conclude with a re-amplification of our central argument regarding the liminal and in-between nature of contemporary societies in transition.

2
Urban Worlds and Global Cities

I am, you see, a lover of learning. Now the people in the street have something to teach me, but the fields and trees won't teach me anything.

(Socrates [cf. Plato, 1977: 26])

While the contemporary city is no longer the Greek polis of ancient times, and although we might dispute the slight disrespect for nature that rings through in his statement, we can still relate easily to the enthusiasm of Socrates for city life. If you want to see what is 'hot', if you want to observe how strangers meet and get on, if you want to listen to and discuss with differing and contradicting voices, indeed, if you want to know about human nature, what better place than the city? Throughout history, scholars of human behaviour have been amazed and fascinated by the city and city life. The importance of the city rests on its role as a 'cultural marketplace' (Hannerz, 1998: 135) and the enduring import-ance of the city is based on this tendency of bringing together variety and difference. The city can be depicted as 'the cradle of invention and creativity and, hence, our hope for their future' (Amin & Thrift, 2004: 159). The idea that the city acts as a *pars pro toto* of society, or a window through which to observe trends in society at large, has gained partic-ular, prominence in the modern age. Weber (1966) focused on the role of the city in the process of rationalization. The city provided an enclave of freedom from the constraints of feudal society ('city air makes free'), but also fostered the conditions for rational conduct particularly through entrepreneurship, the guilds and civic institutions. Simmel (1969) argued that an understanding of the modern metropolis provided the basis for an understanding of modern society. The metropolis was the impersonalized crystallization of all that modernity had developed. Amidst the abundance of commodified culture, the individual felt a deep ambivalence: stimula-tion and challenge on the one hand, loneliness and struggle to (re)gain individuality on the other. The Chicago School, influenced by Simmel,

13

followed the *pars pro toto* idea to such an extent that modern sociology could be equated to urban sociology (Lindner, 1990).

In recent years, there has been an important resurgence of interest in the dynamics underpinning the city and city life. This is perhaps unsurprising given the ambivalence of the contemporary era and the tradition role of the city as *pars pro toto* for society. While urban sociology has lost the privileged position it once held through the dominance of the Chicago School, it could be argued that at the beginning of the new Millennium 'the city is once again emerging as a strategic site for understanding major new trends that are reconfiguring the social order' (Sassen, 2000a: 143). 'Globalization' is the umbrella term that attempts to capture the reconfiguration of society along a sociospatial pattern beyond the nation state. Insofar as this sociospatial order works itself out in and through cities, the city can indeed be seen as an important 'strategic lens' (Sassen, *ibid*: 143) or 'window' (Healey et al., 1995: 13) through which to spotlight the new trends and problems that face contemporary society at large. Furthermore, the world is becoming increasingly urban. Current trends suggest that by 2025, 66 per cent of the global population will live in cities and it thus makes increasing sense to characterize the world as a 'global urban society' (Clark, 1996: 166–187) or an 'urban planet' (Girardet, 2004: 3). Anticipating these developments during the 1970s, Henri Lefèbvre (1990) advanced the hypothesis of an 'urbanized society' based on the functional integration of the hinterland of the city into a wider urban system. The supermarket on a green field site, the summer residence of the urban dweller in the countryside and the motorway that connected the two were presented as part of an increasingly pervasive urban web. History has thus drawn us ever closer to the universalization of the city as the epitiomization of human civilization. As Lewis Mumford (1991), argues: '[history] opens with a city that was, symbolically, a world: it closes with a world that has become . . . a city'. However, the assumption of an urbanized society raises more questions than answers, for while the urban world seems to be increasingly omnipresent, an agreed definition of the city has become increasingly illusive. As Amin & Thrift (2004: 1) suggest, 'the city is everywhere and in everything' yet at the same time 'cities have become extraordinarily intricate, and . . . difficult to generalize'. While there is a tendency towards urban concentration around certain metropolitan hubs on the macro scale, there is at the same time a dispersal of urban functions within urban networks and along metropolitan corridors. The diffusion of urbanism as a way of life well beyond the traditional city environment has changed the form of urban society, and the cognitive mapping of the contemporary urban condition is becoming increasingly difficult. The ubiquity of the urban world has, moreover, important implications with regard to ecological sustainability and thus, rather than being civilization's declaration of independence from nature, the city remains *the* crucial mediator between nature and society.

In this chapter, we explore the main dynamics underpinning the development of the global city and the main contours and functions of the emergent global urban system. We begin by tracing the ecological embeddedness of the city in the global environment and the 'urban footprints' that can be traced in the wake of ecologically unsustainable forms of westernized urban life. We argue that the contemporary debate around the 'sustainable city' highlights the social and cultural dynamics underpinning this crisis of unsustainability and the way in which forms of development and inequality in the global urban system highlight the key dynamics and inequalities in an emergent 'world risk society'. We then explore the divergent patterns of urbanization underpinning the development of the global urban system. We highlight differences between the 'cities of slums' developing in the Global South, the post-socialist cities in Central-Eastern Europe and the winners and losers of post-Fordist restructuring in the developed Global North. These developments highlight the way in which the global urban system is developing through a dynamic premised on the global interconnectedness of local diversity that can be best described as 'nested urbanism'. We then explore the main dynamics and dimensions of the global city as an example of post-metropolis urbanization. We demonstrate the way in which the position of the global city as a nodal point in the global cultural economy results in a complex combination of spatial standardization and social disjuncture and fragmentation. We conclude the chapter by subjecting the concept of 'global city' to rigorous critical analysis: highlighting the ways in which over-generalized and ahistorical applications of the concept have obscured important continuities between the imperial world city and the global city and the complex diversity of the functions undertaken by geographically diverse global world cities.

Urban Footprints: The Ecological Embeddedness of the City

Mumford (1991: 199) speaks of the 'cockney illusion' underpinning urban modernity involving a naïve forgetfulness of the dependence of the city on the countryside. The city has become home to 'amplified (wo)man' (Girardet, *op cit*: 10, 110), a being that has transcended its biological limits by merging with the powers of technology. Few of us know the origins of the energy that fires our computers and microwaves or the destination of our waste. The distant links that support the city and the environmental impact of the urban way of life remain largely invisible to the urban dweller. We imagine the city as a contained unity, marked out by planning and architectural rules, and bound together by transport networks. Yet, if we were to zoom in on the urban landscape from a distance, we would be struck by its 'ecological footprints'. The term serves as a metaphor to highlight the dependence of the contemporary city on a worldwide hinterland and the way the city increasingly takes the form of a 'multi-layered eco-technical system' whose metabolism, mediated through a huge array of technologies, stretches far beyond its built environment (Giradet, *ibid*: 109). For example, London is both a leading global city and a pioneer in unsustainable development. In 1992, Londoners used the energy equivalent of 20,000,000 tonnes of oil per year, or the equivalent of two super tankers per week, and discharged 60,000,000 tonnes of carbon monoxide into the atmosphere. Throughout its colonial history, London developed a global hinterland to facilitate the long-distance importation of food, spice and timber. It is somewhat ironic that the Heathrow area, where cargo planes supply Londoners with fresh fruit and vegetables today, was once a market gardening centre that provided Londoners with fresh local produce. Computer simulated models suggest that London has an 'ecological footprint' 293 times its surface area: in other words, an area of approximately 45,000,000 hectares, somewhere in Kansas (wheat), India (tea and timber) or the Amazon forest (carbon monoxide), is needed to sustain the life of 7,000,000 Londoners (see Girardet, *ibid*: *passim*).

While London may appear to be an extreme example, it is generally accepted that cities are the main culprit for the ecological overdraft of modern society and, consequently, cities are 'almost inherently undesirable in environmental terms' (Haughton & Hunter, 1994: 10). In this context, the environmentalist perspective has developed the model of the 'sustainable city'. In 1987, the United Nations Commission on Environment and Development issued the 'Brundtland Report'. The report raised the issue of 'sustainability' of human economic and social development in the light of its long-term environmental impact. Chapter 9 of this report deals explicitly with the 'urban challenge' to create more sustainable urban communities (Whitehead, 2003: 1185ff.). Inspired by these thoughts, the sustainable city can be defined in the following way:

> A 'sustainable city' enables all citizens to meet their own needs and to enhance their well-being, without degrading the natural world or the lives of other people, now or in the future (quoted in Girardet, *op cit*: 6).

One way to achieve the 'sustainable city' is to replace the linear metabolism of the city by the circular metabolism of nature (Girardet, *op cit*: 123; Haughton & Hunter, *op cit*). There is, however, little agreement on how this could be achieved practically. The options range from a strong environmentalist perspective, that argues for a bioregional decentralization of the urban landscape into self-sufficient communities, to a softer environmentalist perspectives that advocate various versions of the 'compact city'. While the latter may seem more practical, it nonetheless remains ambivalent, for while the compactness of the built environment was, for many years, equated with high-energy efficiency, recent empirical studies no longer seem to support the link (Haughton & Hunter, *op cit*; Jenks et al., 2000). Whatever the solutions to these implementation problems, the existence of the debate highlights the importance of going beyond the purely technical issues of urban metabolisms and urban design to explore the social dimensions of sustainability. As both Andrew Ross (1994: 94) and David Harvey (1996: 391–426) argue, a discussion on sustainability conducted predominantly in ecological and architectural terms could easily turn into 'anti-urban sentiment' and 'rural nostalgia'. The city as a 'cancerous growth' or 'parasite' on the body of nature is just two of the many metaphors that illustrate this anti-urban discourse. Turning the city into a scapegoat for these problems, however, is not a viable option and leaving the city is not really on the agenda for the majority of urban dwellers. A large-scale urban diaspora would have disastrous consequences for the environment, for most of those re-inhabiting rural areas would be ignorant and careless towards the biodiversity and the ecological milieux they found in the countryside. To contemplate seriously such an urban future would require the re-skilling of the urban population (Orr, 1999; Ross, 1994: 130) and the development of new forms of revitalized urban agriculture (Garnet, 1996; Girardet, *op cit*). In essence, we need to find solutions to the problem of sustainability in the city rather than looking for solutions outside it.

In order to discuss the sustainability of the city, we need to consider the diversity of urban worlds in the context of their social, political and cultural ecology (Haughton & Hunter, *op cit*: 26; Whitehead, 2003). The 25 per cent of the global population who live in the urbanized Global North consume 70 per cent of the global energy supply (Clark, *op cit*: 175). Tokyo, a city where just 15 per cent of commuters drive to work by car, stands in stark contrast to Los Angeles, where 90 per cent commute to work by car (Haughton & Hunter, 1994: 13). At the same time, LA is being divided into unequally balanced 'parallel cities': cities based on private car ownership stand alongside cities whose populations are immobilized or reliant on public transport – 'to be car-less in LA is to be faceless' (Hutchinson, cited in Amin & Thrift, *op cit*: 15). While London is heavily reliant on post-colonial global food consumption, local authorities in Shanghai have fostered the development of urban agriculture such that 60 per cent of the vegetables consumed in the city are locally produced. China, the most rapidly urbanizing and industrializing country, is projected to build 400 new cities each with 600,000 inhabitants and with corresponding increases in energy use and consumption levels (Girardet, *op cit*: 8, 241). While these figures and juxtapositions have been selected randomly, they indicate that ecological issues are interwoven with regional pathways of city development and are subject to the policy decisions of national and local authorities, patterns of social and racial inequality within cities and uneven power geometries between city regions. The 'sustainable city' requires more than a technical blueprint for new circular urban meta-bolisms based on the increasing resource productivity of the city as eco-technical system. What really is at stake here is the global sustainability of westernized urban lifestyles and the asymmetries of power and one-sided growth mentality on which they are based (Jenks et al., *op cit*: 4). The city rings the alarm bell for what Beck (1999) has termed '(world) risk society': a society that has to face up to the (unwanted) 'boomerang' effects of modern technology and the modern world view. Haughton & Hunter (*op cit*: 10) highlight the role of cities as 'early warning indicators of more deep-seated, broader reaching environmental crises'. The open radius, both in time and space, of the ecological side effects of urban living make it now virtually impossible to draw a clear-cut distinction between the local, urban and global environment. Thus, if we are to rebalance the relationship between nature and society within 'world risk society', this attempt has a fixed address: the city, home of 'amplified (wo)man' (see Keil, 1995).

Urban Landscapes of Change: Between Local Diversity and Global Interconnectedness

Urbanization is a process that involves the constant reproduction and innovation of urban forms and captures a whole range of processes and dynamics that evade narrow definition and hierarchization. The urban is the most dominant structure that humanity has imposed on Earth, and yet this 'urban planet' is in constant flux, tension and, in recent years, growth (Whitehead, *op cit*: 1203). The contemporary urban population is larger than the total population of the world in 1960. While in 1900, only 15 per cent of the global population lived in cities, by 2000 this had increased to 47 per cent and at some point during 2005 we stepped beyond the 50 per cent threshold to become an urban planet. By 2000, the world contained 200 cities with 1 million inhabitants, a further 100 cities with between 1 and 10 million inhabitants and around 20 mega- or hyper-cities with more than 10 million urban dwellers. Future projections of growth suggest figures like 24.9 million for Jakarta, 25 million for Dhaka and 33 million for Mumbai (Davis, 2004: 5; Girardet, *op cit*: 3). Observing the urban land-scape from a distance and at night, we would see the flickering lights of an almost uninterrupted urban corridor stretching along the major axes of Tokyo–Osaka, Beijing–Tianjin, Rhine–Ruhr, London–Cardiff, New York–Philadelphia, San Francisco–Los Angeles–Miami. A closer look, however, reveals an urban landscape that hardly fits the picture of an urban planet of city lights. In its shadow, there is a 'planet of slums' (Davis, *op cit*) developing in proportions that defy the human imagination. Drawing on United Nations (UN) statistics, Davis (*ibid*: 13), highlights the existence of 921 million slum dwellers in 2001, which approximates to the total world population of the 1840s. These slum dwellers constitute approximately 33 per cent of the global urban population and 78 per cent of the urban population of the least developed countries. In countries such as Ethiopia (99.4 per cent) or Afghanistan (98.5 per cent), slum dwellers make up almost the entire urban population. In consequence, there is now a sprawling 'slum planet' that parallels the 'urban planet':

> There may be more than a quarter of a million slums on earth. The five great metropolises of South Asia (Karachi, Mumbai, Delhi, Kolkata and Dhaka) alone contain about 15,000 distinct slum communities with a total population of more than 30 million. An even larger slum population crowds the urbanizing littoral of West Africa, while other huge conurbations of poverty sprawl across Anatolia and the Ethiopian highlands; hug the base of the Andes and the Himalayas; explode outward from the skyscraper cores of Mexico, Jo-burg, Manila and São Paulo; and, of course, line the banks of the rivers Amazon, Niger, Congo, Nile, Tigris, Ganges, Irrawaddy and Mekong (Davis, *ibid*: 14).

This 'planet of slums' highlights the emergence of a 'new species of urbanism' and an urban landscape in transition. In Lagos – once known as the 'Venice of West Africa' (Gandy, 2005) – Davis detects an extreme form of 'over-urbanization' or a form of urban growth without economic embeddedness, which he describes as 'urban involution' (Davis, *op cit*: 27). This new urban form is the product of supernova-like overdrive and the inward collapse of a former metropolis into a slum-like conurbation. It is characterized by a loss of public space, the decline of public services and the intensification of forms of ethnic polarization. Increasingly, family-based communities fend for themselves in a makeshift informal economy and people are left in a perpetual state of day-to-day survival. Where does this city fit in the overall picture of contemporary society? Gandy provides a succinct answer to this question:

> Eroded modes of service provision persist as a ghostly palimpsest of structures: rusted post boxes, the twisted remains of parking meters and other accoutrements of an *abandoned modernity* litter the urban landscape (Gandy, 2005: 52; our emphasis)

The 'planet of slums' in general, and Lagos in particular, are indications of an 'inverse of the globalization thesis' (Gandy, *ibid*: 38) and their only function in the new global economy consists in 'warehousing the twenty-first century's surplus humanity' (Davis, *op cit*: 28).

There are other, less dramatic, new urban worlds developing within the global urban landscape. An important hotspot of change is provided by urban transformation in the 'countries of transition' in East-Central Europe. Pickvance refers to a 'unique natural experiment' (2002: 195) that is being carried out in the post-socialist city. The experiment raises two important questions. First, to what extent did socialism create divergent forms of urban development? Second, how are the simultaneous processes of post-socialist and global economic restructuring reflected in the partic-ular urban form of post-socialist city? Some commentators suggest that the socialist city was merely a temporary detour from the European city model that ended with the fall of the Berlin Wall. From this perspective, the more (post) socialist urban development is directed towards private sector development, private ownership and market regulation, the more similar cities like Berlin, Warsaw and Budapest will become to their siblings in Western Europe (Szelenyi, 1996). In contrast, other commentators witness the emergence of a 'new urban society' (Harloe, 1996: 2) that contains enduring legacies from the socialist period, including, inter alia, deterior-ated inner city housing and the lack of civic urban milieux. The ecological structure of the post-socialist city highlights the ambivalence inherent in this complex restructuring process. While restructuring involves a revital-ization of inner city living, there is at the same time an 'edge city' emerging in extensive green field developments which, in the context of the 'auto-mobilization' of all sections of the population, are resulting in clusters of shopping malls, car dealerships and petrol stations along-side the suburban homes of the newly rich. While the 'socialist city' is slowly disappearing, the direction in which the 'post-socialist city' is developing is less clear, both in its broad development (Pickvance, 1998; Pickvance, *op cit*; Szelenyi, *op cit*) and in its national variations, as recent studies on urban development in Hungary (Kiss, 2004), Poland (Szymańska & Matczak, 2002) and (East) Germany (Gornig & Häussermann, 2002) illustrate.

These transitional dynamics are particularly evident in Berlin. In Berlin, two societal systems and their respective architectural forms met head on, and urban dwellers are still encouraged to practice 'East meets West' on an everyday basis. However, symbolic struggles are being fought between East- and West-Berliners over the ideological implications of city redevel-opment – especially in the East, with its (un)famous remnants of socialist monumentalist architecture. Berlin finds it difficult to reconnect to its glor-ious past as a metropolis of science, culture and industry that it enjoyed in the 1920s. After 1989, Berlin suffered severe job losses in the manufacturing sector and has been unable to compensate for this with growth in the service sector. During the post-war period, Germany established Frankfurt (finance and banking), Munich (insurance and media) and Hamburg (trade and publishing) as important competitors to Berlin and these cities have developed important advantages in the global market. However, Berlin has retained the image of an eccentric city, with a huge variety of subcultures and an increasing ethnic mix. This makes it attractive to (young) people from the world over. Thus, today it is perhaps best described as 'international gateway between east and west' (Eckardt, 2005; Gornig & Häussermann, *op cit*).

The attentive reader might at this point argue that both the 'slum planet' and the 'post-socialist city' are rather exceptional cases of urban change. However, if we shift our gaze further towards the Global North, to the transatlantic western region which we have routinely in mind when talking about 'the urban' (Amin & Thrift, *op cit*: 5; cf. Robinson, 2004), we also observe movement and change within the urban landscape. The processes of de-industrialization and the onset of ICT-based service sector growth have altered the urban landscape in both Europe and America (MacLeod et al., 2003). The most vivid example is the shift of gravity in the American urban system from the notorious 'rust belt' to the hip and dynamic 'sun belt'. Between the 1970s and 1990s, the combination of free trade arrangements, the cheap import of steel and cars and the subsequent relocation of labour-intensive jobs overseas and to the Mexican border region, led to the steady decline of a band of manufacturing cities stretching between Chicago and New York. Cities like Pittsburgh (steel), Detroit (cars) and Buffalo (locomotives) that were previously the powerhouses of US industry have in recent times contracted rapidly resulting in the out migration of jobs and people and the subsequent deterioration of the inner city built environment. Detroit, the world famous 'Motor City' – symbol of American car-based modernity and the wealth generating power of the Fordist assembly line – was virtually emptied out by 1990, losing 165,000 of its 230,000 jobs and 1 million of its formerly 2 million inhabitants (Sugrue, 2004; Zukin, 1993: 103). In contrast, the 'sun belt' continued its steady growth into the 1980s and 1990s. Based on a bifurcated development of low skill service industries such as tourism and catering and high-tech industries in the computer, defence and media sectors, the 'sun belt' has benefited from foreign investment and the advantages of a mild climate. Consequently, the stretch between Los Angeles and Miami has become the symbol of postmodern urban growth. The Los Angeles region, for example, has benefited from Japanese inward investment and has come to represent a key example of post-Fordist reindustrialization with a clustered diffusion of flexible production in both electronic industries and low skill, labour-intensive sweatshops (Davis, 1998: 135; Soja, 2000: 142–156).

The growth of the 'sun belt' is at least partly a reflection of the spatial logic of an internationalized and flexible regime of post-Fordism capitalism. The boom in the LA region, however, was also a product of the way in which the changing political priorities of the US federal government shifted the gravitational centre of the American urban system towards the South (West). In the post-war period, the hegemonic interests of the US Government shifted from the Atlantic to the Pacific and the LA region, and other sunbelt locations benefited from investment into research and development in aerospace and other high-tech industries. Thus, in the contemporary period 'Aerospace Alley' and 'Silicon Valley' are sustained by the Southern California aerospace-defence-electronics industrial complex (Gottdiener, 2002: 166—171; Soja, *op cit*: 133–143). The examples of LA and Detroit reveal how the transformation of the planetary urban landscape also affects the urban topography within individual cities. Both cities are embodiments of the 'post-metropolis' (Soja, *ibid*; cf. MacLeod et al., 2003: 1660) defined as city regions that are no longer driven by a vibrant and dynamic inner city or downtown area, but thrive instead as an urbanization of suburbia. The post-metropolis is an urban form congruent with post-Fordist economic clustering, but lacks the social and cultural density of urban life associated with inner city living. 'Sixty suburbs in search of a city' became the catchphrase to describe urban development in LA since the 1960s (Soja, *op cit*: 137). Detroit, on the other hand, has experienced the simultaneous growth of its outer area and the erosion of its inner city. The observer, who drives along the new freeways that connect suburb to suburb but bypass the inner city, gets the impression of driving through 'endless plots of nothingness' (Gallagher, 2004: 243). In both cases, the city as we know it has disappeared and has been replaced by 'cities without cities' (Sieverts, 2003).

What we observe when looking across the 'urban planet' is a deeply perspectival and shifting landscape. There may be a planet-wide urban structure, but the urban worlds represented by Lagos, Berlin, Los Angeles and Detroit are very different indeed. While the post-industrial topographies are similar on the surface, the underlying dynamics of local development are highly variable. To paraphrase Therborn (2000: 154–166), there may be one global urban system, but there are plural urbanizations: thus, 'who you are and where you are (within the geography of global urbanization) make crucial differences and give very different grounds and possibilities of action'. This suggest an 'increasingly decentred and complex urban geography' (MacLeod, *op cit*: 1662) and a picture of the urban planet that is reflected in the 'recent turn towards variation, contradiction and complexity' in urban studies (Hill & Fujita, 2003: 207). These developments resonate with a perspective on globalization that demands analytical strategies of *complexification* (Robertson & Khondker, 1998: 27). However, highlighting the differences within and between a plurality of urban worlds in the global arena is only half the story. For as Therborn (*op cit*) and Harvey (1996: 401–129) remind us, while the 'geography of difference' maps an uneven spatio-temporal development, it has emerged within the all-embracing logic of global capitalism. Global urbanization reflects the new spatial logic of global capitalism that leads to a new global division of labour and a process of stratification between and within urban regions and cities. While LA claims to be one of the more innovative centres of the global economy, and Berlin desperately searches to reconnect to the global economy by promoting itself as 'gateway to the East', Lagos is left warehousing surplus population. This, however, is not to suggest that these different city worlds are the straightforward outcome of globalization or global capitalism. Rather, each of these cities and urban regions is embedded in a multi-level sociospatial configuration and, while the global 'level' may be decisive, meso-level dynamics are also important. The Lagos of today is not just the outcome of IMF-led structural adjustment policies, but also the outcome of regional tribalism and the practices of post-colonial elites. Berlin finds itself struggling between global opportunities and post-socialist restraints. LA would not have become the showcase of post-Fordist clustered urban growth in the 1980s if national policy had not already laid the infrastructural foundations during and after Second World War. Thus, it would seem that the metaphor that best depicts this interplay between local diversity and global interconnectivity and dependency within the 'urban planet' is 'nested urbanism': a concept that highlights the complex interplay between 'global niche, regional formation, national developmental model and local historical context' (Hill & Fujita, *op cit*: 212).

The Global City As Post-metropolis

There is an essential ambivalence to the impact of post-Fordist globalization on the restructuring of urban space. The same dynamic leads to both the virtual emptying out of the industrial city and the decline of its 'down town' and the generation of a new type of city that is more powerful than ever and whose down town areas are by no means obsolete. While cities like Liverpool, UK, Detroit, USA, or Osaka, Japan have lost their importance as modern centres of trade and industry, cities like London, Tokyo and Frankfurt have gained new or renewed prominence as centres of global capitalism. The decline of Fordism obviated the need for the spatial agglomeration of production, supply and management. Since the

1970s, the new international division of labour (NIDL) has resulted in a flexible global dispersal of the basic elements of production and supply and the (re)centralization of control, management and innovation in urban centres that have become known as 'global cities' (Castells, 2000a: 409–448; Lash & Urry, 1994: 25; Sassen, 1991: 5; Soja, *op cit*: 192). The central districts of the new global cities have become the locus of transnational management and global prestige. These cities provide the urban meta-system on which the networked world of global capitalism is built. The global city has the characteristics of the 'post-metropolis': an urban form that comes to prominence when the metropolitan inner city is no longer the growth engine of a metropolitan regional economy that powers a national industrial hinterland (MacLeod et al., *op cit*: 1660; Soja, *op cit*). The global city becomes disconnected from its national hinterland and connected to transnational networks of capital accumulation. This disconnection does not apply to the entire city or even the whole downtown area. This transurban world comprises the central business district and the clusters of residential areas and socio-cultural infrastructure related to the transnational elite. This creates an increasingly fragmented and even-fractured urban environment. The reconfiguration of spatial inclusion and exclusion that mark the 'new industrial spaces' of the post-Fordist global economy are paralleled within the new urban form of the global city. Manuel Castells has described this newly fragmented structure of 'city scapes' as the 'dual city' (Castells, *op cit*: 446–448; Mollenkopf & Castells, 1991). These cities are connected externally to global networks and to segments of their own countries, while remaining internally disconnected from local populations that are either functionally unnecessary or socially disruptive.

The global city is a new type post-metropolis in a wider sense that, in the context of globalization, the metropolis has lost the autonomy it enjoyed in the era of colonial imperialism. Fernand Braudel highlighted the way in which world cities functioned as gravitational centres of regional world economies or empires (cf. Jones, 1990: 45). London was the ultimate world city or metropolis, governing an empire that was an almost complete world in itself. The collapse of colonial empires resulted in the end of the modern metropolis. The (self) perception of the metropolis as a centre of gravity of a large territorial universe was challenged by the new post-colonial international division of labour. King (1991: 3, 24) reflects on these developments in his study on the transition of London from imperial to global city. During the 1970s, he suggests, there was a 'major paradigm shift' when cities such as London started to lose industrial jobs to cheap labour regions across the world. At the time, it became apparent that the urbanization processes both at the periphery and the core of what used to be a colonial world were increasingly shaped by the same global economic dynamics beyond national control. The colonial metropolis started to lose control of its own development. Hence:

> We no longer think of the metropolis as an autonomous self-governing polity but rather as an urban agglomeration that is shaped by forces beyond its control (Knight & Gappert, 1989: 16).

Against this backdrop, Friedmann (1986, 1995) has formulated the 'world city hypothesis', which placed world cities or global cities as the 'basing points' in the new spatial division of labour. These cities form a global and hierarchical system of world cities around which the new world economy gravitates. This leads to a repositioning of cities in relation to both the nation state and other cities that become potential competitors and partners. Sassen (*op cit*: 5) suggests that global cities are not just 'nodal points' in the coordination and control of global flows of finance and capital, but also sites of a special type of production focused on 'freestanding industries' such as financial services, management consultancy, head hunting and international legal advice. Moreover, the leading global cities, Tokyo, London and New York provide a 'transterritorial marketplace' (Sassen, *ibid*: 327) which not only covers all the major time zones, but within each of the cities fulfils a distinct role as exporter, processor and receiver of capital. Technological infrastructure is, however, less important in determining the centrality of the global city than the social buzz that is generated in its communicative environments: a 'specialized kind of social connectivity' that comes with the 'bouncing off' of information that become the key feature of the global city (Sassen, 2002: 21). The global city function has been a major dynamic behind the contemporary processes of urban restructuring. A 'global metropolitan culture' has developed (Short & Yeoung-Hyun, 1999) which is marked by a kind of generalized post-metropolis infrastructure of airport, motorways, conference venues, hotels, shopping malls – all appearing in a postmodern architectural style. However, it is exactly this tendency towards convergence that also increases the pressure to develop or maintain the locally or regionally distinctive city culture that is the unique selling point of a city within the global cultural economy. Thus, there is at the same time an intense 'co-presence of homogenizing and heterogenizing trends' that shapes the global urban centres (Short & Yeoung-Hyun, *ibid*: 11).

The global city is of central importance in defining the socio-cultural geography of the post-metropolitan world. Global cities are not just nodal points in the flows of capital, finance and information, but are also the centres of the 'new global cultural economy' (Appadurai, 1992; 1998; Lash & Urry, *op cit*) and are also, therefore, key nodes in the flows of people, social practices, ideas and beliefs. In this context, the global city seems initially to conform to the model of the metropolis developed by Wirth (1969: 61) as an 'orbit' that weaves 'diverse areas, peoples and activities into a cosmos'. However, globalization has altered significantly the cultural configurations of global cities such as London, New York, Sydney and LA. The landscape of global cultural flows is a complex, overlapping, disjunctive order, which can no longer be understood in terms of a centre-periphery model (Appadurai, 1992: 296). The landscape of global cultural flows based on the 'technoscapes' of the new means of transport and communication, implies that different social and cultural worlds intersect but do not necessarily intermingle or mix. The global city is consequently less of a big 'melting pot' (Wirth, *op cit*: 69) and more of a switchboard of global cultural flows that links local urban life worlds with the landscape of global cultural flows. Thus, it bundles, accommodates and refracts global cultural landscapes and juxtaposes global variety and difference. In this way, the global city modifies the perspectival character of the global cultural landscape without dissolving it. The global city is a global cultural economy *en miniature*. The continuous compression and subsequent accommodation of global cultural variety and difference into the everyday rhythms of a global city can be described as 'microglobalization' (Dürrschmidt, 1997; 2000: 12, 132). Soja (*op cit*: 218) describes this reconstruction of the 'inner workings' of the post-metropolis as a 're-worlding of city space'. Accordingly, a 'central feature of the post-metropolitan transition' is that the expanded symbolic universe of the post-metropolis experiences a 'loss in focus', as 'here' and 'elsewhere' are no longer clearly separable in the transnational practices and frames of reference of the urban arena. In other words, there is a growing divergence of presence and belonging, 'roots' and 'routes'. People live in particular localities but do not live place-bound identities, as their sense of belonging is 'rerouted' along globalized life worlds that stretch beyond the neighbourhood and the physical confines of the city. The retreat and closure of local milieux within the global city are premised on sophisticated forms of 'transclusion'. Transclusion refers to the simultaneous balancing of opening and closure, engagement and non-engagement, in a glocalizing landscape of opportunity structures and networks of obligation. The concept highlights a tendency for individuals to have a reduced level of engagement in their place of residence and be more involved and interested in options and obligations elsewhere.

The Notting Hill Carnival in London is an example of this post-metropolitan 'inner reworking' of a global cultural landscape. The festival was organized originally by and for the Afro-Caribbean community but has subsequently broadened out into a community festival. The whole of London is seemingly gathered every year on August Bank Holiday, when the complex history and present of Afro-Caribbean society is re-inscribed into the local setting of Notting Hill. Alleyne-Dettmers (1997) suggests that this is not just a global aesthetic flow of masks and costumes, but also a creative reworking of transregional Afro-Caribbean identity. It brings people together from various spatially dispersed islands to work on themes of their colonial heritage and post-colonial presence. The carnival allows for the playful interpretation of Afro-Caribbean identity from shared symbols within narratives of displacement. The carnival encourages self-assurance in terms of symbolisms of belonging without attempting to enforce a local black British identity. In sum, identities are renegotiated rather than replicated across distance. From Notting Hill, the images and themes on display at the carnival continue to impact further along the transnational cultural networks of the Afro-Caribbean diaspora; the carnival *Mas* (Trinidad) and *Caribana* (Toronto) being the other major reference points in this network (Quinn, 2005: 935).

This transnational 'rerouting' of (post)-metropolitan culture also influences the extent to which urban culture remains an important location for the generation of cosmopolitanism. The city is 'a milieu in which strangers are likely to meet' (Sennett, 1993: 48). Indeed, all global cities, even Tokyo, have experienced a cosmopolitanization of city culture in terms of an influx of foreign residents. However, transnational 'rerouting' of city life can produce a cityscape of comparatively unrelated and non-localized social worlds in which people can move without encountering the other or the stranger. Albrow (1997: 51) has developed the concept of 'sociospheres' to describe this constellation of local co-existence based on mutual non-involvement. Sociospheres are networks of action and social relations that span different time–space horizons and rhythms. In consequence, a new form of socio-cultural stratification has developed within the same city, sometimes even within the same neighbourhood, that does not rely primarily on spatial segmentation, but on the different ways and degrees to which local life worlds are connected to the wider landscape of global flows. Similarly, Hannerz (*op cit*: 127f.) has argued that there has been a shift in the organizing principle of contemporary 'hetero-genetic cities' such that 'the prevailing understandings and relationships would have to do with the technical rather than moral order'. To exaggerate Hannerz' argument slightly, the real stranger in the multi-ethnic global city is not the person of different ethnic or social background, but the one who 'outs' himself/herself by being unfamiliar with technical systems such as parking meters and ticket machines and thereby interferes technically with the smooth running of a series of sociospheres that overlap but yet hardly intermingle. This 'free play' between locally co-existing social worlds has ambiguous cultural consequences. It facilitates both controlled engagement with strangers and the emergence of new and novel cultural forms and the complete detachment of individuals who exist in parallel socio-cultural worlds. In the light of this ambivalence, it is difficult to concur with Mumford's (*op cit*: 652) optimistic view that the key cultural role of the modern metropolis is 'expressing and actualising the new human personality – that of 'One World Man'.

Recomplexifying the Global City

The global city approach developed alongside and has shared the same fate as the globalization paradigm, from the initial enthusiasm in the 1980s and 1990s to the more recent criticism that the concepts have become over-stretched and overused. The concept of 'global city' provided a window through which to observe an urban world that seemed to be disappearing with the processes of post-industrial change. The idea that a network of global cities was developing provided a corset that gave shape to the flows of 'disorganized capitalism' (Lash & Urry, *op cit*). However, in parallel to the call of Robertson for a 'second wave' of more reflexive and empiric-ally inclined globalization theory (Robertson & Khondker, 1998), urban researchers have called for a similar reframing of the global city paradigm. At the height of the global city debate, King (1995: 217) conceded that 'as with any over-ambitious theory, they (the concepts of world or global city) occlude as much, if not more, as they reveal'. Consequently, there is now a greater degree of scepticism with regard to the converging impetus of the global city approach and a greater focus on complexity and vari-ation in the processes of urban formation (Hill & Fujita, *op cit*; Smith, 2001). For example, there have been enduring disagreements about how to measure the globality of the global city. In much of the literature on global cities, Tokyo is placed alongside London and New York in the top echelon of global cities (Friedmann, 1995: 24; Hall, 1996: 18; Sassen, *op cit*: 1991). More recently, this positioning of Tokyo has been questioned. The city attracts limited levels of FDI; has a comparatively small freest-anding service industry; its airports have comparatively low capacity and poor access to the city; the financing of urban development is highly dependent on the state; and the city has a limited ethnic landscape (Saito & Thornley, 2003). The global reach of Japanese capital was thus mistaken for global connectivity and many global headquarters were revealed to be the headquarters of Japanese TNCs and banks. From this perspective, the role of Tokyo in the global economy seems to be that of 'a Japanese city with global reach, rather than a world city' (Saito & Thornley, *ibid*: 680). The world or global city typologies draw heavily on indicators such as where headquarters of large banks and corporations are located in order to generate world city league tables. This approach leads to a distorted image of the 'global city' as a ranking system that displays success or failure in a global competition between cities. The approach assumes rather than demonstrates the interconnection of these cities in a new division of labour, and, therefore, fails to show who actually is doing the networking between cities. The assumption that attributive statistical data can reflect the relations between cities has become associated with what has been labelled as 'dirty little secret of world city research' (Short & Yeoung-Hyun *op cit*: 8).

There has been a new wave of research that attempts to link global city research with network analysis in order to uncover the spatial configurations of the new international division of labour. For example, Alderson & Beckfield (2005) explored 500 of the largest MNCs across 3692 cities and uncovered a close link between the network centrality of cities and their respective nation states. This undermines the assumption that the spatial logic of the global city network is significantly different to the centre/periphery logic of the international system. Taylor (2005) attempted to measure the network location of more than 300 cities through the global network formation of global service firms, non-governmental agencies (NGOs) and agencies of the United Nations. The study highlighted how New York and London lead the world city network, while Tokyo is reduced to the status of a global economic niche city alongside Hong Kong and Singapore. Similar findings are derived from the study by Derudder et al. (2003) on the business strategies of 100 financial and business firms across 234 cities. Again, there was an emphasis on the transatlantic arrangement between London and New York, with Tokyo reduced to second layer status. The overall pattern resembles the older centre/periphery models with a triadic regional core of Northern America, Western Europe and Pacific Asia. This pattern of regionalization was also demonstrated in a study of network connectivity via passenger air travel that detected clear evidence of a persistence of colonial empires, especially in the case of London and Paris (Zook & Brunn, 2005).

This is a pertinent reminder that history matters. However, much of the research on the global city has suffered from methodological 'presentism' (Abu-Lughod, 1999) and has tended to be based on ahistorical 'snapshots' of metropolitan development (Eade, 2000). This has resulted in the emergence of a dominant perspective based on the convergence of global cities according to the spatial logic of post-Fordist flexible accumulation. More recent research, however, has revitalized the idea that the development of global cities is underpinned by 'path dependency' (Brenner, 2001: 128). London, for example, cannot be understood as a global city in isolation from its role as an imperial city and headquarters to the Bank of England. It is this legacy of persisting networks of global reach and established trust and reputation that gives (the City of) London a competitive advantage over competitors such as Frankfurt. The 'big bang' financial deregulation of

1986 reconfigured this legacy but did not abolish it and the importance of this post-imperial legacy has even outlasted the introduction of the Euro currency (Beaverstock et al., 2005; Budd & Whimster, 1992). The overlap of (post)imperial timescapes is not just something that takes place in the imagination of the researcher. In her study of post-colonial spaces in the global city, Jacobs (1996: 38) reports on a redevelopment scheme at Bank Junction, London where a prolonged process of planning permission turned into a symbolic battlefield between supporters of the imperial tradition and supporters of a more European-focused city. This implies that there are formative periods in city development that at least co-determine the entry of the city into the world city system. In a similar vein, Abu-Lughod (1995, 1999) has argued that global cities in the USA went through a formative era that continues to influence their entry and functional niche within the network of global cities: New York as 'mercantile city', Chicago as 'industrial city' and Los Angeles as 'informational city'. The emphasis on path dependency is an important counterargument against the underlying assumption of convergence within the world city hypothesis. This is not to suggest a simple plurality of global cities, however, as the new global division of labour and the new global cultural economy constrain developmental pathways (Brenner, *op cit*: 140). The world city system is not static. Historical contingencies continue to shape the present and the future of world city functions. Brussels, for example, has developed the status of a 'political world city' in the context of NATO and EU headquarters being located there and the city has therefore been transformed into a 'major locus of transnational political centrality' (van Criekingen et al., 2005: 175). Notions of path dependency thus highlight the fact that there are not just differences between urban trajectories, but, more importantly, discontinuities within each city.

Terminological Confusions in the Global City Discourse

The terminology applied in the discourse on world or global cities does not reflect adequately the path dependency of global city functions. Sensitivity to the historicities and trajectories of city development tends to disappear behind the 're-centring metaphor' of the 'global city' (Smith, *op cit*: 2, 50). At the same time, there is a striking terminological lenience within the global city discourse. The terms applied include, for instance, 'major cities' and 'premier cities' (Sassen, 1991), 'world cities' (Friedmann, 1986) and 'supranational key cities' (King, 1991). The interchangeable use 'world city' and 'global city', however, is one of the most irritating and problematic features of the debate on global cities (Brenner, 2001: 29; Keil and Olds,

2001: 119; King, 1995: 219). In this context, the calls for clearer definitions and analytically meaningful distinctions within the global city paradigm have become increasingly marked (Derrudder et al., 2003: 875; Taylor, *op cit*: 1593). On the basis of quantitative measures of world city connectivity, Taylor suggests a distinction between world cities as general term and global cities in the sense of 'especially important cities in the world city network' (Taylor, *ibid*: 1593). Alternatively, King (*op cit,* 2002) suggests that the concept of 'global *city*', with the emphasis on finance, banking and the new service sector, should be reserved for the socio-economic function of major cities. The notion of '*world* city', with the emphasis on the lived presence in the socio-cultural variety within the city, should be used to underline the status of these cities as centres of global cultural flows at the crossroads of life worlds (Dürrschmidt, 2000: 12; cf. Sassen, 2001a: 79). Of course, this is an ideal typical distinction, and not a definition of absolute validity. For example, Tokyo may be a global city, but when compared with London barely registers as a world city. Frankfurt may or may not challenge London as a global city, but certainly not as a world city. While the 'global city' is a recent development, the 'world city' is not. If we were to look for a prototypical case in which both developments complement each other, it would be London, the post-imperial world city that is also a global city. Furthermore, not all global cities fulfil all global city functions. Thus, it is important to specify the functions of a global city in order to gain sight of which cities are actually at the centre of particular functional networks. Brussels, for instance, is not a global city in the sense of London or New York or Frankfurt, but certainly is a 'political global city' (van Criekingen et al., *op cit*). A similar argument could be made with regard to the role of Milan in the world of fashion. However, no matter how much we specify, there comes the point at which it is pointless to call a city a global city. All cities, big and small are irretrievably caught up in the web of global connectivity. In this context, Marcuse & van Kempen (2000: 262) have suggested the term 'globalizing cities'. This is a helpful conceptual hint to the fact that the 'world of cities' does not only consist of 'world cities' or 'global cities' but a plethora of 'ordinary cities' (Robinson, 2004) which are nevertheless part and parcel of the uneven geography of urban globalization.

We could also increase analytical clarity through the differentiation of cities according to their scale or reach. Smith (2001) suggests that on closer inspection most 'global cities' operate on a transnational and perhaps transregional scale, but not on a global scale. So while transnationalization might be the more appropriate term for many aspects of globalization, the term 'transnational city' could be better equipped to grasp the regionally specific concrete transnational interconnectedness of cities like Los Angeles or Sydney, and even more so of 'second tier cities' such as Hong Kong or Miami. Miami is a case in point. The connectivity of Miami is clearly structured by its role as a financial and political centre of the Caribbean basin and a gateway to Latin America (Smith, *ibid*: 60; cf. Grosfoguel, 1995). The concept of 'global city-region' (Scott et al., 2001) is a further attempt to redirect the concept of global city based on scale and territoriality. While the 'transnational city' rests on the concrete structuration of the networks bundled in global cities, the 'global city-region' emphasizes the concrete territoriality of these cities. In contrast to the metropolitan centre of earlier times, the global city-region is 'a highly fragmented chessboard of uneven development sprawling ever outwards' (Scott et al., *ibid*: 20). In this light, it is not a city as an identifiable unity, but a fragmented cluster of a number of cities that produces the synergies that enable a city-region to bundle global networks to its advantage. Clearly, this concept is modelled on LA. These conceptual distinctions and refinements focus on the different functions and locations of the city within the new global economy and society. Accordingly, it depends on what we attempt to analyse as to what analytical tool might be best equipped to guide our investigations. Thus, while the global city concept might be better suited to grasp questions of centrality, power and inequality, the concept of the global city-region is possibly better equipped to highlight issues of scale, distribution and synergy, and in turn the 'transnational city' most suited to the analysis of concrete patterns of 'external' urban interconnectedness (Sassen, 2001a: 80).

These distinctions are ultimately ideal types that guide our analysis by highlighting and maybe at times overemphasizing particular aspects of contemporary post-metropolitan urban development, and thereby neces-sarily neglecting other aspects of the same phenomenon. The ideal type in the Weberian sense of the term is a scientific construct that guides our investigation by constantly reopening cleavages between concept and (urban) reality rather than finding the perfect fit. Ideal types are the means and the medium of scientific investigation rather than its end product. Thus, once we start to equate these ideal types with a scheme for normatively measuring reality, things start to become problematic. The ongoing dispute about the true model of contemporary post-metropolitan development is thus rather pointless. There are various claims as to which city exemplifies the contemporary post-metropolis or global city. While for some this would be New York (Mollenkopf & Castells, *op cit*: 5), for others, it would be the decentred post-metropolis LA (Gottdiener, 2002; Soja, *op cit*: xvii;) and for Europeans it would tend to be London (Eade, 1997). However, as we have seen, this conceptual apparatus is a deeply perspectival construct. Therefore, if we are interested in the continuity and discontinuity between a modern imperial metropolis and a post-metropolitan global city, London might be the most revealing field of research. If, in contrast we were interested in the post-industrial chess-board territoriality of the global city region, LA would provide the principal empirical frame of analysis. In many ways, therefore, world city or global city research continues to have a remarkable degree of vision. However, we should be aware that the world city hypothesis as initially postulated by Friedmann (1995) was first of all a heuristic device designed to open up a vast research terrain. The variety of concepts and contradictory claims as to which city might serve as the paradigmatic world or global city highlights the vast field of questions the concept has opened up. In fact, this heuristic device was perhaps so successful that the conceptual grasp of the 'global city' or 'world city' now has become too narrow for it to integrate meaningfully the changing urban field in all its variety.

Summary and Conclusion

In this chapter, we have explored the way that contemporary patterns of social change are underpinned by processes of hyper-urbanization on a global scale. We noted the plurality of urban forms in the global urban system. We highlighted examples of 'slum cities' in the Global South that seem to illustrate a process of 'urban involution' or a 'reverse globalization'. We explored the post-socialist cities of East-Central Europe as spaces that reflect the ambiguities of post-socialist transformation and neo-liberal globalism. We highlighted the important changes to the urban landscape in the Global North based on the decline of industrial cities such as Detroit and the emergence of a new spatial logic based on the flexible regime post-Fordist capitalism for which LA seems to be emblematic. We then explored the 'global city' as an example of post-metropolis urbanization marked by the detachment of important segments of the city from their surrounding hinterland and their integration into the 'space of flows' constituted by networked global capitalism. So where does this leave us with regard to the related questions of homogenization/heterogenization of social development on the one hand and continuity/rupture of patterns of urbanization on the other?

As Jennifer Robinson (2004: 575) has argued, the challenge for a twenty-first century urban theory will be 'to carve a difficult path between an appreciation of the world of diverse cities, and the distinctive world that is any given urban place'. We have attempted a step in this direction by showing the distinct features of the urban worlds represented by Detroit/LA, Berlin and Lagos, without losing sight of the logic of global capitalism that ties them together in a web of dependencies. The urban involution of Lagos, the de- and reindustrialization observable in Detroit and LA and the proliferation of Berlin as a switchboard between East and

West reflect divergent patterns of urban transformation that in turn reflect adjustments to the logic of globalization. At the same time, however, these divergent patterns of transformation force us to acknowledge the importance of regionally specific subglobal dynamics and the continuity of path-dependent urban trajectories. We share the growing reservations within urban studies as to whether re-centring metaphors such as 'global city' or even 'globalizing cities' can capture the re-complexification of urban worlds that accompany the growing interconnectivity within the global arena. With its emphasis on the transcendence of national and local culture and institutions, the 'global city' model carries a latent theory of convergence that is largely insensitive to the lasting regional and local specifics in which cities are embedded. If, as Saskia Sassen (2000a, 144) has suggested, 'recovering place' in an age of global flows is one of the crucial tasks of twenty-first century urban studies, then the concept of the 'nested city' (Hill & Fujita, 2003) seems to be the most fruitful approach. It implies the need to consider cities in a 'multi-level configuration – global niche, regional formation, national development model, local historical context – in which each city participates' (*ibid*: 212). Such a model would not only capture urban experiences outside the paradigmatic transatlantic 'North', but would also force us to be more precise, and at times perhaps more unsure, about the actual developmental dynamics behind diverse urban worlds, instead of conveniently referring to the seemingly all-embracing logic of 'globalization processes'.

Context-sensitive research and reasoning on urban worlds, as implied by the 'nested city' concept, might also make us more cautious with regard to drastic claims of continuity and discontinuity. Cities are undoubtedly at the centre of a spatial reconfiguration of global capitalism and the global cultural economy, but does that justify claims of a 'radical break in late twentieth-century urbanization' (Beauregard, 2006)? Any account of urban development in keeping with the 'nested city' approach would have to qualify claims of radical rupture. In other words, notions of a radical rupture can never refer to the whole of the city or encompass equally all levels of its spatial, economic, political and cultural embeddedness. The city is thus an uneven and contradictory historical process (cf. Beauregard, *ibid*: 219f). We have attempted to illustrate the oscillation between continuity and rupture by looking at the development of London from the metropolis of a worldwide empire towards a global city within the global cultural economy. What was notable was that while there were dramatic changes in the sociospatial structure as marked by the Docklands redevelopment there was nonetheless a continuity with regard to administrative structures such as the City of London and City of London corporation and with regard to cultural tradition as marked by the city's tolerant and assimilative cosmopolitanism (cf. Eade, 2000). Hence, approaches premised on a radical break tend to disregard this complex historic embed-dedness: the concepts of 'global city' (Sassen, 1991) or 'post-metropolis' (Soja, 2000) tend to overemphasize spatial and economic forms, basing their argument almost entirely on the new geometry of dispersal and cent-rality typical of post-Fordist capitalism, and subsequently, urbanity.

We are not arguing against the notion that urban restructuring and rupture underpin patterns of urbanization, but that the notions of 'global city' and 'post-metropolis' do not leave sufficient room for analysing the configurations of continuities/discontinuities that constitute the complexity of this current urban transformation. This implies more than the need for more nuanced research based on micro-empirical studies that are able to capture and retrieve historic diversity. Rather, we highlight the need to view the future beyond the usual phantasmagorias of transatlantic urban studies. What the brief introduction into the slum lands of Lagos suggests is that the basic question of social order and integration should be as much at the heart of the question of continuity/radical break in urban society as is the concern with spatial centrality and fragmentation. This 'nowhere landscape' populated with 'nowhere people' (Breman, 2006) is indeed a symbolic marker of radical urban and societal restructuring which has largely under-researched consequences. Throughout modern history, the city has always been an integrating milieu to which people more or less voluntarily went in search for a better life, and who more or less could hope for more or less regularized employment. This link between urbanity and social inclusion via industrialization no longer holds for an increasing amount of people in the slumlands of the global South. Here urban worlds develop that have no other function than to sustain the new pattern of social inclusion/exclusion by warehousing the 'wasted lives' of the outcasts of globalizing modernity with unforeseeable consequences for global society as a whole (cf. Bauman, 2004).

Consequently, viewed from this wider global perspective, the question of continuity/rupture goes right to the heart of the debate on the future of urban sociology at the beginning of the twenty-first century (cf. May & Perry, 2005). Couched in these terms the debate is not simply a competing dialogue between different vehicular metaphors within Western urban studies that compete for scholarly attention and interest, but more an overall challenge towards Western-centred scholarship. Hence, when thinking seriously about the future of the city 'the characteristics of urbanism dominant in the world are rapidly being defined outside of the wealthiest countries' (Robinson, 2004: 571).

3

Borders, Border Regions and Post-socialist Transformations: New Geographies of Power and Identity

(And) the human being is likewise the bordering creature who has no border.

(Georg Simmel, 1994: 10)

Simmel reminds us that borders and boundaries are drawn by human beings and their institutions. Borders are not fixed, but are there to be crossed, transgressed and reconfigured. Borders are not a monolithic institution, but a process realized in human interaction. The current phase of global spatial restructuring has brought these points into stark relief by undermining state-centric and territorial understandings of borders and boundaries. Political and administrative borders are becoming unstable, permeable and shifting, while the significance of cultural and symbolic boundaries are increasing. This is linked to an intense process of disembedding and re-embedding of social milieux and cultural identities across nation-state-boundaries. In contrast to earlier times, when political borders appeared solid in a clear-cut territorial landscape of nation-state-societies, the social construction of borders has become increasingly visible. In this context, individuals are both able and forced to navigate political borders and actively construct and negotiate socio-cultural boundaries. The border reveals itself as a transitional space loaded with mediation and ambiguity. In the border region, social and cultural identities meet, converge, coexist or conflict. Different national worlds encounter each other directly and political, economic and cultural tensions are played out in ways that have direct consequences for the everyday life of individuals. Here, individuals find the opportunity spaces for the construction of increasingly complex cultural identities and engage in forms of social interaction that transcend disparate national ideologies. Thus, border regions function in a similar way to global cities as 'microcosms' in which the re-ordering of a global cultural economy is bundled.

The fall of the Berlin Wall in 1989 was *the* event that exemplified the new dynamic of borders and a new phase in the restructuring of global landscapes of power and identity. The Iron Curtain being forced down by the power of the people highlighted the processual and relative character of the border. However, the significance of the events of 1989 went far beyond Germany and Europe. The fall of the Berlin Wall ended the head-to-head confrontation between East and West that determined the geopolitical and cultural landscape of the world between the two world wars: a landscape that extended beyond Europe into those regions of the Third World where the boundary between East and West intersected with the inequalities between North and South. The distinctiveness of East-Central Europe is the way in which this redrawing of the global landscape of power and identity has occurred in the context of the transition from a 'closed' to an 'open' society. The countries of East-Central Europe are a kind of laboratory in which the intersecting and partly conflicting dynamics of globalization and post-socialist transformation can be researched.

In this chapter, we highlight the renewed importance of border regions within the global political and cultural economy. We focus on Europe: the region where Western Modernity and European integration intersects with post-socialist transformation and incomplete European integration. Contemporary Europe provides a unique historical context marked by an acute and accelerated simultaneity of globalization, 'rectifying' modernization and regionalization. We begin by sketching out the structural ambiguity of borders and border regions and develop a typology of different borderlands that highlights the importance of historical and geographical specificity. We then focus in more detail on the interdependent borderlands between Poland and Germany in order to highlight the ambiguous and largely negative effects of globalization on this border region and the absence of cultural integration or a cosmopolitan outlook between people on the two sides of the border. Subsequently, we concentrate on the ambiguous effects of European regional policy on this border region in terms of a disjunction between *institutionalized Europhobia* and *latent Europhobia* and the festivalization of politics. We then explore the extent to which the ambiguous nature of transformation in this region is a result of the legacy of actually existing socialism. We argue that this provides only a partial explanation and that an understanding of *transformation* requires an examination of the complex interplay between globalizing modernity and the legacy of post-socialist development. We conclude with the argument that this complexity can be grasped through the concept of 'transclusion' or the simultaneous patterns of openness and closure, engagement and non-engagement, that mark everyday life in the post-socialist borderlands of East-Central Europe.

Borders and Border Regions: New Landscapes of Power and Identity

Scholarly research on borders has highlighted the significance of borders and border regions with regard to the shifting landscapes of power and identity created by the processes of globalization and European integration (Berezin & Schain, 2004; Donnan &Wilson, 1999; Meinhof, 2002). There is, however, a debate concerning the extent to which globalization dissolves spatial and cultural boundaries. On one side of this debate, are scholars who argue for a structural kinship between real and metaphoric borderlands and who identify both border regions and global cities as hot spots of hybridity and creolization. The formerly neglected border regions gain a new prominence alongside global cities as sites where 'notions of diversity, polyphony, fluidity and complexity have replaced those of purity, boundedness, stability and consent' (Wendl & Rösler, 1999: 10). In this model, the social actors who inhabit border regions live at the intersection of different worlds and cultures. These 'border people' are constantly shifting and renegotiating their identities in ever increasing manoeuvres of power and submission, and often adopt 'multiple realities' which in turn have 'come to be standard human behaviour in the global arena' (Alvarez Jr., 1999: 225–228). As borders become more porous and contested, notions of national belonging and citizenship become increasingly ambiguous. The border becomes rather like a bridge that enables global flows as opposed to a barrier that attempts to stop them (Flynn, 1997). Furthermore, border region status in itself can trigger migration and movements of a cross-border and transnational type. People at the margin of a nation state often face political, economic and social marginality and must consider constantly the question of whether 'to stay or to go' (Wastl-Walter et al., 2003). Border cities are often sites both of 'commuter migrants' who cross the border on a daily or weekly basis in search for work and 'long distance migrants' for whom the border city serves as a stop over on their way to a better life elsewhere (Cornelius, 2001: 662). On the other side of the argument, however, are scholars who adopt a more cautious approach to the dissolution of borders in the global cultural economy. These scholars reject the simplifying rhetoric of 'global flows' and 'borderless world' to argue that while boundaries and borders have become more flexible and overlapping in the context of globalization, they nevertheless remain an important means of organizing social space and cultural identity (Anderson & O'Dowd, 1999). While borders as highly visible, state-administered lines of demarcation between economic, political and cultural spaces might have lost in significance in many places across the world, the 'process of bordering', or the continuous process of maintaining distinctions between 'us' and 'them' or between the 'included' and the 'excluded', has become ever more prevalent and important in global society. During the 1980s and 1990s, there was a clear tendency towards the economic and political opening of borders in the wake of projects of transregional economic growth and development associated with the development and expansion of the European Union (EU) and the North American Free Trade Agreement (NAFTA). More recently, however, observers have detected a tendency towards the social and ideological 're-closing of borders' in a new 'securitization discourse'. This has been induced by the events following 9/11/2001 in New York and the increasingly intense and desperate debates about the provision of welfare in a mobilized society (Newman, 2006). In this context, there has been a shift in the dominant perception of borders from borders as a mechanism for surveilling state territory towards the role of borders in segregating and governing (il)legitimate mobilities (Amoore, 2006).

Despite this divergent emphasis on the dissolution of borders in the context of globalization, these approaches share the view that borders and boundaries are not 'fixed lines', but an ongoing and complex social and cultural process through which territories and identities are produced and reproduced (Paasi, 2001: 23, 16). Consequently, borderlands have become an analytic laboratory that rejects a one-sided approach:

> The study of state borders and border regions . . . . . challenges state centric predis-positions. However, it also has the potential to challenge facile assumptions about globalization. (Anderson & O'Dowd, *op cit*: 598)

In essence, there are two reasons why researchers on borders and border regions are reluctant to embrace fully the idea of a 'borderless world' of hybrid identities. First, borders are sites of structural ambiguity in their role as both a 'bridge' or entry point and 'door' or point of exclusion. This inherent ambiguity of borders underpins the structural ambivalence of the 'border experience'. The experience of inhabiting the borderlands can often result in social tolerance and important synergy effects can develop from looking over the fence and engaging with the 'other'. In contrast, the direct engagement with otherness in the borderlands can also produce cultural conservatism and more intense forms of 'pure identity'. Second, there are important regional specificities and contextualities with regard to border regions in disparate global locations. The development of a 'border culture', as an everyday culture with a unique cross-border pattern of meaning and identity that is significantly different from the two parent societies, is not axiomatic and depends on a range of contingent factors and circumstances. These include the (non)complementarities of the neighbouring societies, the (a)symmetry of cross-border patterns of development and the historic legacy of the border. Thus, a spectrum of national and transnational border relations can be imagined from which Martinez (1994, 1997) has developed the classic typology of 'alienated' (i.e. the Middle East, North/South Korea), 'co-existent' (i.e. Ecuador/Peru, Russia/China), 'interdependent' (i.e. USA/Mexico, Germany/Poland) and 'integrated' (i.e. Western Europe) borderlands.

The overriding effect of economic and cultural globalization has been to render borders increasingly permeable and to encourage convergence within border regions. However, it is important to be sensitive to the unique regional and historic dynamics that underpin particular border regions. The USA/Mexico border has become established as the 'paradigm case' in border research (Alvarez Jr., 1995: 449). This border stretches 3100 kilometres and is an excellent illustration of an 'interdependent' borderland. Despite substantial economic asymmetries between Mexico and the United States and a rather harsh border regime, a 'border culture' has nonetheless developed; most notably around the San Diego–Tijuan metropolitan region where Texan Anglo-Saxon culture intermingles with Mexican *norteño* culture. For Martinez (1997: 294), this *Tex-Mex* culture constitutes a distinct border way of life. Cross-border interaction is 'normal and routine' and includes the cross-borrowing of language, religion, customs, traditions, foods, clothing and architecture. Tex-Mex culture finds symbolic expression in *Tex-Mex* music: a cultural hybrid formed in the nineteenth century as the music of Scottish and German immigrants was played by Mexicans in the *Tejano* style. There are, however, a number of factors that put this rather idealized picture of synergetic border culture into perspective (Sadowski-Smith, 2002; Wood, 2004). First, *Tex-Mex* culture is rooted in the deep and enduring economic inequalities between the United States and Mexico. The border marks the meeting place between First and the Third World. This is highlighted by the recent intensification of the *maquiladora* or *Border Industrialization Program*, which is based on a combination of cheap Mexican labour and US advanced technology. Tex-Mex culture is thus a rather asymmetrical form of interdependence. While the Mexican *fronterizos* look across the border for employment opportunities, on the US side it is mainly the Mexican Americans that engage in Tex-Mex culture. In this context, cross-border stereotyping is as prevalent as ever (Fernandez Kelly, 1981: 260; Schmidt, 1997). The coexistence of Tex-Mex culture and cross-border stereotyping is only seemingly a contradiction. In fact, it reveals the ambivalence of the border as 'bridge' and 'door'. Closeness and contact do not necessarily foster a cosmopolitan attitude and, in certain circumstances, direct contact can result in the reinforcement of long standing cultural barriers. The example of *Tex-Mex* culture also highlights the importance of 'double' or 'twin cities' within border regions. Border culture is most vibrant within border cities, and Tex-Mex culture is indeed focused on the San Diego–Tijuan region (Martinez, *op cit*: 295; Sparrow, 2001). However, the lived reality in these border cities is far from the idealized picture of a distinct border culture derived from the formula 'Mexicans and Americans: two worlds, one border' (cited in Fernandez-Kelly, 1981: 261). Observers stress the structural and cultural varieties that exist within the Mexico–USA border region. There are the local 'commuter migrants' whose lifestyle is rather different from the temporary population of 'long distance migrants' drawn from regions such as Mixtec. Then there are the 'metropolitan artisans' and the 'cultural tourists' who visit the region for erotic escapades in the honky-tonks of the tourist strip. Thus, in the light of the various Mexican and non-Mexican subcultures in this example, it would seem apt to refer to border cities as 'evolving from bipolar communities (in)to complex, pluralistic places' (Arreola, 1996). It is also important to analyse border regions within a wider context of social and cultural change. Martinez (*op cit*: 295) argues that 'border culture' is not confined to the actual border region corridor and highlights examples of people migrating from Guadelajara and Mexico City to Denver and Chicago, who maintain links with their home regions and thus produce a type of translocal or transregional border culture. This culture is maintained through circular patterns of migration within 'transnational social spaces' (Pries, 1998). Hence, 'border culture' does indeed intersect with the wider landscape of global flows that constitute the disjunctive order of a 'new global cultural economy' (Appadurai, 1992). In the context of NAFTA and the development of a transnational regional economy, the United States has attempted to seal its south-western border from the entry of undocumented labour and to channel the benefits of integration between the United States and Mexico according to the needs and interests of the US economy. Since the beginning of the new Millennium, short but significant corridors of the border have been cordoned off by a range of strategies including intensified border patrols armed with infrared night scopes, high steel fencing and biometric scanning (Cornelius, 2001; Eschbach et al., 1999). The US–Mexican border thus epitomizes the paradigm shift in contemporary border regimes from the controlling of territory towards the governing of unwanted mobilities. It reveals clearly the way in which the border exists as a heavily contested site amidst a growing web of (unbalanced) interdependencies between two countries embedded within the global economy.

A somewhat different border dynamic presents itself in respect of 'the world's longest undefended border' – the Canadian–American border (Gibbins, 1997). This border does not manifest the harsh economic, social or cultural barriers that characterize many other international borders and the 8000 km border has always been very porous. However, owing to important historical and geographical dynamics, there is no evidence of a distinct border region between Canada and the United States nor has any discernible 'border culture' developed. American culture is interwoven deeply and irrevocably into Canadian life and this is a cause of great concern for many Canadians with regard to the maintenance of cultural autonomy. However, the effect is not limited to a narrow border corridor, but is prevalent throughout Canadian society. Owing to climatic factors, Canadian society is concentrated along a narrow strip within 150 km of the US/Canadian border. Culture on the USA side of the border is focused predominantly on the heartland rather than on Canada and thus, 'Canada at large can be seen as a borderlands society' (Gibbins, *ibid*: 321) that lacks a counterpart on the USA side of the border. However, recent developments have had a lasting impact here too. Observes argue that in the wake of 'securitization', the USA–Canada boundary which has 'traditionally (been) seen as a "soft" boundary, has become much more difficult to cross' (Newman, 2006: 149). This examination of the contrasting border regions in North America has highlighted the extent to which 'every state border, every border region, is unique' (O'Dowd, 1999: 594) and the problem of generalizing the outcome of the globalization processes for border regions. Rather, the sub-global regional dynamics that intersect with the processes of globalization are of crucial importance in detecting concrete patterns of de- and re-bordering and grasping the role that respective border regions play within the resulting uneven geography of global transformation. In this respect, it might be said that the American–Canadian border is unlikely to turn into a 'hot spot' of societal transition, even though changes in USA border policy in the wake of 9/11 have accentuated the visibility of this 'friendly border' for those that inhabit the border region (Konrad & Nicol, 2004). The German–Polish borderland, on the other hand, owing to its role in articulating post-socialist developments within a global cultural economy, can certainly be described as such a hotspot and we now turn our focus towards this comparatively small, but analytically significant, borderland.

'Interdependent Borderlands' or 'Wild Zone'? The German–Polish Border Region

The German–Polish border is part of a larger border strip that traverses the middle of Europe and marks the former 'system border' between East and West. Following the events of 1989, and in a context of an emerging discourse of European integration, this corridor – stretching from the Russian-Finish border down to the border of Slovenia with Austria and Italy – has become an intense focus of academic research (Meinhof, 2003; Paasi, 1999; Wastl-Walter et al., 2003). However, the re-unification of Germany in 1990 altered significantly the landscape of this border corridor by shifting a comparatively small, but historically significant, part of the East–West border further to the East. In this context, the socio-cultural and socio-economic dynamics of the German–Polish border have become a particular focus of interest (Bürkner & Matthiesen, 2001; Dürrschmidt, 2006; Galasiński & Meinhof, 2002; Krätke, 1996). Between 1945 and 1989, the border between the German Democratic Republic (GDR) and Poland had many characteristics of an 'iron curtain' itself, despite being a border between two aligned socialist countries. In the period following 1989, this border region has become an important 'social laboratory' in at least two ways. First, the border is positioned at the intersection between global restructuring and European transformation and, as a consequence, is a hot spot of intense disembedding and re-embedding processes with regard to institutional transfer and social mobility. The region highlights the way transnationalism as a broader social trend is not confined to the (trans)migrant experience, but also includes more complex forms of local cross-border life (Kennedy & Roudometof, 2002: 1). Second, while 'Europe' remains an abstract term of identification for most Europeans, the imme-diate encounter of Polish and German culture and society in the region has created a situation in which the borderlanders have the opportunity to engage with Europe as a 'lived place' (Paasi, 2001: 10). This borderland should, therefore, be an ideal setting for an exploration of whether the emerging transboundary culture is inclined towards 'cosmopolitan place' and 'cosmopolitan citizenship' (Entrikin, 1999; Held, 2000: 402). However, while the border has become semi-open and cross-border interaction has developed at various levels, the border has lost little of its significance, either for the people living in the border region or for wider German and Polish society. On the contrary, it is in the context of a clear-cut border becoming porous and contested that complex border issues have mater-ialized and a complex 'geography of difference' (Harvey, 1996) has been revealed. This highlights the relevance of what Beck (2002, 2004: 134) has referred to as 'passive cosmopolitanism' or the latent and unintended cosmopolitanization of everyday life, which is particularly likely to occur where landscapes of national identity and affiliation have been redrawn. In this context, finding a sense of belonging and cultural identity implies 'literally looking across at the other' (Galasiński & Meinhof, *op cit*: 23).

Prior to 1945, the German–Polish border region of today was a unified economic and socio-cultural space. Following the Second World War, the current border was re-drawn between Germany and Poland and the contemporary socio-cultural make up of the region still reflects a 'culture of displacement' that goes back to the resettlement policies on both sides during and after the Second World War (Galsińksi & Meinhof, *op cit*; Gruchman & Walk, 1997: 177; Krätke, 1999: 638). On the Polish side, people came mainly from what are now Russian territories, while on the German side many came from parts of pre-war Germany that became part of Poland in 1945 (Meinhof, 2003: 785; Jajeśniak-Quast & Stokłosa, 2000). These ethno-spatial cleavages were suppressed by political closure and socialist ideology in the post-war period, but maintained a lingering presence in the collective consciousness. The border is marked by one of the harshest language barriers in Europe and, on the German-side Polish language competence is almost nonexistent. Thus, despite the brave work of some 'boundary brokers' in regional politics and local civil society, the prevailing 'low trust environment' (Krätke, 1998: 250–258) appears to be a serious developmental blockage with regard to the emergence of forms of cross-border cooperation embedded in everyday culture. Empirical studies have highlighted that the increasingly permeable state border has not diluted the rigid stereotyping between the neighbouring communities (Dolinska & Falkowski, 2001; Lisiecki, 1996). Cross-border integration is also undermined by the way that two divergent post-socialist pathways (Stark & Bruszt, 1998) collide within the region. Important 'path dependencies' have developed based on the divergent strategies that Poland and the former-GDR have pursued with regard to the transformation towards liberal democracy and a market economy. The legacy of socialism has had a differential impact on life world, civil society and institutional restructuring on the two sides of the border. While the East German pathway is framed by the 'silent' accession to the EU through German reunification, Poland has followed a strategy inspired by the neo-liberal doctrines of the International Monetary Fund (IMF). In East Germany, this resulted in a 'gradualist' transformation through the transfer of a functioning welfare system and bureaucratic elite from West Germany. In contrast, Polish society has experienced social change as a 'big bang', with the rapid introduction of market mechanisms, a minimal welfare net and an emphasis on private initiative from below (Offe, 1996: 131; Zukrowska, 2000). The existence of a substantial differential in wage levels in Germany and Poland of between 10:1 and 8:1 throughout the 1990s (Gruchman & Walk, *op cit*; Krätke 1996: 660; 1998: 254) highlights the embeddedness of the different pathways of socio-economic transformation (Gorzelak & Jałowiecki, 2002). These framing conditions tend not to favour cross-border cooperation, even, or especially, within the twin cities along the border where these differences are manifested in daily life (Matthiesen, 2002; Meinhof, *op cit*).

These path-dependent trajectories of transition intersect with wider patterns of socio-economic and cultural restructuring to inhibit the process of cross-border integration. The German–Polish border region is located at the heart of multi-layered processes of restructuring whereby European space(s) are being transformed within a globalized socio-economic and cultural landscape (Paasi, *op cit*; Therborn, 2000). The Eastward expansion of the EU highlights the way in which new geometries of power are emerging around both visible and invisible boundaries. While this process is framed in terms of the integration and connectivity of Eastern Europe, it also provides a way of managing the European region in the interests of the established members of the EU. This has involved the tightening of borders to unwanted neighbours (and potential new members) and generating new 'winners' and 'losers' within the 'European House'. The attempt to generate a globally competitive pan-European space has resulted in both shifting political and economic boundaries and a new spatial pattern of regional centres and peripheries (Heidenreich, 2003; Hudson, 2003). In this respect, the German–Polish border region finds itself in danger of becoming 'leapfrogged' by new patterns of transregional cooperation (Krätke, 1999: 632; 1996: 655). Thus, as the region is bypassed by global flows and regional transport corridors it appears as a 'black hole of marginality' within the new global division of labour (Castells, 2001a: 410). The restructuring of the traditional industrial base of the border region, with its emphasis on clothing, textiles, furniture and steel, has resulted in plant closures or redundancies. Unemployment on both sides of the border is above the respective national average(s) with levels hovering around 20 per cent along the border corridor. Unemployment on the German side would be even higher were it not for the existence of a state-sponsored, secondary labour market in the form of the ABM (*Arbeitsbesuchaffungs-massnahmen*) programme. Consequently, outward migration has become a serious problem for the border region and this has undermined both its demographic base and the urban and civic culture of its border cities. This has been particularly serious on the German side because of the comparative attractiveness of relocating to the more prosperous regions of Western Germany. The everyday discourse thus speaks of 'dying cities' and encourages the young generation to leave the region in order to pursue a brighter future elsewhere. Many of the border towns have lost up to 30 per cent of their population since 1989 (Matthiesen, 2005). The impact of this on civic culture cannot be overstated, as it is usually the best qualified and most talented people who take the exit option.

This thinning out of civic culture and civil society is not an encouraging precondition for the development of a transborder culture. The softening of the territorial and administrative border between Germany and Poland has not encouraged the formation of a cultural and social environment that could be described as a synergetic transborder community. Serious structural problems and a deep awareness of being part of a 'loser' region have failed to encourage joint activities and strategies. The border region thus provides evidence that 'overlapping communities of fate' do not necessarily foster the 'cosmopolitan project' of a genuine interest in 'the other' or the perception of the border situation as one of 'relevant community' (Held, *op cit*: 399).

Between 'Europhoria' and 'Europhobia': The Festivalization of Borderland Politics

The impact of globalization and Europeanization on the German–Polish border region has failed to result in the generation of a shared cosmopolitan or European culture in this zone of transition. The two border societies, and their respective everyday cultures, have drifted apart despite their spatial proximity, the existence of a softened state border and the shared fate of peripheralization. The only shared communicative horizon can be found in the discourse of the 'dying region', which is prevalent in everyday discourse and culture on both sides of the border. In this context, there have been attempts by local and regional political elites to counteract the threat of disjuncture between the two sides of the border region. During the 1990s, the Council of Europe sponsored the formation of 'Euroregions' which were subsequently established in order to promote common interests and cooperation between contiguous territories in two or more European countries. These Euroregions established an institutional framework for cross-border cooperation and integration between 'Europe' and 'Not-Yet-Europe'. However, a decade after their foundation, observers had come to the somewhat sobering assessment that, with their emphasis on infrastructural projects such as water refinement plants and their adherence to national and local administrative hierarchies, Euroregions have contributed little to cultural integration. A significant gap has developed between programmatic objectives, which include the promotion of a sense of European identity, and observable results (Chessa, 2004; Krätke, 1996: 651; Scott, 1999). The identity-generating power of the 'Euroregions' and the declaration of twin cities as 'Model-Eurotowns' have been overestimated and these political projects have become increasingly self-referential and have failed to generate grassroots support. What is increasingly visible is a disjuncture between political discourse and everyday life discourse, between *institutionalized Europhoria* and *latent Europhobia*. This is also reflected in the sensitivity of the local life world to the changing vibes of the European political project, marked by a generalized reduction in enthusiasm for the grand political project of European integration. Hence, the notion of constructing a 'European House' based on cultural integration and pan-European values has been transformed into a narrow neo-liberal project of economic integration. Hence, the initial enthusiasm of the accession countries to European integration has given way to more ambivalent feelings associated with 'having to make the grade' in terms of quantifiable convergence criteria (Agnew, 2001: 32–34; Boxhorn, 1996). This new framing of the European project has had a counterproductive impact on the 'border crossing capacity' of those living in the border region (Anderson & O'Dowd, *op cit*: 598). Thus, the German–Polish border region highlights how the decline of the border as a clear-cut line of demarcation between neighbouring political and social spaces is being replaced by a more sophisticated 'bordering process'. This process has developed along the various scales and levels of political governance and is experienced by inhabitants of the border region through its impact on sociospatial activity in the everyday life of border towns (Newman, 2006: 144).

The laudable attempts of local and regional politicians to promote European integration as a source of identity formation have thus been emptied out and transformed into a form of 'symbolic politics' or, more prosaically, a 'festivalization of politics' (Häußermann & Siebel, 1993). European Integration and the enlargement of the EU eastwards have become important tools in the toolbox of 'symbolic politics'. We can illustrate this point by looking at the various symbolisms of Europeanized local politics that twin cities were able to attain during the 1990s. There was a plethora of *European Medals, European Diplomas and European Flags* with which border cities could be decorated. Several have been proudly declared 'Model Experiment Euro Town' (Matthiesen, *op cit*: 79). Marked emphasis is placed on the location of these cities at the heart of a 'Euroregion' and there are various types of European funding attached to this status. However, this governance approach has proved ambivalent, for while the symbolic discourse of 'Europeanization' is aimed primarily at attracting investors to the region, the lack of success in this respect has undermined popular enthusiasm for the European project on both sides of the border. Indeed, the increasing gap between ambition and results has had counterproductive effects as far as the relationship between political discourse and the culture of everyday life. The discursive image of a 'Euroregion' and a 'Euro Town' playing a pioneering role in the process European integration and restructuring, stands in stark contrast to the popular self-perception of everyday life in a dying and forgotten region. This has resulted in a second dimension to 'symbolic politics': namely, its 'festivalization' proper. In the context of a lack of tangible results, it becomes vital to relieve the tension between expectation and results through the orchestration of popular events. The border and twin cities along the German–Polish border are the stage for well-organized and well-attended cross-border festivities and festivals, with folklore, drink and food in abundance. However, these events can only temporarily mask the growing disjuncture between the claims of symbolic politics and the harsh reality of a border region trapped in the process of 'cumulative peripheralization' (Matthiesen, *ibid*: 75). The problems surfacing in the German–Polish border region are not just of theoretical interest, but have important implications for public policy. What is at stake here is the configuration of inclusion/exclusion, or rather the pattern of *inclusion/integration* associated with the process of EU-enlargement to the East. While integration at the level of economic system and political institutions appears to have occurred with ease and speed, the cultural inclusion of member societies with all their various collective identities is lagging far behind (Spohn, 2000). This mismatch within the EU-enlargement process manifests itself in the translocal everyday culture of the border region. The long-term cost of this cleavage between inclusion and integration and between (local) people and a transnational elites is already being paid in terms of heightened levels of public disaffection and an increase in political populism (Grzymała-Busse & Innes, 2003; Mudde, 2000).

The Legacy of (Post-) Socialism or the Victory Crisis of Western Modernity?

Behind the disjuncture between Europhoria and Europhobia in the East–West European border region, another far-reaching problem of transition and change reveals itself. The failure to generate an active and vibrant Europeanized border culture, alongside the administrative and institutional preparations for European unity, is only the most visible aspect of a general tendency towards a declining enthusiasm for change and transition in the post-socialist societies of East-Central Europe. This 'ten years after' or 'nostalgia syndrome' (Kostecki, 2000) is an interesting and puzzling question. The initial enthusiasm and pioneering spirit that underpinned the project of transforming post-socialist societies into open and democratic societies and active and vibrant building blocks in a global cosmopolitan order has become increasingly less prominent. Piotr Sztompka, a prominent analytical voice from that region, asks:

> Why is all this so awfully difficult? What bad fortunes keep us – Eastern and Central Europeans – from attaining the goal of democratic polity, market economy and open culture, once the proverbial Wall has crumbled? (Sztompka, 1993: 86)

The answers to this question generally tend to point in two directions. The first highlights the civilizational legacy of socialism and the persistence of a socialist mentality long after the break down of socialist society. The second, questions the efficiency of the full-scale transfer of western institutional structures into the transition countries of East-Central Europe. The positions meet in the assumption that there is a misfit between the 'new' modernizing institutional framework and 'old' socialist attitudes: that is, between structure and agency. In essence, the first position argues that 'civilizational incompetence' produced a blockage and a paralysis of entrepreneurial, civic and discursive culture during state socialism. The paternalist features of state socialism resulted in a decline in civic virtues and a thinning out of self-organizing civil society. Some commentators argue that behind this 'civilizational incompetence' is the lasting impact of two fundamental pathways of social development within Europe itself. The line between comparatively successful (e.g. the Baltic States, Poland, Slovakia and Hungary) and comparatively unsuccessful (e.g. Russia, Rumania and Yugoslavia) post-socialist transformation is said to coincide with the old dividing line between Roman and Byzantine civilizations with their divergent urban cultures and civic traditions (Gorzelak & Jałowiecki, 2002; Panther, 1998). Thus, somewhat ironically, an effective cultural barrier has come to the fore only after the actual Wall has crumbled. This is particularly lamentable as a functioning civil society is essential to bridge the gap between 'new' institutions and 'old' everyday life cultures (Srubar, 1994; Sztompka, *op cit*).).

Thus, 'homo sovieticus' with entrenched habits of passivity and state dependency, has survived despite the introduction of market forces and institutions of liberal democracy (Bryant, 1994: 66). There is, of course, an element of truth in this position particularly in the context of the (so far) limited time horizon of post-socialist transformation. Developments in East-Central Europe highlight the extent to which mentalities, attitudes and habits have their own cultural logic and persistence. There are limits to the extent that mental patterns can be altered swiftly or new civic patterns fostered by institutional design and framing. Dahrendorf (1990) has argued that a time span of 60 years will need to elapse before a rooted civil society will once again be functioning in East-Central Europe. Thus, while the 'hard' structures of organizational and institutional frameworks have been transferred with comparative ease, the 'soft' infrastructure of the post-socialist life world constitutes a real obstacle to post-socialist development (Sztompka, *op cit*: 86).

A second and alternative interpretation of the barriers that have developed to social change in East-Central Europe would argue that the focus on the mental legacy of socialism obscures the way in which the costs associated with the transformation process militate against change. This includes the intrinsic devaluation of biographies and social milieux within the transformation process (Kostecki, *op cit*; Wingens, 1999: 257). There is an increasing awareness that the ongoing process of post-socialist transformation implies a continuing 'status insecurity' for many individuals and a new polarization of 'winners' and 'losers'. Furthermore, the period of 'extraordinary' and charismatic politics is giving way to an ongoing period of time consuming and complex reforms marked by increasing bureaucratisation. There have been few visible improvements for the masses, who are exhorted regularly to new levels of delayed gratification. In this context, there has been an increase in social dissatisfaction and resistance and a new gap is opening up between what the new elites can realistically offer and what the people expect (Balcerowicz, 2000; Bauman 1994; Grzymała-Busse & Innes, 2003; Kostecki, *op cit*).

This raises a series of important and interesting questions with regard to the ambiguous effects of the wholesale transfer of Western institutions into Central and Eastern Europe in the period since 1989. Stark & Bruszt (1998: 81) argue that the people of East-Central Europe have an understandably healthy scepticism of large scale, top-down experiments in social engineering (Bryant, *op cit*). Moreover, it could be suggested that the misfit between 'new' institutions and 'old' everyday cultures is due, at least partly, to the large-scale institutional transfer from West to East. The 'cook book' style transfer of a 'modern' institutional model that was already itself in crisis and in transition towards 'reflexive modernity' has triggered something of a 'victory crisis' (Beck, 1997). The events of 1989 forced Western Modernity to fill what seemed like an institutional void in East-Central Europe with its own outdated and worn out institutional blueprint. However, there are serious doubts as to whether this wholesale transfer was the right medicine for the patient, particularly in the light of the divergent historical conditions between 1989 and 1945 when most of the Western European institutional framework started to emerge. Moreover, the new democracies of East-Central Europe have to deal with problems of a hybrid character. These societies face simultaneously the challenges of globalization and rectifying the problems associated with an undeveloped technological and communicative infrastructure. In other words, these societies have to deal with problems of First *and* Second Modernity in the unique conditions of post-socialism. In the light of this consideration, it is perhaps more appropriate to talk of an 'institutional legacy of the transition process' rather than simply referring back to the 'legacy of socialism'.

There is 'neither model nor precedent for the transition from real existing socialism to democracy and capitalism' (Bryant & Mokrzycki, 1994: 3). This applies, not only to the divergent conditions in East and Western Europe, but also to the continuity between the transitions to democracy in Southern Europe (Portugal, Spain and Greece) during the 1970s, South America (Argentina, Brazil, Uruguay, Chile and Paraguay) in the 1980s and the post-communist transitions in East-Central Europe from 1989 onwards (Linz & Stephan, 1996). In contrast to the political focus of earlier transitions, the transformations in East-Central Europe have important economic and cultural dynamics. In the context of the obvious blockages and the variety and complexity of change faced by the post-socialist countries, it is perhaps more appropriate to see this process of change as a new 'great transformation' (Balcerowicz, 2000: 234; Bryant & Mokrzycki, *op cit*: 1994). The emphasis here is on the complexity and the uncharted character of transformation. There are no 'comprehensive blueprints' to facilitate an all-encompassing process of institutional change and thus each country and region has forged its own 'pathway' from state socialism to open society (Grabher & Stark, 1997; Stark & Bruszt, *op cit*: 82). While the term *transition* implies a rather fixed process, with a clearly defined starting point and destination, the notion of *transformation* shifts the emphasis towards the processual nature of change and emphasizes its hybrid and open-ended outcomes. Framed in this way, the regions of East-Central Europe remain a social laboratory in which new forms of society might emerge and, following Bauman, it could be argued that the post-socialist transformational societies are 'sunk in the liminal condition'.

The abandoned structure does not survive the movement; and the arrived-at structure is not in any real sense fixed before the movement starts. (Bauman, 1994: 16f)

Few people expected this state of liminality to endure for so long. This state of liminality or no-mans-land of the betwixt and between, neither socialism nor capitalism, neither state-authoritarianism nor civil society is puzzling to both the politicians, who are in desperate need of realistic policies, and the masses who are in search of the historical embeddednes of their individual and collective biographies.

Thus, the persistence of post-socialist mentalities, habits and milieux is too simplistic an explanation for the ambiguous patterns of social and cultural change in post-socialist societies. While there is evidence that, in conditions of prolonged liminality, people refrain from political discourse and retreat into the relative stability of a familiar milieux, it is too simplistic to subsume these tendencies under the formula 'resorting to the orientations of real socialism' (Srubar, 1994: 200). Rather than speaking of the continued existence of 'homo sovieticus', it is perhaps more accurate to refer to those caught in a situation of multiple transformation and undertaking an ongoing journey through uncharted waters as 'homo liminalitus' or 'threshold people' (Turner, 1997: 95). Paraphrasing Beck (*op cit*: 90), we could ask: how much transition and liminality can a person survive? In the light of the continuing change in all spheres of life, and no obvious policy solution to a complex cluster of pressing

socio-economic and environmental problems, is not the retreat from political discourse and civic engagement into the relative stability of the private
milieu rather normal? This process of individual retreat and collective withdrawal could be subsumed under what Castells (*op cit*: 402) has described
as the 'defensive spaces' generated by those marginalized by a globalizing
post-industrial modernity. However, this is also a rather simplistic explanation based on the dichotomy between mobilized/globalized and tradi-
tional/localized milieux (Giddens, 1994: 100). The hybrid element in these
seemingly passive tendencies of withdrawal do not derive simply from the
persistence of a stubborn socialist tradition, but are also the outcome of
an active and reflexive positioning towards the demands of a radicalized
modernity that has gripped every aspect of society. This process involves an
active counter-balancing of unprecedented demands in terms of learning,
adaptability and mobility. These tendencies are thus the outcome of both
radicalized modernity and the legacy of state socialism. Perhaps it is more
appropriate to relate the ambiguous realities of post-socialist everyday life
culture to a 'modern counter-modern milieu' (Keim, 1997: 390) and ponder
Keim's admittedly provocative question as to whether these hybrid post-
socialist/modern milieux perhaps provide the right answer to the wrong
type of modernization.

Strategies of Transclusion: Hypermobility and Symbolisms of Belonging

It can be argued that the retreat and closure of local milieux within
post-socialist society is premised on sophisticated forms of 'transclusion'.
Transclusion refers to the simultaneous balancing of opening and closure,
engagement and non-engagement, in a glocalizing landscape of opportunity structures and networks of obligation. The concept highlights a
tendency, common in many forms of transnational migration, towards a
reduced engagement in the place of residence in order to be more attuned
to options and obligations elsewhere. It is linked to ideas of 'presence
availability' (Giddens, 1986) and 'absentee landlordism' (Bauman, 1998b).
In the specific context of marginalized post-socialist borderlands discussed
here, it draws attention to how the processes of post-socialist transformation overlap with more general processes of structural disembedding.
Post-socialist socio-economic stratification is marked by the intertwining
processes of professional relocation, the rupturing of vocational careers,
the relocation of social status, geographical and symbolic mobility, the
opening and closure of new opportunity structures and accelerated individualization tendencies. What people experience is thus a rupturing of
old frames of reference and familiar socioscapes, whilst being confronted

with the options and challenges of globalizing sociospheres. The same ambivalence can also be expressed in less cosy terms: people have lost the social security of socialist society and gained the freedom/obligation to find their place in a globalizing post-industrial society. There are two partially complementary coping strategies that are not peculiar to the peripheralized German–Polish borderlands, but make themselves disproportionately felt there – *hypermobility* and the retreat into the *symbolisms of belonging*.

We illustrated the first process earlier in relation to the loss of demographic stability in the German–Polish border region. However, it is not just the sheer number of those leaving the region that highlights the hypermobility associated with post-industrial restructuring. The new patterns of mobility have also affected those who decided to stay. There are people in their late-1950s/early-1960s that commute on a weekly basis across Germany in order to work in The Netherlands, but who remain committed to maintaining their 'home' in the German–Polish border region. Hence, these people are increasingly, and often involuntarily, detached from developments in the community. In this context, events on the Polish side of the border are not a major consideration. There is, therefore, a new type of 'absentee landlordism' (Bauman, *ibid*) that accounts for the blasé attitude towards the neighbour on the other side of the border. Here we see the enforced mobility of the lower layers of society, where absence from the daily life of the border community is a forced freedom rather than a choice. The point here is not to lament the mobility demands of a post-industrial society, but to indicate the costs that this interplay of presence/absence can have for civil society.

Alternatively, there are those individuals who are unable or refuse to comply with the increased levels of mobility imposed by radicalized modernity. Here we encounter a celebration of place in a narrower sense. In the context of a prevailing affective detachment from the region and the city, there is often an intense focussing on the immediate surroundings of home and the daily routines in which individuals are embedded. As Sennett (1999: 14; see also Häußermann, 1997: 24) argues, the celebration of place plays an important role in the separation of an individual's 'sense of self' from the negative consequences of workplace restructuring in the context of post-Fordist flexibility and its associated culture of (personal) failure and dislocation. Sennett (*op cit*: 23), however, suggests that this retreat into the 'symbolism of belonging' presupposes a vibrant civic urban culture that helps to preserve a sense of self-worth. If that urbanity is lacking, as is the case in the German–Polish border region, place tends to be celebrated on more exclusionary terms. Well-ordered daily routines and spatial arrangements underpin the drawing of a line between the familiar 'world inside' and a hostile 'world outside'. This 'world outside' encompasses public space and neighbourly relations in both the narrow (street neighbours) and wider (Polish neighbours) meaning of the term. Nevertheless, the people who experience this 'closure' more or less frequently cross the border. They do so in order to acquire cheap goods and services, and in the process often develop sufficient language competency for trade-related conversation. In the context of enduring disparities in costs of living and living standards between Germany and Poland, this trade helps to stretch the comparatively low income of the East German borderlanders. More important, however, is the symbolic upgrading of the milieu, for each time these German boundary-crossers return from the Polish side they claim, with a kind of sorry relief: 'they're worse off than us' (Dürrschmidt, 2002).

There is a further example of the interplay between pathways of post-socialist transformation and wider processes of global disembedding that helps to illustrate emerging patterns of 'transclusion'. It concerns the local elite on the Polish side of the border. These 'self-made social climbers' have flourished in the golden years of a booming bazaar economy, some directly as traders and others more indirectly through related services jobs such as tax advisers. This pattern of social mobility tends to reflect the 'big bang' pathway of Polish transformation, which has resulted in marked patterns of polarization within Polish society. As 'winners' in this process, the biographical trajectories of this elite have started to resemble the American experience of the *self-made man* (or woman!) rather than the reality on the German side of the border which is marked by a 'gradualist' pathway of transformation embedded in the German welfare system. There are, therefore, indications that the Polish elite are developing an affinity for the American way of life. This is reflected both in their desire for symbolically charged consumer items and in their striving to achieve a standard of living comparable to the United States rather than Germany. Thus, the American way of life tend to replace the German 'neighbour' from across the border when it comes to comparing living standards, measuring social achievement and allocating true affinities. This affinity is reflected in the way this elite have established their younger generation onto American-style career paths. Through the Internet, placement agencies and elite networking, children are sent to the United States for 'gap years' where they undertake language courses and placements in American banks and companies and are encouraged to maintain social contacts across the Atlantic on their return. This process is underpinned by the influence of print and television media and through narrative and personal contact (Dürrschmidt, *op cit*) and results in an orientation towards the global socio-cultural landscape rather than towards the immediate neighbour. This can be described as an affinity-based 'globalized west drift' of the regional elite that operates in the opposite direction to the institutional process of European integration (Dürrschmidt & Matthiesen, 2002).

In this context, it is unsurprising that cross-border contacts are kept to a necessary minimum by this segment of Polish border society. While those who work for local or regional government are obliged to conform to the official discourse of European integration, as private people they have failed to develop into pioneers of a border-crossing everyday life culture.

Owing to these developments, the German–Polish border region remains an important social laboratory with regard to the prospects for cosmo-politan order and citizenship. Cosmopolitan citizenship is defined by its capability to mediate national and transnational structures of belonging, loyalties, rights and obligations (Albrow & O'Byrne, 2000; Held, *op cit*: 402). The case of the German–Polish border region raises important questions concerning the extent to which this form of citizenship can be generated and sustained in the less favourable context of post-socialist transform-ation and post-industrial peripheralization. More generally, how sustain-able is a social fabric that establishes transnational connections between distant localities across nation states (Germany/Netherlands, Poland/US) but where translocal connections that cross state borders and cultural boundaries remain weak and undeveloped? There is clearly a disjunc-ture between the politically enforced 'institutionalized cosmopolitanism' of regional and local political elites and the 'actually existing cosmo-politanization' in the everyday life strategies of the borderlanders (cf. Beck, 2004). These forms of disjunctive cosmopolitanism and patterns of 'cultural transclosure' in the German–Polish border region reveal complex coping strategies that are not amenable to simple categorization and moral censure. Rather, they are part of a complex and intermingling geography of rejection, engagement and approved detachment that defies simple notions of cosmopolitanism or the diametric opposition of transnational elite and xenophobic locals (Dürrschmidt, *op cit* ; Paasi, *op cit*).

Summary and Conclusion

In this chapter, we have highlighted the way in which the analysis of border regions provides key insights into the shifting landscapes of power and identity in the global cultural economy. We argued that the trans-formation of the border regions is underpinned by the same dynamics of disembedding and re-embedding that underpin the development of the global city. Both are social microcosms which bundle together the prin-cipal dynamics and consequences of contemporary social change. Both are sites of increasingly complex social interaction and contested identity formation and intense sites of migration flows and attempts to channel them. With regard to the overarching question of continuity and change, borders have maintained continuity with regard to their inherent quality of generating both mediation and closure. Thus, despite borders becoming more porous through processes of globalization, the ambiguous status of borders as 'bridge' and 'door' continue to produce complex patterns of openness and closure, engagement and non-engagement. However, we can also observe crucial discontinuities with regard to the form and function of borders since the onset of globalization processes. The initial tendency towards increasingly open borders emerged as part of the neo-liberal project of globalism during the 1980s and 1990s. More recently, however, there has been a tendency towards the re-closing of borders as a result of the securitization discourse associated with the aftermath of 9/11. However, this does not imply that we have returned to the modern system of clearly demarcated nation state territories with clear-cut and continuous borderlines. Rather we see a tendency towards borders being reconfigured along newly emerging patterns of migration networks and transport corridors that attempt to control mobility rather than territory. This implies an overall shift of emphasis from 'the border' as a state-administered line of demarcation to the border as a 'bordering process' that involves a multitude of actors operating across a variety of scales and levels. Of particular interest in this context is the question as to what extent the border regions themselves retain significance for the reordering of the global cultural economy.

In the second part of the chapter, we focused in particular detail on the unique structural dynamic of a border region that has become a hot spot of intense social change. We explored the German–Polish border to highlight how the border dynamic operates in tandem with the broader changes associated with post-socialist transformation, European integration and neo-liberal globalism. We observed that these dynamics were combining to produce a situation marked by wide scale industrial decline, symbolic and largely unsuccessful forms of cross-border political engagement focused on reversing this decline and an intense process of transclusion based on new patterns of translocal hypermobility and the retreat into the symbolisms of belonging. It was particularly noticeable that this setting did not induce the utopia of a synergetic cross-border culture, and in this context, we argued that the complex socio-cultural geography of rejection, detachment and yet also engagement within the region did indeed reflect the complex 'this-as-well-as-that-realities' of a society in transition.

4

The Workplace in Transition: Labour, Time and Space

For the majority of people, other than the chosen few, in the present day flexible labour market, embracing one's work as a vocation carries enormous risks and is a recipe for psychological and emotional disaster.

(Zygmunt Bauman, 1998a: 35)

The workplace is an important 'hotspot' of transition. The central dynamic underpinning this transition is a prolonged period of capitalist restructuring on a global scale and the development and application of information and communications technology (ICT). The development of the 'networked' transnational corporation (TNC) has changed fundamentally the nature of the production process and the organizational form of the productive enterprise. The networked organization is less bound by the constraints of geography and the rigid and hierarchical Fordist enterprise of the industrial age has morphed into the flexible and footloose 'networked enterprise' of the informational age. The application of ICT to the production process has thus deepened the new international division of labour that first emerged during the 1970s, enabling TNCs to outsource an increasing range of both manufacturing and service functions in order to exploit cheap labour in Asia, Africa and Latin America. As Bauman (ibid) suggests, work in the industrial societies of Europe and North America has become increasingly flexible and insecure and, in this context, increasingly 'de-centred' as a source of social meaning and social identity. This tendency has been encouraged and to some extent facilitated by new 'unitary' management techniques that attempt to marginalize and bypass established forms of industrial democracy and forms of workplace representation based on autonomous and independent trade unions.

The interplay between globalization and capital accumulation has produced patterns of complexity and ambiguity with regard to contemporary production processes. According to Scholte (2005: 159–184), there are three interrelated developments associated with the globalization of

57

production. First, globalization has strengthened capitalism as the world structure of production. The development of global product and financial flows, in the context of the development and consolidation of the information, marketing, communications and biotechnology industries, has both expanded and entrenched capitalism as a system of production operating at an increasingly world scale. Second, the development of transplanetary and supraterritorial social spaces has facilitated intensified surplus accumulation and commodification in the areas of primary production and heavy industry, and the expansion of surplus accumulation and commodification into new sectors and industries including finance, retail, communications, caring, education and bio- and nanotechnology. Third, the expansion of 'transworld' links has encouraged significant shifts in the organization of capitalism including the development of TNCs, global outsourcing and the development of 'export processing zones'(EPZs), off-shore financial centres and global mergers and acquisitions. The central argument of this chapter is that the sociological consequences of this complexity cannot be grasped adequately through the application of simplistic models of workplace change that presuppose a linear shift from industrial to post-industrial society, from Fordism to post-Fordism or from modern to postmodern workplace identity. Indeed, a cursory glace at contemporary production networks highlights the way in which globalization has not encouraged a straightforward shift from an 'industrial' to a 'post-industrial' economy. The contemporary production of motor vehicles, for example, combines one of the most Fordist industries in the form of steel production and processing with advanced processes of computer-aided design and software engineering. Thus, the old sectors have survived on an increasingly global organizational scale while new industries and sectors have developed and proliferated alongside them. In this context, we attempt to make sense of recent changes in the organization of production through the concepts of 'reflexive accumulation' and 'informational' or 'virtual' capitalism that in its scope and intensity can be most usefully described as a form of 'hyper-capitalism' (Scholte, *ibid*: 160).

In this chapter, we focus on the non-linear and complex changes that have marked the recent phase of workplace restructuring. As in the previous chapters, we approach this through an empirical investigation of an area that is a 'hotspot' of disembedding and re-embedding, in this case an exploration of the global financial services industry with a particular focus on the phenomenon of business process outsourcing (BPO) associated with the growth and development of 'call centres'. We suggest that current trends in contemporary work and employment resonate with the trends that we can observe in the call centre workplace (for a broader and more detailed discussion of contemporary trends see Bradley et al., 2000; Castells, 2000a; Eaton, 2000; Noon & Blyton, 2002). The consumer, finance and information sectors are increasingly dominant in terms of market capitalization and shareholder returns and mark out the geographic 'hotspots' and 'wastelands' of the contemporary global economy (Scholte, *op cit*: 176). Hence, we follow the logic of this book to suggest that call centre employment in the financial services industry is an intense 'hotspot' of social change that can provide crucial insights into more general trends and developments in the area of workplace restructuring and changing forms of workplace identity and culture.

We begin by outlining the principal dynamics and forms underpinning the development of the global economy and the ways in which this process combined with the development and application of ICT is transforming the nature of work and employment in the developed and developing world. We suggest that capitalism is indeed becoming increasingly informational and reflexive and that this raises a number of important questions with regard to contemporary trajectories of workplace restructuring. First, does the form of work and employment typified by the call centre environment mark the end or reversal of the model of scientific management or 'Taylorism' that dominated workplace relations in the modern era? Does the increasing reflexivity of work in 'second' modernity result in the re-skilling and upgrading of work within the labour processes of informational capitalism? Second, does the informational or reflexive workplace reconstitute the subjectivity of workers or result in the transformation of workplace culture and identities? In particular, does the informational workplace encourage individualistic orientations amongst workers and thereby undermine the forms of collective workplace culture associated with modern trade unionism? How does the informational workplace reconstitute relations of power within the workplace or make power less visible by embedding power within the networks of informational capitalism? Does this imply a rejection of Weberian and Marxian models of workplace relations in favour of a model based on the Foucauldian notion that workplace control is increasingly secured through inter-subjective self-discipline? Third, how does the reflexive nature and affective content of informational labour transform gender relations within the workplace and to what extent do these developments result in the 'feminization' of work and employment? In particular, does the performance of 'emotional labour' redefine gender relations within the workplace or make the performance of sexuality more central to workplace culture and identity? Fourth, how does the outsourcing of call centre work to places such as India impact on workers in the developing world and the relations between Indian workers and their colleagues and customers in places such as the United States and the United Kingdom? Do such developments highlight the placelessness and virtuality of informational capitalism or is it possible to highlight tensions and disjuncture between divergent places in global production networks? Finally, what are the prospects for established forms of industrial democracy and the strength and vitality of trade unions in the informational and reflexive workplace? In the context of powerful dynamics of disembedding and re-embedding, what are the prospects for the emergence of new networks of obligation and collective cultures of resistance within sectors such as the global call centre industry? We begin with an exploration of the reflexive and informational character of contemporary capitalism.

Work and Employment in the Networked Society

The most important and influential attempt to explore the 'informational' and 'reflexive' nature of contemporary capitalism can be found in the work of Manuel Castells (Castells, 1997, 2000a,b). There is agreement amongst commentators on contemporary social change that the transition from modernity to 'second', 'high' or 'post' modernity involves an increase in both individual and institutional reflexivity (Beck, 1992; Giddens, 1990; Lash & Urry, 1994). However, the source of reflexivity in the analyses of these commentators tends to be somewhat vague and unspecified and this makes it difficult to apply the concept of reflexivity to substantive social change associated with institutions such as the contemporary workplace. The analytical power and importance of Castells work on informational capitalism derives from the way in which he highlights the importance of ICT in the development of individual and institutional reflexivity and the ways in which ICT underpins the processes of time–space distanciation and social disembedding (Bromley, 1999). Castells provides an important discussion of the linkages between the transformation of work and employment through the development and application of ICT and broader patterns of societal transformation. Specifically, Castells suggests that the development of 'informational capitalism' and the resulting 'network society' involves the individualization of work and the fragmentation of society. Castells rejects linear models of post-industrialization that highlight the societal implications of a service-based knowledge economy (Bell, 1973, 1976; Touraine, 1974) in order to highlight the uneven and disruptive effects of a new mode of informational development premised on the maximization of knowledge-based productivity. Castells highlights the distinction between the 'industrial mode of development' and the 'informational mode of development'. While in the former, technology and knowledge played a key role in shaping the production process, the informational mode of development is distinctive to the extent that knowledge is used primarily to generate new knowledge that then becomes the catalyst for further economic development. Knowledge has become *the* resource that is capable of transforming any type of economic activity. Gibbons et al. (1994) have argued that this requires a shift in the dominant form of knowledge from 'mode one' profession-based expert skill towards 'mode two' project-dependent skill. Every sector of the economy has been affected by information processing technology including health, telecommunications, banking and insurance. Indeed, information has increasingly become a commodity in its own right that is bought and sold on the market. Information has become increasingly important in improving economic performance within both manufacturing and services and this has resulted in the development of the informational economy. Castells argues that there are important social and economic implications resulting from the development of the informational economy including new forms of organizational design and new configurations of power.

The 'networked enterprise' (Castells, 2000a: 163–215) is a new form of organizational design facilitated by the application of information technology to communications, management and production within TNCs. The application of this design has enabled TNCs to operate in a decentralized and 'footloose' way in order to exploit cost advantages and specialized labour markets on an increasingly global scale. Castells cites the example of the Pontiac Le Mans car built in the United States, but involving South Korean routine assembly, Japanese advanced components, German design engineering, small components from Taiwan and Singapore, UK-based advertising and marketing and data processing in Ireland. In this context, loose networks of companies and agencies form loose-knit and temporary partnerships around a succession of temporary projects. These developments have produced new configurations of power through the concentration of 'informational power' amongst a 'knowledge elite' within corporations and the automation of low-skilled jobs – particularly amongst blue-collar, unionized workers in manufacturing. The restructuring of the global economy has combined with this informational mode of development to transform all areas of social and personal life according to the social logic of the network. This logic is premised on the decline of place-bound power as 'flows of power' are superseded by the 'power of flows' between nodes in the network and the elites that control the network. This is not to suggest that the post-Fordist TNC is placeless. As we demonstrated in Chapter 2, the control functions of the post-Fordist organization and its controlling elite are agglomerated in the centralized and hierarchical configurations of the global city. This creates an increasing disjuncture between the meaning and experience of everyday life and work in local places and the constitution of power and knowledge in the 'space of flows' through a culture of 'real virtuality'. The result is social disintegration and the individualization of work.

Castells highlights changes in the occupational structure of the G7 economies towards a growth in managerial, technical and service roles and an increasing polarization, not between skilled and unskilled occupations, but between different positions of similar occupations across sectors and between firms based on gender, age and ethnicity. Changes in the occupational structure are variable between the advanced economies owing to the ways in which the process of informationalization has been managed by state officials and TNC managers. Castells highlights an important distinction between the 'service economy' informational model that has developed in the United States and the United Kingdom and the 'industrial production' informational model that has developed in Germany and Japan. Castells argues that these divergent forms constitute different positions in the global economy. These developments do not imply the existence of a global labour force. There are certain types of elite workers that circulate within the global networks including the executives of TNCs, computer software consultants and the executives of transnational agencies and organizations. The majority of workers, however, do not circulate within global networks but are dependent on them. The diffusion of ICT in the workplace has made labour interdependent and this interdependence has opened up a range of restructuring strategies for MNCs including downsizing, subcontracting, flexibilization, automation and relocation. In reality, MNCs combine these strategies and the result has been transformation of labour and labour institutions marked by the integration of the labour process and the disintegration of the workforce.

The impact of ICT on the labour process is presented by Castells as being essentially positive and empowering. In contrast to Braverman (1974), he argues that it is not the introduction of technology *per se* that results in the de-skilling and degradation of labour, but the social organization of production. He presents a range of case studies that suggest that the deep penetration of ICT into the labour process has in places resulted in the emergence of the highly skilled 'networker' (Castells, *op cit*: 257): an autonomous and educated worker able and willing to programme and decide entire sequences of work. This is made possible through the way in which the application of ICT tends to result in the abolition of the types of routine and repetitive tasks that can be pre-coded, pre-programmed and automated. This process has produced similar effects across factories, offices and service organizations. The result has been the emergence of a new informational division of labour and organizational hierarchies that reward the ability to add value to organizations through the innovative use of ICT. Castells differentiates between the 'commanders', 'researchers' and 'designers' who act as 'networkers'; the 'integrators' and 'operators' who are 'networked' and execute tasks under their own initiative; and the 'human robots' that undertake the ancillary tasks that cannot be automated and who are 'switched off' from the network. While these represent the main task-positions in the informational workplace, they are not an inevitable product of post-industrialization. Castells highlights the importance of managerial decisions around issues of training and trade union participation in the development of the 'high performance workplace'. However, Castells falls back to a more technologically determinist position when discussing changes in office work and service employment. We will discuss this in more detail as it is important to our analysis of call centre employment.

According to Castells (*op cit*: 262), the process of office automation has gone through three phases. The first phase, during the 1960s and 1970s, involved the batch processing of data through mainframe computers and was characterized by the hierarchical control of information flows and a labour process marked by high levels of de-skilling and routinization. The second phase involved the processing of information through micro-computers. During this phase, clerical workers were given control over their immediate work processes with support provided by centralized data-bases. During the 1980s, improvements in telecommunications resulted in the networking of workstations, and the third phase has involved the integration of networked office systems with 'multiple microcomputers interacting amongst themselves and with mainframes, forming an inter-active web that is capable of processing information, communicating and making decisions in real time' (Belt et al., 2000: 386). This has resulted in the routinization and automation of low-level office work and the potential for the up-skilling and up-grading of higher-level professionals and clerical workers who can work autonomously and make decisions based on information stored on their computers. This process has the potential to eliminate middle management supervision as procedures can be standardized and stored within computer networks. Castells also highlights the possibility of a fourth phase premised around the 'virtual office' of networked and autonomous 'portfolio workers' (cf. Handy, 1994, 1995). However, in industries such as financial services, automation has generally taken place in the context of deregulation and an intensification of global competition and the main managerial objective has thus been a reduction in production costs based on the introduction of flexible working practices. Consequently, the main tendency has been the automation of unskilled data entering tasks, the multi-skilling of clerical work and the fragmentation and polarization of professional work. These occupational changes have reproduced and intensified existing divisions around gender, age and ethnicity. For Castells, therefore, the development of 'dual' labour markets and the polarization of workers around levels of skill and autonomy are central to the logic of the networked society. Power and knowledge reside in the 'space of flows' in 'timeless time' and the resulting culture of 'real virtuality' results in the solidification of social differentiation.

This has deeply negative consequences for established forms of industrial democracy based on the representation of workers by independent and autonomous trade unions. In the network society, the claims of organized labour become increasingly defensive, protective, territorially bounded and ultimately incommunicable. In the informational workplace, it becomes increasingly difficult to challenge the symbolic power of the network owing to the individualization of workplace relations. As we will illustrate through our exploration of call centre employment, in the informational workplace workers interact with the network but are increasingly isolated from each other. In contrast to the NSM politics of the women's and environment movement, the trade unions have found it difficult to move beyond a nationally determined and bureaucratic form and consequently have found it difficult to contest the logic of the network by assuming the reflexive form of the network (Castells, 1997). The logic of informational capitalism is thus to exclude organized labour from the workplace and demobilize labour as a social movement.

Castells presents an empirically rich and theoretically challenging analysis of the dynamics underpinning the transformation of the contemporary workplace and the important linkages between workplace restructuring and the wider transformation of society. There are, however, a number of problems and weaknesses that have been highlighted with regard to his analysis. First, while Castells focuses on the importance of 'informational capitalism' he also seems to privilege the 'informational mode of development' as the principal dynamic of change. There is, therefore, a danger that Castells ignores important continuities with industrial capitalism particularly with regard to the material power of capital and the state (Bromley, 1999: 12–15). Second, many studies have demonstrated the enduring importance of place and the entrenched institutional and social arrangements associated with local habits, customs and environment in defining the form of the global economy (Amin & Thrift, 1997). The transformation of work and employment is more complex than Castells suggests and requires a sensitivity to the way in which the disembedding and re-embedding of workplace relations is taking place in the context of capital and state restructuring in geographically diverse locations. We will illustrate this points through an exploration of 'business process outsourcing' (BPO) with a particular focus on the global call centre industry – the exemplary example of globalized informational capitalism (Taylor & Bain, 2005: 262).

Beyond Taylorism? Skill, Control and the Informational Labour Process

According to Castells (2000a) the development and application of ICT in the contemporary workplace contains the potential to reverse the de-skilling effects of Taylorism and Fordism. While Castells highlights important differences in the potential for re-skilling and autonomy between privileged and marginal workers, he nonetheless highlights an important trend towards the emergence of more autonomous and educated workers in the networked society. In this section, we explore the levels of skill and autonomy of call centre employees and thus the complex patterns of change between the Fordist and the informational workplace. The development of the informational service sector is associated with the increasing popularity and dominance of business process reengineering (BPR) as a model of managerial restructuring. In contrast to 'total quality management' and 'lean production' that dominated managerial discourse and practice in manufacturing industries during the 1980s and 1990s, BPR is particularly relevant to management restructuring in the service sector. BPR involves the dismantling of managerial hierarchies and functional demarcations within organizations to enable managers to respond more efficiently and effectively to the demands of fragmented markets. Within the BPR model, production or service failures are presented as a failure of management rather than as a reflection of an inefficient, unmotivated or defective workforce. The solution to low efficiency or a lack of effectiveness is a process of managerial restructuring, led by visionary management leadership, based on a fundamental change in business processes in which ICT is used to facilitate change, achieve flexibility and increase customer responsiveness (Hammer & Champy, 1993). The focus of visionary management within the BPR model is the elaboration of a management discourse that presents the company or organizations a 'team' and, indeed, a commitment to 'team work' is a key component of this managerial approach. However, commentators have detected a key tension and ambiguity in the practice of BPR between this focus on team-oriented restructuring and the ultimate objective of BPR that is to increase efficiency. The team-ethos of BPR is undermined by the focus on rationalization and the reduction of duplication and unnecessary complexity that tends to lead to work intensification and insecure employment (Sewell, 1998: 402). In many ways, therefore, these tensions and ambiguities highlight important continuities between BPR and the 'lean production' paradigm developed in manufacturing during the 1990s, particularly in relation to a polarization of skills and autonomy between elite and routine workers (Ashton & Green, 1996; Machin & Wilkinson,

1995). The ambiguities of 'flexible Taylorism' (Berggren, 1989) are reflected in workplace relations that combine unitary managerial strategies based on 'goal hegemony' with enduring examples of workplace disruption, symbolic acts of resistance or workers that display 'cynical compliance' rather than 'emotional engagement' in response to unitary managerial discourses (Delbridge, 1998; Knights et al., 1985). We need to be aware, therefore, that the rhetoric of unitary management paradigms such as 'lean production' and BPR may obscure important continuities between the Fordist and informational labour process.

There is a growing recognition that the ambiguity of call centre employment derives from the distinctiveness of the call centre labour process. This distinctiveness is based on the mechanisms of control underpinning workplace relations. In *Labor and Monopoly Capital,* Harry Braverman (1974) focused on the 'direct control' of workers within the capitalist labour process and, as sympathetic critics later pointed out, this tended to ignore the way in which the capitalist labour process was also underpinned by various forms of structural control (Edwards, 1979, 1984). According to Richard Edwards, these structural forms of control included 'bureaucratic control', where control was embedded in the formal structure of the organization, and 'technical control' where control was embedded in the mechanical and informational systems of the workplace. The work of Edwards has been developed in order to explore the extent to which the networked informational workplace involves the application of an intensified form of structural control, in which technical and administrative control is embedded within networked ICT-based systems. However, the notion that the 'reflexive' workplace is governed by structural control is somewhat problematic, as this would ignore the processes of individual and institutional reflexivity generated by the informational labour process. This is recognized by Callaghan & Thompson (2001) who suggest that call centre management involves both 'structural control' and innovative forms of 'normative' and 'emotional' control that combine to produce a complex and highly ambiguous form of managerial control.

This complexity was explored by Callaghan & Thompson in a study of a financial services call centre in the United Kingdom. The study focused on a call centre operated by 'Telebank' in Scotland, UK that was located on an out of town industrial estate and employed 500 staff on a shift work rota system between 8.00am and 10.00pm. The call centre agents were employed in large open-plan offices and their principal work task was attending to incoming calls from the bank's customers on routine issues such as balance enquiries, balance transfers and overdraft facilities. Each customer service representative (CSR) received approximately 120 calls per day each lasting approximately 180 seconds broken down into 'talk time' (160 seconds) and 'post-call wrap up time' (20 seconds). The key technological development within the call centre is automated call distribution (ACD) that automatically processes and distributes in-coming calls to agents. ACD systems are connected to a range of databases through computer telephony integration (CTI) that allows a customer's record or account details to be displayed on the computer screen along with the call. The call centre utilized ACD to distribute incoming calls to CSRs by placing calls in a queue and allocating calls when CSRs became available, while other software enabled managers access to sophisticated information gathering techniques relating to call waiting times, length of calls and the ability to 'listen-in' to the calls taken by CSRs. As Callaghan & Thompson demonstrate, this facilitated the 'technical control' of the pace and direction of work undertaken by the CSRs.

The technology of the call centre is designed to limit the autonomy of CSRs and maximize the pace of work through the constant 'firing' of calls to operators through the ACD technology. The pace of work appears to be embedded within the technology rather than set by managers and supervisors. In the case study, the monitoring and evaluation of CSRs took the form of the visualization of call queues and average waiting times on LCD panels hanging from the call centre ceiling and the ability of managers to 'listen-in' to telephone conversations and compile performance statistics. These statistics were displayed prominently in the workplace, aiding the lateral displacement of worker-manager conflict and generating a powerful dynamic of self-control. When CSRs failed to meet targets, they were described as 'out of line with the system'. This highlights the way that technological choice can produce seemingly objective control mechanisms. The disciplinary aspects of technical control were achieved through the self-disciplinary effects of surveillance, the public sharing of performance statistics and the ways in which management information was used in the formal appraisal system. Bureaucratic control complemented technical control through the encouragement of desirable behaviour patterns and performance standards and the institutionalization of values and norms as specific criteria for self-management and self-evaluation. These forms of structural control were complemented by normative and emotional forms of control. Normative control specified the 'right attitude' with regard to respect for hierarchy, the importance of customer service and appropriate standards of behaviour, dress, appearance and personal conduct. The notion of 'attitude as work' highlighted the extent to which the CSRs were required to undertake emotional labour (Hochschild, 1983) or 'feelings rules' (Leidner, 1993) in order to deliver high quality customer service. CSRs were encouraged to 'manage their emotions' in order to 'build rapport' with customers. This involved both 'conversational control' and the 'management of the self' in order to (self-)regulate levels of energy and enthusiasm.

The case study highlights the ways in which the combination of technical and bureaucratic control did indeed diffuse conflict laterally: CSRs vented their anger against 'the stats' rather than management. The workforce was organized into teams even though team work was not part of the technical division of labour. Rather, team work functioned as a mechanism of social control by offsetting the isolation and individualization of call centre work with a degree of sociability and generating a competitive mechanism designed to boost productivity (van den Broek et al., 2004). Despite these mechanisms of control, there was evidence of individual and collective resistance amongst the CSRs. This included CSRs identifying and exploiting 'blind spots', such as the use of codes, to disengage from call queues and thus regain a measure of control over the pace and intensity of work. CSRs often abandoned or manipulated conversational scripts in order to alleviate boredom and frustration or to develop sympathetic dialogue with customers. This was possible as most CSRs knew when their calls were being monitored. There was, however, no formal or organized bargaining over the labour process at Telebank. The call centre was non-unionized and the main way that employees voiced their dissatisfaction was through 'exit'. This is part of a broader trend in call centre employment as labour turnover is as high as 35 per cent per annum in many UK call centres (Welsh, 1997). The workplace clearly remains a 'contested terrain' (Edwards, 1979) marked by complex patterns of control and resistance. This terrain has undoubtedly been transformed, however, by what Castells (2000a) has termed integration of the labour process and the disintegration of the workforce. Reflexive self-control was the principal managerial dynamic in the call centre environment and, while this was resisted when it threatened the self-autonomy and self-actualization of the CSRs, resistance, including the ultimate resistance of 'exit', was a highly individualized form of behaviour. Indeed, the ability of managers to construct workgroups for their own purposes highlights the way the workforce is fragmented by the logic of the network and the increasing barriers to collective workplace culture or resistance. We will now explore the extent to which this process of individualization is premised on more fundamental changes in the nature of power in the workplace.

Identity, Subjectivity and Control in the Informational Workplace

While the workplace has remained a 'contested terrain', contestation increasingly takes the form of an individualistic reflexive accommodation with or rejection of the logic of the network. The development of ICT falsifies the traditional organizational premise of the economic system by enabling the technical refutation of technological determinism through reflexive critique (Beck, 1992: 216). This process of reflexive moderniza- tion has resulted in the 'de-centring of work', the increasing importance of consumption in the process of identity formation and a shift in polit- ical alignment from the labour movement towards new social movements. Similarly, Bauman (1998a) argues that the shift from Fordism to post- Fordism involves a movement away from a society of producers based on the 'work ethic' towards a society of consumers based on the 'aesthetic of consumption'. In post-Fordist society, the majority of workers no longer have a stable job and so building a stable identity based on employment is increasingly problematic. In this context, individuals tend to build their identities from the things they consume and, as a result, identities have become temporary, changeable, volatile and disposable. It is, therefore, argued widely that work remains a central and stable source of identity only for elite workers (Bauman, *ibid*; Castells, *op cit*). This de-centring of work has led corporations to pursue strategies based on the re-centring or recuperation of individual identities through corporate and managerial strategies that attempt to reconstitute the 'class self' in the image of the corporation (Casey, 1995). In the context of a HRM paradigm that stresses attitude, emotion and empowerment, workers are increasingly expected to put their 'whole' self into the job. This includes their emotional labour and, in the context of an increasing pressure to attend social events, ceremonies or team nights out, the boundaries between 'work' and 'life' have become increasingly blurred and imploded (Scase, 2002) – a process that Urry (2004: 121) refers to as the 'Starbuck-ization of work-leisure relations'. The demands of greater involvement and commitment from staff have developed alongside a tendency towards increasingly complex and demanding domestic arrangements for many workers particularly the growth in one-parent families (Crow & Hardey, 1999). This has resulted in many workers experiencing life as a 'multi-variable balancing act' with marked levels of stress and tension (Cooper et al., 2001: 50) or having to manage the detrimental effects of a culture of 'presenteeism' on family life (Simpson, 2000).

We will explore these tendencies in the context of recent surveys of call centre employment. In recent years, Foucauldian concepts have been applied to the analysis of the workplace and this has led commentators to describe workplace settings such as the call centre as 'electronic sweat- shops' marked by the perfection of 'panoptic power' and a mode of surveillance that gives management 'ultimate' or 'total' power (Fernie & Metcalf, 1988). According to this perspective, the invisibility of surveil- lance renders it perfect, as workers are unsure when they are being watched and 'the surveillance is permanent in its effects, even if it is discontinuous in action' (Foucault, 1977: 201). The result is a frictionless workplace in which direct supervisory power is redundant or rendered 'perfect' and its use unnecessary (Fernie & Metcalf, *op cit*: 9). However, as we witnessed in the above case study, call centre workers are able to resist this form of control and consequently this somewhat deterministic formulation has been modified to take into account the social relations of accommod-ation and resistance in the workplace. This is reflected in the work of Sewell (1998), who argues that the call centre marks the emergence of a new form of 'chimerical control' in which existing forms of control are augmented through the interaction of electronic surveillance and the peer group scrutiny of team work. Team working is a central component of the call centre labour process and is presented as a key mechanism in the shift from direct, objective forms of workplace control to subjective, indirect forms of workplace control. This suggests that management is increasingly focused on the reconstitution of subjectivity and forms of 'government-ability' that link subjectivity and power in order that individual lives can be rationally administered and regulated at a distance (Knights & McCabe, 2003). Management thus becomes a 'technology' through which author-ities shape, normalize and instrumentalize the conduct, thought and aspir-ations of individuals (Miller & Rose, 1990: 8). Following Foucault's 'capil-lary' model of power, these technologies are not totalizing 'as we live not so much in a governed world as in a world traversed by the 'will to govern' (Miller & Rose, *ibid*: 19). The disciplining technologies of power/knowledge are embedded within social relations so that those against whom power is targeted are themselves active participants in its production, reproduc-tion and potential demise through transgression, dissent and resistance (Knights & McCabe, *op cit*: 1593).

These forms of control and power are deeply embedded within the call centre workplace. The development of semi-autonomous workgroups is an important mechanism by which individual subjectivities are aligned with the strategic goals and objectives of management (Frenkel et al., 1995). The call centre can be seen as a site of 'info-normative' control that involves self-regulation and a shift from 'direct control' of supervisors to the role of supervisor as a supportive 'coach' (Korczynski et al., 2000). This supportive mode of management is based on the need for constant improvements in customer service, but is constantly compromised by the pressures of competition. In this context, management becomes an increas-ingly ambiguous discourse and practice as it constantly shifts between coercion and cooperation (Knights & Odih, 2002). While subjective control involves individualization, it does not imply support for individualism and, indeed, ambivalent attitudes towards collectivism and individualism allow workers to develop the concept of autonomy against itself as a form of 'auto-critique' that secures the conditions for collective action and resistance.

These tendencies were uncovered by Knights & McCabe (*op cit*) in a study of the introduction of customer process reengineering (CPR) in the call centre in a large building society in the United Kingdom. The organization had recently undergone a protracted period of restructuring; including the introduction of a 'team work' approach throughout the organization and the introduction of a new appraisal system designed to encourage autonomy and responsibility. This produced a tension in the organization owing to the way in which autonomy and responsibility were mediated by the power relations embedded in a hierarchical management structure. In this context, staff were expected to prioritize work according to the business demands of the organization and the appraisal system became a 'dividing practice' (Foucault, 1977) that divided staff into 'team players' and 'non-team players'. The discourse of autonomy was thus an attempt to secure 'self-regulation at a distance' which failed ultimately as CSRs were as likely to exercise power in an attempt to resist management attempts to 'mould' them as to allow themselves to be compliantly moulded. There were, therefore, tensions around productivity figures and their continuing use as a mechanism of discipline; tensions between the individual reward structure and the collective discourse of 'team work'; and a tension between the 'team lives' and the 'private lives' of call centre workers.

The study highlights the ongoing resistance of individual workers to the subjective forms of domination embedded within the management and information systems of the call centre workplace. In the context of an ongoing reflexive critique, call centre workers were able to refute the technological determinism of management discourse. Despite the discursive power articulated within the new management technologies, workplace identity remained 'de-centred' and subordinate to non-work sources of meaning and identity. This was highlighted in a study of four call centres in Scotland by Hyman et al. (2003) who explored the extent of work-related incursions into family life. The study explored both tangible incursions, such as having to work paid or unpaid overtime, unexpected and inconvenient shift patterns and having to take work home, and intangible incursions such as exhaustion, stress and disturbed sleep patterns. The survey discovered that for call centre workers, work was not the most important aspect of life and that the most important sources of individual satisfaction were derived from leisure activities or family. The most prominent incursion of work into private lives was reported as 'feeling stressed' or thinking about work whilst at home. Rather than work becoming more central to everyday life, the study highlighted the way in which the boundaries between work and home are becoming increasingly fluid and dynamic and the way that establishing a normative balance between these spheres creates considerable conceptual and practical difficulties for call centre staff. What we have here is the implosion of boundaries or boundaries becoming increasingly porous. We will explore this further through the breakdown of the boundaries between male and female work and employment.

Gendered Informationalism? Occupational Segregation and Emotional Labour in Call Centres

An important consequence of the development and application of ICT in the workplace is the substitution of male by female workers across many sectors and industries. (Castells, 2000a: 271) Castells (1997: 134–242) attributes this to the 'end of patriarchalism' engendered by the political success of the women's movement in challenging the patriarchal family and the rapid increase of women into paid employment. Both these developments are related intimately to the process of globalization. According to Castells, feminism contested successfully the 'space of flows' through demands for the reintegration of knowledge/experience and power/identity in a way that contested the logic of the network from within and assumed the reflexive form of the network (Bromley, 1999). This reflexivity is based on the fragmentation of the feminist movement into a multiplicity of feminist identities that, for many, is the principal definition of the movement (Castells, *op cit*: 199). In the global South, developments such as the internationalization of the electronics industry increased the demand for young unskilled women with 'nimble fingers'. In the global North, the demand for female labour has been a result of its relative cheapness and flexibility in the context of intensified global competition. Castells (2000a) does not suggest that these developments are irreversible or uncontested by men, nor does he suggest that women workers are necessarily undertaking de-skilled employment. Indeed, he highlights the contrary trend of women's work requiring increasing levels of skill, initiative and autonomy. Castells (1997) does highlight, however, the cultural importance of the breakdown of the patriarchal family and within the workplace the process of 'role redefinition' around flexible personalities and the 'normalization of sexuality'. The evidence from call centres suggests a complex combination of role redefinition and important continuities with established gender roles and occupational segmentation resulting in an increasingly complex and ambiguous range of gendered and sexual workplace identities.

Call centres constitute a rapidly growing sector of the economy and projected trends suggest that women will take the majority of jobs in this sector. Women are presented as having the necessary 'life skills' and 'communication skills' that are at a premium in the new service economy (Schnabel & Webster, 1999) and the decoupling of time and location facilitated by ICT has been described as particularly beneficial for women to achieve a better balance between work and non-work activities including childcare (Stanworth, 2000: 21). There is, however, evidence of enduring occupational segregation within the call centre sector. In a study of call centres in the United Kingdom, Netherlands and Ireland covering both financial services and IT, Belt et al. (2000) found that women constituted between 70 and 90 per cent of the workforce in the former but only between 46 and 60 per cent in the latter. The work process in the financial services call centres required less skill and tended to be monitored and controlled more intensively with the result that it was experienced as repetitive, stressful and tiring. The most important skill within the financial services call centre was the ability to handle customers in a patient and efficient way and convey the right image to the public. This required the performance of 'emotional labour at a distance' or 'smiling down the telephone' (Marshall & Richardson, 1996). While the majority of women expressed a desire to secure promotion and around 50 per cent of managers were women, the opportunities for progression beyond team leader were limited owing to the flat organizational structure of the call centre and there were considerable role gaps between team leaders and managers with few opportunities for team leaders to develop managerial skills. These difficulties were compounded by the difficulty that many women faced in combining domestic life and a management career.

There are enduring patterns of occupational segregation and workplace inequality within the informational workplace. There are also examples of 'role redefinition' and evidence of new gendered workplace identities. The increasing importance of services and 'customer care' has privileged feminine traits within the workplace, including the increasing importance of 'sexual' (Adkins, 1995) and 'emotional' (Hochschild, 1983) labour in the delivery of services. The extent to which this has resulted in the feminization of employment or more feminine styles of management is, however, problematic in the light of both the enduring material inequalities outlined above and the enduring domination of workplace culture by a discourse of masculinity (Collinson & Hearn, 1996; Wajcman, 1998). In this context, the performance of emotional labour has ambiguous consequences. Emotional labour can be defined as a form of service employment in which the 'service and its mode of delivery are inextricably combined' (Filby, 1992: 37) and 'the emotional style of offering the service is part of the service itself' (Hochschild, 1983: 5). Emotional labour involves 'the management of feeling in order to create a publicly observable facial and bodily display that becomes an integral part of the service being offered (Hochschild, *ibid*: 7). In her seminal study of the airline industry,

Hochschild noted the negative consequences of performing this type of labour in terms of the 'emotional dissonance' that resulted from prolonged or inappropriate emotional display or the management of emotions in the context of rude, aggressive or angry customers.

In a study of call centres in Australia and the United States, Korczynski (2003) outlines the ways in which frontline service work can be a source of both pleasure and pain for call centre workers. The ambiguities of emotional labour derive from the complex relationship between call centre workers and customers. The discourse of customer sovereignty is central to service work. The 'enchanting myth' of their own sovereignty is a key 'sign value' consumed by the customer in the service encounter (Korczynski, 2002). Owing to the fragile nature of the service encounter (Edwards, 2000), enchantment may be transformed into disillusion when customers face the bureaucratic and rationalizing reality of the service encounter (Ritzer, 2003) and when this occurs call centre staff are likely to experience real and meaningful pain (Bitner et al., 1994). This pain has become particularly marked as staff are increasingly recruited on the basis of their pro-customer attitudes (Korczynski et al., 2000) and society has become dominated by consumption-based identities (Bauman, 1998a; du Gay, 1996). However, this becomes problematic in a context of 'real virtuality' for as Bauman (1989) has also noted, social and technological distance increase the likelihood of inhuman and disrespectful behaviour between individuals. In this context, customers and customer contact has become an increasing source of meaning and pleasure in service employment and a source of pain when staff are abused by customers. Korczynski (2003) argues that in recoiling from this pain, call centre staff are likely to form 'communities of coping'. These informal communities are formed both within the labour process and in 'back stage' areas, and may be functional for management or may spill over into direct and indirect acts of resistance. This resistance can be seen as a form of 'tacit collectivism' (Taylor & Bain, 1999) that could nurture embryonic forms of collective or trade union activism. Managers were aware of the contradictions and ambiguities this produced and attempted to promote individualized ways of dealing with the consequences of abuse; including the development of mental and emotional distance between body, ears and voice and emotions. This produced the contradiction of prioritizing impartiality in a role where personality was central and, in this context, CSRs turned to their colleagues for emotional support. Management rhetoric on the importance of 'team work' served to strengthen these lateral links and gender played a central role in these 'communities of coping' as the majority of abusers were men and the majority of the workforce was female.

There is therefore an essential ambivalence with regard to the gender relations underpinning the informational workplace. Knights & McCabe

(2001) present a study of the introduction of BPO at a major UK retail bank that employed 3000 mainly female employees. The study highlights how the introduction of call centres and the shifting 'back office' functions from high street branches undermined the power and prestige of (predominantly male) branch managers. The discourse of paternalistic patriarchy that had dominated gender relations in the branch network was increasingly marginalized as branches were closed down and back-office functions shifted to large business processing centres. BPR involves the de-layering and dismantling of managerial hierarchies and a shift from functional to process forms of work organization including the introduction of multi-skilled teams. In the case study, BPR produced a tension between the need to approach organizational change in an aggressive, rationalist and controlled (masculine) way and the need to develop a human-centred (feminine) team work approach. This was manifested as the application of a 'macho' management style to the qualitative traits of female staff in an instrumental way that could be managed, manipulated and moulded into a form desired by the Bank. This resulted in a tension between the need for managers to display assertiveness and the need to display emotion in the new team-oriented environment. The gendered identities associated with the workplace in transition are thus fundamentally ambiguous and involve continuities with the 'macho' discourse of managerial science and elements of new 'softer' and 'feminized' discourse associated with the post-industrial, informational workplace. As we have seen, this ambiguity can often spill over into various forms of resistance, non-engagement and exit. In the face of resistance and the pressure to reduce costs there is, however, another option open to the executives of corporations: outsource to the Global South. We will now explore the main features of call centre work in India to see how the disembedding and re-embedding of call centre work transforms the organization and experience of the call centre labour process.

India Calling! Cyber-coolies in Cyber-Space?

India has become a particularly important location for business process outsourcing (BPO). The growth in outsourcing has been facilitated by advances in ICT and is a key component of 'business process reengineering' (BPR) marked by de-layered organizational structures, 'open' management styles and a stress on worker empowerment (Hammer & Champy, *op cit*). Household names that have recently outsourced to India include Dell Computers, Citibank, HSBC, AXA Sun Life, British Airways and Prudential; by the end of 2003, it was estimated that more than half of the world's top 500 companies outsourced either IT or business processes to

India. In 2005, it was estimated that 348,000 workers were employed in the BPO industry in India and it is estimated that by 2008 India will earn $24bn p.a. from this industry (Seabrook, 2003). Corporations derive clear economic advantages from this type of outsourcing and can expect to cut costs by between 40 and 50 per cent. India produces around 1.3 million English-speaking graduates per year and with starting salaries of around 10,000 rupees ($230) per month, the BPO industry has emerged as an attractive first destination for many Indian graduates. The development of BPO involves the transfer of call centre and other backroom operations by large MNCs. The main trend has been the transfer of business processes from corporate headquarters in Europe and North America to South East Asia; although there have also been important BPO transfers within Europe and North America and to locations such as South Africa.

In a study of Indian call centre work, Mirchandani (2004) argues that the main practices associated with work of this kind are 'scripting', 'synchronicity' and 'locational masking'. While these processes highlight the importance of a culture of 'real virtuality' (Castells, 2000a), a careful examination of the substantive consequences of these processes allows an insight into the 'gaps' and 'margins' of global capitalism (Bergeron, 2001: 999) and the practices through which 'economic globalization' and global control are constituted (Sassen, 2001b: 196). The study of Indian call centres highlights the existence of 'hidden transcripts of power' that deviate from the 'script' of neo-liberal globalism. In the context of call centres, scripting refers to the use of 'standardized service scripts' which outline the detailed specification of conduct expected from CSRs including the scripting of 'feeling rules' or 'emotional labour'. The impetus for this form of scripting is the live or synchronous nature of call centre contact with customers. Indian workers receive both generic training focused on accent, grammar and customer service and product specific training. The neutralization of Indian accent is particularly important. In Mirchandani's study, the client group were customers in the United States and the CSRs experienced training as the 'Americanization' of their English and the reproduction of a racist hierarchy in which American English is presented as superior to Indian English. The scripting produced ambiguous results. While on occasions service scripts may remove the CSR from disagreeable situations or awkward clients (Leidner, 1999), the CSRs in Mirchandani's study found the scripts to be de-skilling, tedious and repetitive. The result was a form of 'cultural dissonance' through which difficult and often-hostile encounters with American clients resulted in the representation of Americans as 'rich but stupid'. In response to the dominant discourse of customer sovereignty and the idea that 'customers are gods', the CSRs were thus able to pity rather than revere their American clients and thereby subvert the discourse of Western superiority and colonial mimicry (Bhabha, 1994: 86).

The practice of synchronicity refers to the way in which the Indian workers are required to operate according to American or European daylight hours and thus predominantly through the night in relation to Indian time. This amounts to a conflation of 'national time' and 'capitalist time' (Sassen, 2000b: 222) or the 'colonization of time' by which Western time is exported across the globe as standard (Adam, 2002: 21). The lure of India as a location for BPO lies in its potential to offer a 24/7 'business service platform'. Typical shifts in Indian call centres are 8pm–4am, Midnight–8am and 4am–Noon. The gap between global and local time has a profound impact on the health, well-being and family life of call centre workers. Call centre workers live in India but organize their lives around the time in the United States or the United Kingdom and the holidays, celebrations, and communication styles in these countries. The resulting strain, however, highlights the enduring immobility of time and its embeddedness in local social context. Hence, rather than 'time–space compression' (Harvey, 1989) the experience in Indian call centres highlights the importance of 'time–space expansion' (Katz, 2001: 1224): the experience of life becoming bigger in marginalized places. In the case of the call centres in India, workers were detached from the spaces of social life such as markets, households and transportation links that occur during the day (Mirchandani, *op cit*: 365).

The practice of locational masking is an illusion created by transnational production processes that mask translocal capital, transnational earning flows and far away workers (Appadurai, 1998: 41). In Mirchandani's study, locational masking was an attempt, only ever partially successful, to protect American TNCs from the racism of their customers in the United States. The result was a form of workplace resistance that went far beyond direct confrontations between management and employees. Through interaction with difficult and often hostile clients in conditions of tight supervision and control, workers were able to challenge the conception of their work as privileged, skilled and desirable. Indian workers were aware of the comparatively higher wages earned by less qualified and less educated call centre workers in the West and this resulted in a lack of organizational commitment and high levels of labour turnover. The example of Indian call centre employment provides a general corrective to forms of 'transnational centrism' (Grewal & Kaplan, 1994) in which TNCs are portrayed as invincible hegemonic structures that dominate the global stage. Indian workers manage, and at times deny, their scripting as passive and grateful workers and 'craft' themselves in the light of shifting fields of power (Kondo, 1990: 260). There is an essential ambivalence in respect to the position of Indian call centre workers: neither cyber-coolies nor privileged skilled workers but the products of a complex process of social change developing from an engagement with the power/knowledge embedded within the global economic regime (Sarker & Niyogi, 2002: 2). Evidence of this can be found in both the resistance of Indian workers to the controlled and scripted nature of call centre work and signs that in the face of resistance some call centres are moving back to the United States and Europe. We see again therefore the ambiguity and cultural dissonance produced by the complex process of disembedding and re-embedding on a global scale. The resulting dissonance amplifies resistance in the workplace. In the light of Castells (2000a) argument, earlier, however, to what extent is this likely to find collective expression in the form of trade union affiliation and action?

Globalization and Organized Labour: The Ambiguities of Identity in the Informational Workplace

In the discussion above, we have highlighted the complex patterns of involvement and non-involvement in the call centre labour process. This is producing increasingly ambivalent workplace identities that inhibit the (re)formation of the types of collective identity that underpinned modern trade unionism. We believe that this provides a more sophisticated and detailed account of trade union decline and the limits to trade union reorientation than recourse to simplistic theories of individualization (Beck, 1992), disorganized capitalism (Lash & Urry, 1987) or exclusion from the 'space of flows' (Castells, 2000a). The source of liminality in the informational workplace is the ambiguity produced by educated reflexive workers living simultaneously the managerial discourse of autonomy, responsibility and empowerment and the everyday reality of control, domination and disempowerment. We are not arguing that the new workplace is somewhere between Fordism and post-Fordism or that new forms of flexible production are somehow mythical (Bradley et al., 2000). Rather that the working arrangements associated with the call centre represent a qualitatively different organization of the capitalist labour process (Taylor & Bain, 2005: 263). In this context, it is maybe best to see these ambiguities as arising from the position of call centre employees as networked workers living the contradiction of managerial discourses that simultaneously promise and deny universal connectivity and autonomy. This raises fundamental questions with regard to changing workplace identities in general and the future of organized labour in particular. As we mentioned in earlier chapters, transclusion relates to the simultaneous balancing of engagement and non-engagement, openness and closure in a glocalizing landscape of opportunity structures and networks of obligation. We highlighted two important manifestations of transclusion in the form of hypermobility and symbolisms of belonging. We will now focus on these processes in the context of the global call centre industry.

We have seen how hypermobility is manifested in the high rates of attrition and labour turnover in the call centre sector; often a product of the high-volume induced burnout and tedium associated with the call centre labour process. In India, call centre workers work unsociable hours and often spend several hours a day being transported to and from work in special forms of transport organized by their employer. In this context, Indian workers have minimal involvement with their neighbourhood community and are denied meaningful workplace interaction with colleagues owing to the fractured and fragmented nature of the call centre labour process. These workers spend their nine-hour (night) shifts interacting with disembodied, disembedded and potentially hostile 'voices' from distant continents through scripted and masked forms of real virtuality. Despite this almost classical expression of alienated labour, the social organization of production in the informational workplace militates against the formal collective organization of workers in trade unions. A dynamic trade union movement requires the articulation of collective forms of identity between a vibrant workplace community and a wider collectively inspired movement in civil society. While accepting that the relationship between these two elements has varied across time and space (Hyman, 1994, 2001), it is nonetheless revealing that the 'social movement' role of the labour movement has been particularly important in the less developed societies of the Global South (Robinson, 2002). In India, for example, approximately 90 per cent of workers are employed in the informal sector and trade unionism is concentrated in the small but politically significant public sector (Sinha, 1984). Thus, while there are ongoing attempts to organize Indian call centre workers, particularly through Union Network International (UNI) – a global network of 900 unions with 15 million members – these attempts have so far been unsuccessful. The difficulty of organizing these workers has been compounded by the policies of the Indian state which for several decades has been a staunch supporter of the 'Washington Consensus' agenda of liberalization, privatization and neo-liberal globalism (see Chapter 6) and the executives of MNCs and Indian outsourcing companies that see unionization as a threat to the competitiveness of the industry. In the context of these broader economic and political dynamics and the specificity of the call centre labour process, we see a tendency towards the symbolism of belonging. In the workplace, the process of locational masking heightens feelings of Indian nationalism. Outside the workplace, the newly affluent call centre workers are the most enthusiastic visitors to India's fast growing shopping malls and Westernized fast food outlets. The process of globalization is producing new solidarities and individualities in India, but it is doubtful that these can be harnessed to either the organization of Indian workers or solidarity networks between call centres in India and the Global North.

The process is not so marked in the Global North but we can, nonetheless, see the same tendencies. In the United Kingdom, for example, the call centre industry is concentrated in the post-industrial wastelands of South Wales, Central Scotland, South and West Yorkshire and North East England. The workers in these call centres face the constant threat that their jobs will be relocated to India or elsewhere in the Global South. In contrast to India, there is a tradition of workplace trade unionism in the United Kingdom. However, the profile of the call centre workforce is inhospitable to trade unionism: a white-collar, two-thirds female, one-third part-time workforce in the private service sector (Taylor & Bain, 2001) combines the type of worker and the type of sector where trade union coverage has been minimal. This is compounded by the political and economic context in which UK call centres have developed. The restrictive anti-union legislation of the Thatcher administration has only been reversed partially by the post-1997 New Labour Government and both MNCs and UK companies have pursued a range of strategies to exclude or minimize union organization including single union 'sweetheart' deals and no strike agreements and relocation to non-union green field sites. Despite these developments, there is evidence of enduring collectivist orientations in UK call centres marked by oppositional attitudes and successful recognition and recruitment campaigns by trade unions (Taylor & Bain, 2001; Bain & Taylor, 2002). There have been an array of trade union campaigns focused primarily on preventing the export of jobs to India and highlighting the higher levels of quality and security in UK call centres. Recognition and coverage remains uneven and patchy and membership is lowest amongst younger workers where labour turnover is highest. In this context, trade union growth in the UK call centre industry does not appear sustainable in the long term. As we have seen, call centre workers construct other 'symbolisms of belonging' whether this is through emotional ties with immediate work colleagues, a strong affinity with home, family and consumption or in many cases the immediate environment of the call centre office. For example, van den Broek et al. (*op cit*: 208) give examples of management 'team building' strategies that allowed teams to choose the colour of the walls that surrounded them or decorate them with themes such as Walt Disney, give their work teams 'themed' names such as 'ALLSTARS' and 'BEEGEES' and themed days when workers wore fancy dress. The resulting identities are more than anything marked by fluidity, complexity and ambiguity.

In the context of declining union density, trade unions are adopting the alternative strategy of mobilizing in civil society and have become an important component in the anti-globalization movement. However, given the ambiguous form of workplace culture and identity in both the UK and Indian call centre industry, it is difficult to see how this could be translated into a form of cosmopolitan industrial democracy based on transnational networks of obligation between workers in the developed and developing world. The interests of labour are, therefore, rather place-bound and incommunicable in the 'space of flows' (cf. Castells, 1997). We have highlighted the gaps and chinks in the network and the cultural dissonance that develop as a result. The resulting patterns of openness and closure, engagement and non-engagement are complex, ambiguous and create forms of workplace individualism and solidarity that will remain difficult for a labour movement that remains hierarchically and nationally organized to (re)capture. While the call centre is something of an extreme example, it is emblematic of the dominant trend in the current phase of industrial restructuring. In this context, the prognosis for the ailing worker's movement is not good.

Summary and Conclusion

We have explored the globalization of the financial services industry and the organization of call centres in this sector owing to its importance as a hotspot of intense social change. The informational workplace provides an insight into the current phase of workplace restructuring which highlights the increasingly complex and ambiguous nature of workplace organization and workplace identity. The liminality of the contemporary workplace is a product of a complex pattern of continuity and change between the industrial and the informational workplace. First, the informational labour process is a capitalist labour process and the workplace remains a 'contested terrain'. We have illustrated the tendency towards a seamless and totalizing system of control within the informational workplace marked by a combination of direct, structural and subjective forms of control. However, we have also demonstrated the ongoing contradictions produced by this system of control and the forms of resistance and conflict that result from these contradictions. These contractions result from the irresolvable problem of capitalist management that maximum efficiency is premised on both the control and motivation of workers. The case studies explored in this chapter highlights that this problem is not resolved within the informational workplace. An important manifestation of this is the tendency towards labour market dualism and a polarization between autonomous and upsklilled 'net workers' and increasingly de-skilled and precarious human 'robots'. Second, informational capitalism is not place-less and both transcends and limits the 'real virtuality' outlined in the work of Castells. The logic of the network and the power embedded within the 'space of flows' is subject to constant challenge and disruption from the 'place of space'. The case studies explored in this chapter highlighted how local cultures and vernacular repertoires of meaning both negotiated and contested the logic of the network and provided the basis for both collectivist and individualist forms of workplace resistance and struggle.

In the context of global restructuring and flexible employment strategies, both the workplace and work-based identities have become increasingly precarious and challenged by risk-generating social change. In this context, work has been increasingly 'de-centred' as a source of meaning and identity and replaced by individualized forms of meaning and identity based on consumption and the family. The tendency towards individualization is amplified by the specificity of the informational labour process that simultaneously integrates the labour process within the logic of the network while fragmenting and disintegrating the workforce. In this sense, power has become embedded within the logic of the network and this has produced an important tendency towards reflexive self-monitoring and self-control. The tendency towards individualization is, however, complicated by an important tendency towards the implosion of workplace boundaries as the boundaries between home and work, work and leisure and between 'male' and 'female' work become increasingly contested and porous. In this context, 'emotional labour' has become an increasingly important component of the informational labour process and forms of 'communities of caring' have developed as important components of workplace culture. We have highlighted the way in which these ambiguous forms of workplace organization provide an inhospitable climate for established forms of industrial democracy based on autonomous trade unionism. In essence, the informational workplace is a liminal space premised on and reproducing a complex culture of transclusion. The hypermobility of informational capitalism has produced ambiguous 'symbolisms of belonging' that correspond to neither the collective solidarity demanded by the modern trade union movement nor the fragmented individualism that is celebrated by postmodern social theory.

5

Consumption: Money and Identity in the Postmodern World

The compulsion to consume is not the consequence of some psychological determinant etc., nor is it simply the power of emulation. If consumption appears to be irrepressible, this is because it is a total idealist practice which has no longer anything to do ... with the satisfaction of needs nor with the reality principle.

(Jean Baudrillard, 1998: 24–25)

In recent decades, everyday life has become increasingly dominated by the social practice of consumption. The social practice of shopping has been transformed from a mundane and practical means of physical reproduction into an important source of leisure and entertainment. In the previous chapter, we highlighted how changes in the nature of employment have resulted in work becoming increasingly 'de-centred' and marginalized and how consumption and the ideology of consumerism have played an increasingly pivotal role in the construction and reproduction of social meaning and social identity. As the quotation from Baudrillard suggests, consumption has become something of an irrepressible urge or insatiable compulsion for increasing numbers of individuals in both the developed and developing world. However, when we observe the practical organization and personal experience of contemporary consumption it becomes immediately obvious that we are dealing with a deeply ambiguous phenomenon. The new 'cathedrals of consumption', as the new mega-malls, hyper-stores and theme parks have been labelled, appear increasingly prison-like: an inside-out world where public activity is privately monitored, manipulated and controlled. These dynamics of manipulation and control are also apparent in relation to other areas of consumption such as tourism, media and communications and increasingly in areas such as health, education and personal care. Paradoxically, however,

83

there seems to be no limits to the growth, expansion and popularity of consumption. The cathedrals of consumption originated in the USA but now, following the dynamic of globalization, have spread through Europe, India, China and throughout the world, and form a central component of the social and spatial infrastructure of the global city.

It is possible to isolate a range of broad themes from the growing literature on the sociology of consumption that might throw some light on the issue of why consumption should have emerged as a central 'hotspot of transition' towards the end of the twentieth century. The dominant explanation is based on the argument that consumption articulates the cultural, political and economic logic of postmodernity and, therefore, has become increasingly important and dominant as the shift from modernity to postmodernity has intensified. The focus here is on the increasingly non-foundational or 'idealist' nature of postmodern consumption (Baudrillard, *op cit*) and the tendency towards the 'aestheticization of everyday life' (Featherstone, 1992) and for social meaning and identity to be produced and reproduced through the exercise of 'aesthetic reflexivity' (Lash & Urry, 1994). On the other hand, there have been attempts to explain contemporary consumption based on an intensification and globalization of the tendencies and dynamics that were deeply inscribed within modernity. The focus here is on the control, manipulation and alienation that is produced by the dynamics of rationalization (Ritzer, 2005) and/or commodification (Harvey, 1989) and the ways in which these tendencies are obscured by the legitimating 'ideology of consumerism' (Sklair, 2002). In essence, the two dominant approaches each provide a partial and one-sided analysis that fails to engage adequately with the deeply ambiguous and complex nature of contemporary consumption. In contrast, we explore contemporary consumption as a site of intense and complex liminality or in-betweenness that reflects the specific contradictions and tensions of reflexive modernity. Liminal spaces have developed in places like the contemporary shopping mall which is a space between the 'real' and the 'imagined' or between the promise of ultimate satisfaction and happiness and its denial by the insatiable appetite for ever-expanding consumption by the 'desiring machine' (Deleuze & Guattari, 2004). In the sphere of consumption, the dynamics of reflexive modernization (Beck et al., 1994) can be traced back to the basic ambiguities of money as a social form, which is further obscured and complexified by the restructuring of the global cultural economy through the application of ICT to the social practice of consumption. Hence, while we would agree with Bauman (2000) that reflexive modernity is essentially 'liquid', we suggest that the ambiguities of this liquidity can be found in the intensification of the contradictions of monetary relations by ICT on a global scale.

The secret and ambiguous world of money has long been a source of fascination for sociologists. Karl Marx, for example, was interested in the magical or transformative qualities of money, while for Georg Simmel money resulted in the objectification of human personality and human culture. These tendencies were inscribed deeply into capitalist modernity but an important and difficult question we now must face is how have these tendencies interacted with the development and intensification of reflexive modernity? In the context of reflexive modernity, many of the central categories of modern society such as social class and the nation state have become 'zombie categories' that have died but live on (Beck & Beck-Gernsheim, 2002: 27). With the category of money, however, we have a phenomenon that is far more enigmatic for money has always been a 'zombie category'. Marx described money as a 'shadowy ghost' or a reified 'thing' that conjured up illusions, simulacra and appearances (Derrida, 1994: 37). For Marx, however, these illusions were generated by the 'fetishism of commodities' which obscured the dynamic role of money in the process of capital accumulation and the way in which the social power of money is underpinned by the social relations of capitalism (Marx, 1976: 163–177). This is complemented by what Appadurai (1990) has termed the 'fetishism of the consumer', a process through which the consumer is lured in a false sense of agency which masks the real seat of agency in the global cultural economy. The process of globalization and the intensified reflexivity associated with the application of ICT to the marketing and sale of commodities has intensified the speed and expanded the scale of the networks through which money circulates. Increasingly, money capital has become liberated from the geographical constraints of nationally bounded economies and inhabits the 'space of flows' managed by networks of information systems (Castells, 2000a: 106). To the extent that capital accumulation is a real process of abstraction, the development of 'reflexive capitalism' could be seen to intensify the tension between the 'real' and the 'abstract' and to posit individuals in the growing gap of 'liminality' between the 'real' and the 'abstract'. In this liminal world, contemporary consumption is simultaneously seductive and controlling, magical and alienating, real and illusory. The tension between these polar opposites is amplified by the 'hypermobility' associated with globaliz-ation, and 'symbolisms of belonging' are increasingly anchored to the discourse and practice of contemporary consumption – a dream world of mythologized past, nihilistic present and limitless future. In other words, the 'idealist world' of hyper-reality outlined by commentators like Jean Baudrillard (1998) is in fact grounded in the changing forms of sociality associated with the global cultural economy.

In this chapter, we explore how the ambiguities of money have been intensified by the dynamics of globalization and reflexive modernity. We begin with a discussion on the seemingly magical and ambiguous properties of modern money and the way in which these properties have become intensified by the increasingly fluid and intense flow of money on a global scale to produce a hyper-commodified world of hyper-reality. In the following section, we explore the physical manifestations of 'hyperconsumption' through an analysis of the increasingly global reach of the new 'cathedrals of consumption' associated with the 'new means of consumption' (Ritzer, 2005). We then turn to a discussion of how the tension between the 'real' and the 'illusory' is embedded with the contemporary practice of consumption and how this is manifested in intense feeling of disenchantment and re-enchantment in the everyday experiences of consumers. We then turn to a discussion of how the dynamic of hyperconsumption is affecting the social and spatial boundaries of the global city and the ways in which this is resulting in new forms of urban inequality and new forms of social inclusion and exclusion in the urban environment. We conclude with an assessment of the intensity and direction of social change associated with hyperconsumption and highlight how the forms of identity associated with contemporary patterns of consumption provide an insight into the essentially 'liquid' character of reflexive modernity.

Money, Commodification and Identity: Fragments in a Fragmented World?

The relationship between money, commodification and identity was anticipated in the work of Marx and discussed explicitly in the work of Simmel. For Marx, the commodification of human needs and capacities, and their mediation by money, resulted in the alienation and estrangement of human labour. This alienation was obscured owing to the way in which the material relations between individuals appeared as a social relationship between things (Marx, *op cit*: 166). The dynamism of this process resulted from the dual role of money as a means of exchange and as money capital, the motive energy in an endless process of expanded reproduction (Marx, *ibid*: 247–257). The fetishism of commodities obscured the role of money both as a source of alienation and as a dynamic motor of development (Marx: *ibid*: 163–177) and resulted in the reification and objectification of human culture in a way that made it appear as if money had magical or supernatural powers (Neary & Taylor, 1998). Money became an 'alien mediator' that subjugated human activity into a state of slavery (Marx, 1975: 260–261) and in the process, developed apparently magical and creative powers. Through these powers, money is able to transform the contents of individual imagination into sensuous reality, or as Marx suggests somewhat more prosaically:

The properties of money are my . . . properties and essential powers. Therefore, what I *am* and what I *can do* is by no means determined by my individuality. I *am* ugly, but I can buy the *most beautiful* woman. Which means to say that I am not *ugly*, for the effect of my ugliness, its repelling power, is destroyed by money . . . I am a wicked, dishonest, unscrupulous and stupid individual, but money is respected and so is its owner . . . Through money, I can have anything the human heart desires. (Marx, *ibid*: original italics)

Marx, therefore, anticipates the focus of postmodernism on the way in which hyper-commodification creates an abstract and idealized world of signification:

Money turns the imagination into reality and reality into mere imagina-tion . . . real, human, natural powers into purely abstract representations and tormenting phantoms, just as it turns real imperfections and phantoms . . . into real essential powers and abilities. Thus characterised money is the universal inversion of individualities. (Marx, *ibid*: 387)

The idea that money and the process of commodification objectifies and inverts human subjectivity was later developed by Walter Benjamin in his survey of arcades and department stores in early twentieth century Paris and Berlin (Benjamin, 1983). Benjamin found much that prefigured the contemporary age. According to Benjamin, events such as the 'World Exhibition' held in Paris during 1889 were resulting in 'enthronement of the commodity'. The display of commodities as 'objects of desire' allowed their original uses and origins to be forgotten or eclipsed in order to produce 'dream worlds' and 'phantasmagoria'. Individuals entered these false worlds in order to be distracted by folk festivals of capitalism. The development of the entertainment industry had made this easier by redu-cing individuals themselves to the status of commodities, and in the process, individuals had become alienated both from themselves and from others. For Benjamin, the world of exchange values stood in opposition to the organic world and prostituted the living body to the inorganic world. In relation to the living, it represented the rights of the corpse. The way in which this objectification was linked to forms of human sociality was the focus of Georg Simmel (1989) who provides an important link between Marx, Benjamin and more recent analyses of commodification and consumption.

According to Simmel the value of a commodity is a product of both its use value as an object and a measure of the 'desire' that individuals have to obtain it. While the market economy frees the individual from the compulsion of forced labour and liberates the individual personality, it also forces the individual back into the market. Here the individual becomes part of a complex and specialized division of labour, which results in the separation between man as a personality and man as an instrument of special performance as both labourer and as consumer (Simmel, 1978: 293). There is, therefore, nothing new in the liminality of consumption as it is intrinsic to the generalization of the money form. The generalization and intensification of monetary relations in society tends to result in the objectification of culture as individuals are increasingly valued in monetary terms and social relations are increasingly transformed into money relations. Money increasingly determines the rhythm of life, as emotional life gives way to intellectual calculability and the creativity of the mind is subject to a process of reification. These tendencies develop most intensely in the metropolis, which constitutes the seat of the money economy. The emergence of romantic ideals and strong emotions are a reaction against this monetarization of culture in which money and intellect are interchangeable and people and culture can be bought. Through money, all can be bought, all is related, all is in constant motion – the world is in total flux (Deflem, 2003: 72–73). The phenomenon of money and the objectification of culture thus result in the fluidity and fragmentation of identity along the myriad of monetary relations that constitute the social totality.

There is a similar focus on the way in which commodification results in the objectification of culture in the work of the *Frankfurt School*. The Frankfurt School further developed the work of Lukács on 'reification' (Lukács, 1971, 1978). According to Lukács, the forms of consciousness and personality that are developed by individuals in capitalist society are transformed or reified into rationalized, autonomous and objective processes that confront individuals as objective things to which they must submit. The analysis of the culture industry developed by Horkheimer and Adorno (1972) and Marcuse (1964) highlighted the ways in which the development and consolidation of Fordism involved the expansion of markets and the 'education' of the public to become 'consumers' through advertising and the media. This involved the application of instrumental rationality and commodity logic to the sphere of production and the reification of culture. Arts and leisure activities were increasingly filtered through the culture industry and their consumption by the public was increasingly mediated by exchange-value. The result was a mass-produced commodity culture targeted at the lowest common denominator. The domination of exchange value allowed the original use-value of the commodity to be forgotten and, for Adorno (1991), allowed commodities to express a secondary or *ersatz* use-value. Commodities came to be associated with a wide range of cultural associations and illusions and enabled advertisers to attribute images of romance, beauty, desire and exotica to mundane objects such as washing powder, soap and motor cars. The conflation of need and desire harnessed the subjectivity of consumers to the objective reproduction of capitalism through the constant generation of 'false needs' (Marcuse, *op cit*).

The work of Marx, Simmel and the Frankfurt School on money and commodification anticipates many of the themes that have been developed by post-structuralist commentators to highlight the distinctiveness of postmodernity. This is particularly evident with regard to the focus of earlier commentators on the fragmentation of identity around monetary relations and the ways in which the resulting objectification and reification of culture generates phantasmagoria and dream worlds. These tendencies were inscribed deeply into the modern condition. However, the discussion of money and commodification in these accounts was foundational. The ambiguities and contradictions of money were generated by the tensions between the real and the abstract or between desire and compulsion or between 'true' and 'false' needs. These dualities are rejected by post-structuralist analyses of money and consumption, which reject foundationalism and present consumption as an 'idealist practice'. Baudrillard (1998), for example, is critical of the notion of true/false needs developed by the Frankfurt School and argues that a need is not a need for a particular object as much as a desire for *difference* or a desire for social meaning. According to Baudrillard, the shift from modernity to postmodernity has resulted in the *sign value* of a commodity becoming the most important marker of its value. The expansion of capitalism has been so dynamic that sign values have proliferated and become increasingly arbitrary and self-referential. In this context, the global communications media has developed as a self-referential system of signification. Consumption is increasingly constituted as a code or system of signs, and as the sign system has proliferated these signs increasingly have no original, they are *simulacra* – simulated copies without an original. In this super-abundance of signs, reality recedes and is ultimately lost, as the boundaries between phenomena implode and then dissolve into a single undifferentiated mass (Baudrillard, 1983b). This process of homogenization or hyper-differentiation leading to the implosion of boundaries brings art, poetry and ultimately our bodies into the realm of consumption. The profusion of simulacra and simulation has resulted in reality melting into the hyper-real: a reality more real than the reality itself. The signs speak to and of one another, not of anything outside themselves – a closed self-referential system that increasingly signify nothing. In this context, individuals increasingly desire the idea of consuming rather than the consumption of a particular object and the desire to consume is, therefore, abstract and ultimately insatiable.

The saturation of society with simulations has contributed to the erosion of the distinction between the real and the imaginary or between the true and the false. Indeed, the unreal has become the reality and the real imitates the imitation. This is reflected in the growing importance of fake, synthetic and simulated architecture (Huxtable, 1997) which has been described as 'karaoke architecture' (Evans cited in Quinn, 2005). Examples of this include the way in which *Disney World* has become the model, not only for Disney's town of *Celebration*, but communities such as *Seaside*, Florida and *Kentland's*, Maryland that have emulated the ersatz small town America championed by the *Disney Corporation* (Ritzer, 2005: 102). The everyday world emulates the theme park and is increasingly saturated with fantasy and illusion. The interactions within these theme parks are increasingly fake, whether in the form of meeting Mickey Mouse at *Disney World* or the scripted encounter with the cashier at *Wal-Mart*. Increasingly, it appears as if there is no reality – everything is simulation and simulations can be made more spectacular than the real thing. The sphinx at the *Luxor Hotel*, Las Vegas is taller and more spectacular than the 'real' one in Egypt. Restaurants are saturated with simulation, particularly when they take the form of themed restaurants such as the *Roy Rogers* or *Treasure Island* chains in the USA. In the UK, and indeed across Europe, there are Irish themed pubs with names such as *Scruffy Murphey's*, *Nelly Kelly's* and *Durty Nelly's*. There are also examples of 'English' and 'Australian' pubs in town centres, malls and airports across the world.

Baudrillard paints a depressing and pessimistic picture of postmodern consumption. Whilst the process of hyper-commodification has expanded the range of choices open to individual consumers and, whilst these choices have become disarticulated from any material grounding in class position or biological needs, the consumption of simulations in hyper-reality deepens the objectification of culture and intensifies the fragment-ation and alienation of the individual. The sign system leads individuals into believing that as long as they have the signs of happiness then they are happy. Yet this 'abstract happiness' is a product of the total homogen-ization of everyday life and the total control of body, mind, imagination and desire by a totalizing system of reified culture. As we highlight in the following section, the seductive promise of postmodern consumption to increase individual choice and autonomy is ultimately illusive and illusory. This is evident through the disenchantment and alienation experienced by the consumer in the new cathedrals of consumption. The fact that 'abstract happiness' and the enchantment of hyper-reality are constantly ruptured by the disenchanting reality of contemporary consumption suggests that the closed, self-referential world of hyper-reality is not as 'closed' as Baudrillard suggests. Moreover, the tendencies outlined by Baudrillard were inscribed deeply into capitalist modernity. The 'dream factories' of Fordism generated high levels of simulation and spectacle, as the examples of Hollywood movies and mass advertising demonstrate amply. Moreover, the institutional solidity of modernity was always fragile and liable to implode and premised ultimately on the institutional power of the nation state to define and uphold the boundaries between 'work' and 'leisure' or 'public' and 'private'. In this context, it would seem more fruitful to understand the developments outlined by Baudrillard as part of an intensification of the cultural contradictions of modernity stimulated by globalization and the increasingly reflexive nature of contemporary capitalism. We will now explore how the principles of simulation, spectacle and implosion are implicated deeply in the new 'cathedral of consumption' and the ways in which this has been facilitated by the deep penetration of ICT into contemporary consumption.

Cathedrals of Consumption: The Origins of Hyperconsumption

The past few decades have witnessed a massive increase in the size, scale and diversity of what George Ritzer (2005: 1–24) has termed the 'new means of consumption'. This refers to the innovative and revolutionary new ways of consuming commodities that have developed in recent decades that include TV and Internet shopping, credit cards and vast 'mega-malls' and 'hyper-stores'. The shopping mall is emblematic of this development owing to the way in which postmodern 'pilgrims' visit these 'cathedrals of consumption' to practice the new religion of consumption (Kowinski, 1985: 218). Describing shopping malls as 'cathedrals' provides an important insight into the increasingly enchanted, sacred and religious character of consumption in postmodern society and the way in which this enchantment dominates the spatial fabric of the global city. Shopping malls have grown in both importance and size culminating in the development of 'mega-malls' such as the *Mall of America* in Minneapolis, Minnesota, USA. Important departures have been the 'entertainmentization of retailing' which has involved the increasing focus on entertainment in shopping malls, the development of 'speciality malls' in resorts and tourist destinations and the spread of malls into other settings such as airports, train stations, cruise ships, universities and hospitals. Within the mall are other examples of the new means of consumption including franchised fast food restaurants such as *McDonalds*, *KFC*, *Burger King* and *Starbucks*. There has also been a growth in out-of-town chain stores such as *Wal-Mart* in the USA and *Tesco* in the UK and 'big box' superstores such as *Toys 'R Us*, *Home Depot* and *IKEA*. In addition, a range of 'virtual' shopping spaces have developed ranging from established home shopping catalogues to new electronic cybermalls such as *Amazon* and TV networks such as *QVC*. In addition, Ritzer (*op cit*: 16–23) highlights the increasing importance of cruise ships, casinos and sites that emulate the new means of consumption including sports grounds, universities and schools, hospitals, museums and mega-churches.

The growth of the new means of consumption can be explained by a range of economic, social and cultural changes that have occurred in the post-war period. The maintenance of high levels of mass consumption was a central component of Keynesian macro-economic management associated with the Fordist regime of capitalist growth (Harvey, 1989). The crisis of Keynesianism resulted in the deregulation and liberalization of markets and the exposure of corporations to the pressures of global competition. Lash and Urry (1994) argue that this shift towards a post- or neo-Fordist political economy involves a general aestheticization of the overall process of social reproduction. The 'new core' of disorganized capitalism is to be found in the new 'culture industries' of media and publishing, as well as entertainment and tourism. In places where manufacturing remains important, the process has nevertheless become increasingly 'information- and hence culture-intensive' through the important role played by lifestyle-oriented market research and the 'branding' of products such as shoes, clothes, furniture, cars and electronic goods. Thus, there is a clear tendency towards the 'societalization of culture' or 'Kulturgesellschaft' (Lash and Urry, *ibid*: 143). These developments have made consumption a crucial part of social reproduction. As Sklair (2002) has argued, the all-embracing 'culture-ideology of consumerism' has become central to the smooth running of global capitalism. Consumerism has become an all-embracing ideology that guides the conduct of life and provides a set of values and an ethos that makes the consumption of goods meaningful in an ever shifting and reinvented landscape of subcultures and lifestyles. Individuals are compelled to consume owing to their need to reinvent themselves constantly, but 'with only an indirect regard for their ability to pay for what they are consuming' (Sklair, *ibid*: 166). Indeed, intensive forms of advertising and marketing have encouraged individuals to view shopping as an important form of recreation (Zukin, 2004). The emergence of this powerful global culture-ideology has been supported by several additional factors. First, it has occurred at a time when leisure time is expanding owing to shorter working hours, earlier retirement and expanded life expectancy. Second, there have been important cultural changes associated with the 'life cycle' including the development of 'youth', 'child' and 'grey' subcultures resulting in the emergence of specific markets and commodities aimed at children, adolescents and elders. In economic terms, a virtuous circle has developed in which the interests of corporations and banks have converged with the needs and desires of consumers. This virtuous circle has been manifested in two important developments. First, the collapse of state socialism in Eastern Europe, the commercial transformation of China and intense levels of growth in India has extended the global reach of American consumer culture and provided new markets for the expansion of shopping malls and theme parks. Second, the liberalization of the financial services sector has increased the availability of loans and credit. Credit cards have been a particularly important innovation in enabling individuals to consume goods and services when and where they desire, including the development and expansion of TV shopping and shopping on the Internet (Ritzer, 1995). The most important dynamic, however, is the rapid development and application of ICT. Computer technology is central to the maintenance of complex franchising networks and the complex sourcing, distribution and inventory procedures of large stores and supermarkets. Microprocessor technology underpins TV home shopping and Internet shopping as well as a myriad of other developments that are central to the new means of consumption such as ATMs, EPOS and supermarket loyalty cards. This technology is also responsible for a new generation of consumable objects of desire including MP3 players, DVD players, mobile phones and digital cameras.

The development of the new means of consumption is linked to the phenomenon of 'hyperconsumption' as defined by heightened levels of individual and collective obsession with the ideology and practice of consumerism. In the USA, the practical consequences of hyperconsumption are reflected in a society in which individuals spend three to four times longer shopping than individuals in Western Europe, consume twice as many commodities than forty years ago and work increasingly long hours to support this level of consumption in an increasingly frenetic 'work and spend' syndrome (Schor, 1991). The new cathedrals of consumption are designed artistically and scientifically to encourage hyperconsumption. The layout of malls, airports and stores are arranged in ways that encourage the passer-by to browse and purchase the commodities on display. In supermarkets, odours of bread and other fresh produce are channelled to the entrance in order to entice shoppers with the promise of fresh produce. Hyperconsumption involves changes to the way people shop. The development of 'one-stop' shopping in the 'hyper-store' or 'super centre' maximizes the efficiency of a shopping trip. A visit to a *Wal-Mart* super centre in the USA could involve a one-stop shopping expedition for clothes, shoes, electrical goods and even hand guns and rifles. There is an increasing tendency for the shopper to do more for him or herself in the act of consumption. This tendency started with motorists filling their own fuel tanks and has rapidly expanded to shoppers checking out their own goods in the supermarket or buying goods from home through the TV or Internet. This highlights the shift towards a post-social world in which individuals increasingly interact with 'things' rather than people (Knorr-Cetina, 2001).

The cathedrals of consumption and the related process of hyper-consumption developed initially in the USA but there is evidence that the model is being exported vigorously throughout the rest of the world, with signs of hyperconsumption evident in places such as Japan (Clammer, 1997) and China (Watson, 1997). American culture and consumer goods are exported by American-based MNCs and the logos associated with American consumer goods have become highly valued objects of desire throughout the world. There are many examples of the increasingly global reach of American 'cathedrals of consumption' (Ritzer, 2005: 40–44). In 2004, the *Golden Resources Shopping Mall* opened in Beijing, China. When completed this shopping mall was the largest in the world with over 1000 stores on six levels and 560,000 m^2 of retail space enclosed in an overall area of 680,000 m^2. The mall is the largest of an estimated 400 shopping malls that have opened recently in China. Shopping malls under construction in Wenzhou and Qingdao, China, with projected total areas of 930,000 m^2 will be significantly larger than *Golden Resources* when completed. China is not an isolated example. American-style shopping malls have opened in the former state socialist societies of Eastern Europe, including the *Polus Centre* in Budapest, Hungary, the *Palác Flóra Mall* in Prague, Czech Republic and the *Arkadia Mall* in Warsaw, Poland, which has 287,000 m^2 of commercial space and is currently the largest shopping mall in Central Europe. The UK has a marked concentration of American-style super malls including *The Lakeside Shopping Centre* near Thurrock, Essex that boasts 300 stores, 13,000 parking spaces and a nearby retail park containing American giants such as *Toys 'R Us, TFI Fridays* and *Benny's and Jerry's*.

There is also the phenomenal global success of McDonalds and other fast food franchises and multiple outlets such as *Burger King, Pizza Hut, KFC, Subway* and *Starbucks*. In 2003, McDonalds had a presence in 119 nations, a remarkable increase in relation to 1991 where it had a presence in just 59. Global sales have increased from \$12.4 billion in 1986 to \$41.5 billion in 2004. By the end of this period, international sales exceeded US sales by \$14 billion per annum (figures quoted in Ritzer, *ibid*: 40). The example of *McDonalds* illustrates a further tendency produced by the globalization: 'glocalization' and the development and proliferation of 'hybrids'. In India, the religious and cultural pressures of Hinduism have resulted in *McDonalds* marketing the 'Maharaja Mac' – with 100 per cent mutton in the recipe – and 'Vegetable McNuggets'. There are, moreover, numerous examples of national variants of Americanized means of consumption. Examples include the *Harry Ramsden* Fish and Chips franchise owned by the *Compas Group* in the UK. This chain has over 170 owned and franchised outlets internationally and serves around 10 million people annually. It has international locations in Saudi Arabia, *Charles de Gaulle Airport* in Paris, France and even at Epcot in the *Walt Disney World Resort* in Florida, USA. The phenomenal success of the *TESCO* supermarket chain in the UK is partly due to the way in which it has emulated American giants such as *Wal-Mart*.

The development and increasingly global reach of the new 'cathedrals of consumption' has unleashed a powerful universalizing dynamic that has exported the forms of shopping and the styles of consumption that are dominant in the USA to disparate parts of the developed and developing world. This suggests that the multi-directional model of cultural globalization as developed, inter alia, by Featherstone (1991) is becoming increasingly problematic and that the dynamics of globalized hyper-commodification are leading towards forms of global standardization and homogenization that is best described as 'Americanisation' (Ritzer, 2004). However, there are many gaps and disjuncture in this process and the strength of local traditions and the prevalence of vernacular tastes have resulted in the generation of cultural hybrids in many places. In other cases, the processes of hyperconsumption and post-sociality are being resisted vigorously. In Western Europe, for example, there is enduring resistance to 'coca-colonization' (Kuisel, 1993) and there have been important campaigns against the opening of McDonald's stores in historic European cities. In many Islamic societies, the hyperconsumption associated with neo-liberal globalism is resisted fiercely by forms of religious tribalism that perceive it as a threat to traditional forms of religious identity (Barber, 1996). These developments have transformed and in some cases strengthened individual and collective identities in complex and often ambiguous ways. Thus, while the 'new means of consumption' and their associated lifestyles originated in the USA, they have become increasingly globalized through a complex and ambiguous process of cultural homogenization and heterogenization. The ambiguities created by this process have resulted in a constant and increasingly intensified tension between the generation of increasingly spectacular forms of consumption that blend and manipulate simulation and implosion and the generation of alienation, disappointment and disenchantment as the new means of consumption are experienced by increasingly reflexive individual consumers.

Rationalization and Its Discontents: From the Iron Cage to the Castle of Romantic Dreams?

The new means of consumption are clear manifestations of the application of formal rationality to the process of social reproduction. Global corporations require formal mechanisms of bureaucratic control in order to be effective and are underpinned by a formal logic of profit maximization in order to ensure maximum efficiency. The changes currently occurring in the area of consumption mark the culmination and intensification of the process of rationalization outlined by Max Weber (1948). For Weber, the development of modernity involved the increasing domination of modern social institutions by an 'iron cage' formal rationality. The institutions of bureaucracy and capitalism were rational structures through which individuals were constrained in material ways. These constraints contributed to a growing disenchantment in modern societies as 'magical elements of thought' were increasingly displaced by the icy darkness of modern rationalism. George Ritzer (2003) has explored the way in which the dominant forms of contemporary consumption are underpinned by formal rationality. The 'McDonaldization thesis' highlights how the McDonalds fast food franchise represents a paradigm case of a wider process of rationalization. The organizational form of McDonalds conforms to the 'ideal type' model of bureaucracy developed by Weber: efficiency, quantifiability, predictability and control. The efficiency of a 'Big Mac meal' derives from its instantaneous delivery in a society in which individuals are increasingly 'time poor' but 'cash rich'. McDonalds offer large amounts of food at what appear to be comparatively low prices and a *Big Mac* will taste the same at all branches of McDonalds and on each visit. Customers are controlled in the limited menu offered and uncomfortable seats mean customers do what managers want them to do – eat quickly and leave. Ritzer (*ibid: passim*) argues that the principles of McDonalds are spreading from the consumption of fast food to many other areas of consumption including education, childcare, banking and car maintenance. The new cathedrals of consumption clearly articulate the 'icy cold' principles of formal rationality, but this leaves the problem of explaining how and why these new means of consumption and the commodities that are sold within them are a key object of desire for so many individuals around the world. For example, the familiar Golden arches of *McDonalds,* and the symbols of other fast food outlets, have increasingly become cultural icons. They are deeply embedded in North American popular culture and many individuals identify with *McDonalds* with an almost sacred and quasi-religious intensity.

The tendency for individuals to maintain simultaneously positive and negative orientations towards the capitalist economy is a function of the ambiguous and contradictory qualities of money that we outlined earlier. The objectification of culture enables individual desire to flourish in a context of material compulsion. This tendency has been built into the economy from the early days of capitalism but has recently been intensified by ICT-led globalization and the development of reflexive modernization. In an exploration of the origins of this tendency, Colin Campbell (1989) contrasts the early Calvanists, that were the focus of Weber's analysis of the origins of the 'spirit of capitalism', and who sought signs of salvation in their good works, with later non-conformist Christians who sought evidence of their salvation in their good taste. The latter were responsible for the modern association between pleasure-seeking and good character and, in their eagerness to follow fashion, laid the basis, however unwittingly, for the spirit of modern consumerism. This spirit embraced a world of daydreams, illusions and fantasies and stood in stark contrast to the asceticism of the early Calvinist. From the beginning, therefore, capitalism embodied both 'rational' and 'romantic' dynamics. Rational capitalism became associated with production and the world of work and represented an 'iron cage' of economic necessity, whilst romantic capitalism became associated with consumption and the world of shopping and represented a 'castle of romantic dreams' (Campbell, *ibid*: 227). Modern individuals are engaged in a constant struggle to turn the former into the latter: a constant struggle owing to the way in which the fantasies produced by romantic capitalism are materially insatiable and lead to the constant regeneration of new needs and desires. This has important implications for understanding changes in the world of consumption. If rational capitalism resulted in disenchantment then romantic capitalism involved a parallel process of re-enchantment. To the extent that consumption is replacing work as the key source of identity and meaning, re-enchantment is likely to have become the principal cultural product of late capitalism. According to Ritzer (2005: 93–148), the development of the new means of consumption highlights the increasing centrality of re-enchantment in contemporary economic life.

The new 'cathedrals of consumption' involve the re-enchantment of consumption in several ways. As we saw in the work of Baudrillard, one of the principal ways that consumption has been re-enchanted is through the proliferation of simulation, spectacle and implosion. While the modern world was subject to differentiation, the postmodern world is subject to dedifferentiation or hyper-differentiation as phenomena are becoming interpenetrated and dissolving into one another. This tendency creates a different form of often-unintended spectacle that encourages consumption. The supermarket, for example, brings together the business of the grocer, the butcher, the fishmonger, the baker and the chemist under one roof. The shopping mall dissolves the geographical boundaries between shops and increasingly breaks down the boundaries between shopping and fun. A trip to the mall is increasingly seen as a leisure pursuit and malls are increasingly being combined with entertainment facilities such as multi-screen cinemas, themed restaurants such as *Dave and Buster's* and, in the case of large malls such as the *Mall of America,* encompass amusement parks. Postmodern consumption accelerates and intensifies the process of time–space compression (Harvey, 1989) as this results in both disorientation and disruption and the generation of spectacle and phantasmagoria. The boundary between home and shopping has always been porous, as the enduring tradi-tions of door-to-door sales, *Tupperware* and *Anne Summer's* parties, home shopping catalogues and telephone sales aptly demonstrates. However, the development of television and Internet shopping has increasingly dissolved the boundary between home and shopping. Television shopping channels such as *The Shopping Channel*, *QVC* and *HSN* blend entertainment and advert-ising in the form of *infomercials,* often using celebrities to endorse or pros-elytize about goods. Celebrities often sell their own range of goods, such as the ex-boxer George Foreman and his *Lean Mean Fat-Reducing Grilling Machine*. The development of cybermalls has intensified the process of time–space compression still further. Internet shopping is growing at a phenomenal rate. It is forecast that global online retail spending will increase from \$81 billion in 2005 to \$144 billion in 2010 and that the Internet will influence nearly half of total retail sales in 2010 compared to just 27 per cent in 2005 (Jupiter Research, 2006). The explosion of Internet shopping creates spectacle owing to the sheer magic of having the entire world of commodities available to us in our own homes, seven days a week, 24 hours a day (Ritzer, *op cit*: 130–132). These developments have also been encouraged, or indeed facilitated, by the implosion of past, present and future earning in the form of the credit card.

The new forms of consumption embody and articulate high levels of rationality and efficiency and have contributed greatly to the process of 'time–space compression' and profit maximization in an era of flexible accumulation (Harvey, *op cit*). The 'icy cold' effects of this process of rationalization, however, have been countered by a powerful process of re-enchantment whereby the new means of consumption and the commod-ities which pass through them have become increasingly aestheticized through their association with spectacle, simulation and implosion. The intensification of re-enchantment in the context of intense rationaliza-tion and disenchantment would suggest a situation in which individuals experienced everyday life accompanied by a gnawing sense of ambiguity and ontological insecurity. In the next section, we explore further how these feelings of ambiguity and ontological insecurity become manifest in the globalized spaces of the shopping mall and the city.

Postmodern Space and Consumption: Ambiguity, Ontological Insecurity and the Shopping Mall

The global city has created an increasing polarized, fragmented and frac-tured urban environment that can be described as the 'dual city' (Castells,

2000a). The globalized cityscapes of gleaming shopping malls, airport departure lounges, casino hotels and theme parks tend to be disconnected from the functionally unnecessary or socially disruptive populations by which they are surrounded. However, as polarization has increased these marginal populations tend to be excluded physically from globalized space through the walls, barriers, fences, gates and guards of the 'fortress city' (Davis, 1998: 223–264). Here at the heart of the 'space of flows' we see the construction and reinforcement of borders and boundaries. In other words, the global city and its marginalized borderlands are connected inextricably and form a ubiquitous feature of the geographical and social landscape of the global cultural economy. The alienating and ambiguous tendencies of postmodern culture are thus inscribed deeply into the built environment. This phenomenon has been explored by Fredric Jameson through the concept of 'postmodern space' (Jameson, 1984, 1998), which he describes as a mutation of the built environment resulting from the confluence of 'high art' and 'commercial forms' in the era of late capitalism. In the resulting hyperspace, individuals become physically disoriented, as they do not have the perceptual equipment to negotiate the new spaces. The origins of this hyperspace can be traced to the domination of the economy by 'finance capital' and the way this results in capital becoming 'free-floating' and separated from the 'concrete text of productive geography'. In this context, money takes on a second degree of abstraction and, in the context of the increasingly sophisticated communications systems of post-industrial society, finance capital takes the form of a 'butterfly stirring within a chrysalis' that 'separates itself off from that concrete breeding ground and prepares to take flight' (Jameson, *ibid*: 142). The 'dissonant' and 'scandalous' forms of abstraction associated with cultural modernism have entered the mainstream of cultural consumption and both commodity production and commodity consumption are increasingly underpinned by the resulting anti-social modernist forms (Jameson, *ibid*: 149).

Jameson explored this new hyperspace in the postmodern buildings of downtown Los Angeles, focusing in particular on the *Westin Bonaventure Hotel*. The hotel is a futuristic structure comprising three mirror-glassed towers with glass elevators rising up through a circular lobby towards the hotel rooms, a shopping complex, an indoor lake and a rotating rooftop lounge (Berger, 2004). This postmodern edifice does not attempt to insert a distinct or elevated language into the commercial sign system by which it is surrounded, but speaks the same language or commercialized syntax. The building does not aspire to be part of the city but to replace it as a 'total space' or a 'complete world' (Jameson, *op cit*: 11–12). The hotel does not seek to distinguish itself from the commercialism by which it is surrounded, but to reflect back its surroundings in a distorted form. The building is thus a physical manifestation of late capitalism. It forms a city within a city and is conceptually distinct from the 'deterrence machine' (Baudrillard, 1994a) constituted by Disneyland and other theme parks that radiate an 'ideological blanket' of the imaginary in order to render the outside 'real'. The imaginary of Disneyland is neither true nor false, it is a deterrence machine set up in order to rejuvenate the fiction of the real in the realm of fantasy (Baudrillard, *ibid*: 13)

In the absence of this deterrence machine, the design of the hotel reinforces the idea of total space. The lobby is below all the entrances and has to be reached by elevator or escalator, thus cutting off the lobby from the rest of the hotel and the rest of the city and producing a synchronic or timeless 'experience' in which a single 'new world' eclipses the diachronic or historically grounded experience of the outside world. The space makes it impossible to use the language of volume. The space is designed to make emptiness appear busy and evokes feelings of total immersion and submission. Postmodern hyperspace is thus able to achieve the same suppression of depth as postmodern painting or literature. The space is the art and lacks the regular world of references in which to size or ground perception. The resulting sense of disorientation is so intense that shoppers are unable to locate the stores or residents their rooms. In this context, colour coding and directional signs have been added to sustain the businesses within the building, thus deconstructing the hyperspace and adding a simulated sense of referentiality (Jameson, *ibid*: 15). Postmodern space is a reflection of the de-territorialized space inhabited by finance capital in the phase of neo-liberal capital accumulation and a representation of the postmodern perception to which it gives rise. This space distorts perceptions of self, other and the world and to the extent that it undermines and disrupts business, late capitalism creates resistance within itself. This resistance is, however, concealed and reincorporated through a process of 're-narrativization' through which late capitalism is able to re-endow the fragments of the postmodern world with cultural and mediatic meaning.

Los Angeles is often presented as *the* postmodern city. There are darker aspects to the development of postmodern space that have also been highlighted in the context of the recent redevelopment of LA. Mike Davis (1998) highlights the powerful forces of control, separation and manipulation are being inscribed within what has become a hard, quartz-like fortress city. The development of the Westin Bonaventure was part of a massive redevelopment of Downtown LA, which has involved billions of dollars of tax subsidies being used to attract financial and corporate headquarters, developers and off-shore investors to LA. This has resulted in the development of a series of block-square complexes such as the Bonaventure Hotel, the World Trade Center, California Plaza and the Arco Center. These privatized plazas combine corporate offices with high-class and luxury boutiques and middle-class housing and hotel space. These developments have resulted in the privatization of public space and the brutalization of spaces that remain outside these middle-class enclaves. Hence, the LA of free benches, luxurious parks and 'cruising strips' is virtually extinct. The pleasure domes of the elite Westside rely on the social imprisonment of a third world proletariat in increasingly repressive ghettos and barrios. The new privatized plazas form a dense and self-contained circulation system that forms a self-referential 'hyper-structure' separated off from the outside where the denigration of street life has resulted in the sequestration of the vital energies of the centre within a hermetically sealed fortress.

The redevelopment of downtown LA has involved the destruction of public space. The process of urban redevelopment has converted once vital urban streets into traffic sewers and transformed public parks into temporary receptacles for the homeless and wretched. Davies noted that street furniture had become sadistic, fear had become the dominant logic of public space, and surveillance had emerged as the dominant means of monitoring behaviour (Davis, 1998). Davis spotted benches that could not be laid on or even sat on but for short space of time, the destruction or privatization of public toilets, the locking of rubbish bins and even sprinkler systems placed on the outside of buildings to prevent rough-sleepers loitering. Public spaces such as parks were either locked or policed heavily. Those who used public space were stigmatized because of their homelessness, poverty, ethnicity or deviance, or a rabid combination of them all. The LAPD were engaged in a process of 'containment' by which the homeless were displaced into an area along Fifth Street known as Skid Row, transforming the neighbourhood into an outdoor poorhouse and probably the most dangerous ten blocks in the world. In the face of the fear of the inner city, the wealthy retreat either to gated estates or to areas patrolled by private security guards and electronic security systems. Increasingly, Davis (2000) notes the ubiquitous use of video surveillance of public spaces producing what he describes as a *scanscape* – a space of protective visibility that increasingly defines where white-collar office workers and middle-class tourists feel safe. This 'ecology of fear' is produced by the discourse of security not by violence or crime itself. The social perception of threat becomes a function of the security mobilization itself. In the fevered imagination of rampant crime, the middle-class elites flee the streets into the new privatized public spaces that have replaced the street – the shopping mall, the gated community and the downtown plaza.

The processes of rationalization and re-enchantment associated with contemporary consumption are not, therefore, universal processes. The implosion of boundaries within the new cathedrals of consumption has been paralleled by the intensification of boundaries between the happy shoppers within and the wretched and marginalized outside.

The hyperspaces that Jameson and Davis explored in LA are spreading throughout the globe. As we highlighted at the beginning of this chapter, the shopping mall is becoming universalized as a means of consumption. Increasingly shopping is confined within secure environments and monitored by private security guards and state-of-the-art CCTV. Every purchase and every action is captured by the all-seeing 'gaze' of security cameras. Anyone 'troublesome' is removed, and those who are not serious in their intent to consume are removed or deterred from entering in the first place. In these spaces we find the benches, the toilets and the decorations that are missing from outside. In the controlled, rationalized, homogenized space of the shopping centre or supermarket, individuals are 'free' to pursue their 'leisure'. The artefacts of the street have retreated behind the glass and cameras of private, consumption spaces. The guarded shopping mall is a highly controlled environment: closed at night and in the day to 'undesirables'. The mall is guarded from the dangers and disturbances of the street and the street increasingly becomes the preserve of the marginalized: the homeless, the mentally ill, drug addicts, alcoholics and the ethnic underclasses. The development of the shopping mall highlights the way in which postmodern space separates different types of people based on their consumption status: shoppers and non-shoppers in the shopping mall, residents and non-residents in the gated housing development and the tourist and non-tourist in the theme parks and beauty spots of the global tourist industry. The intense flows of the global cultural economy are thus reinforcing the borders and boundaries within the global spaces that house the new means of consumption.

As Georg Simmel noted, the city is not a spatial entity with sociological consequences but a sociological entity that is formed spatially (Simmel, 1971). The shopping mall, along with the other cathedrals of consumption, articulates the ambiguities and contradictions of a form of consumption that is simultaneously beyond modernity and yet continues to be underpinned by its icy grip. Contemporary consumption is neither modern nor postmodern but a liminal form that articulates a profound sense of betweenness that defies categorization. The shopping mall is awash with a cornucopia of images, symbols and values that always threaten to implode into a homogeneous black hole. The spectacles and simulacra that constitute these hyper-real spaces are both constitutive of identity and simultaneously deny the possibility of identity. These spaces are simultaneously forums of sociality and a social form that demonstrates the superfluity and impossibility of sociality. The softness of the mall's privatized interior walls is externalized as a city of quartz and the brutalization and exclusion of those who refuse or are unable to be seduced by its undoubted charms. In order to understand more precisely the impact of these processes on contemporary patterns of identity formation and social marginalization, we need to explore in more detail the complex pattern of disembedding underpinning the ambiguities of contemporary consumption.

Aporetic Consumption? Postmodernism, Ambiguity and Social Change

The postmodern world is defined by consumption (Bauman, 1992). The 'cultural turn' has marginalized the rational world of production and work and turned the economy into culture and culture into the transient and disposable world of goods (Illouz, 1997). This suggests that as modernity is transformed into postmodernity, 'icy cold' rationality is replaced by the warm embrace of emotion, mysticism, magic, myth, religiosity and reflection. The 'rational exchange' of commodities is replaced by 'symbolic exchange', a form of exchange that is potentially both unproductive and limitless (Baudrillard, 1973). In the synthetic world of hyper-reality, seduction underpins the power and play of illusion and the re-enchantment of everyday life (Baudrillard, 1983b). The centrality of seduction and illusion provides the basis for the re-dignification of irrationality and the re-learning of respect for ambiguity and emotion. Postmodernism has been defined as 'neo-medievalism' and postmodern consumption is often presented as containing the liminal forms of pre-modern society. This suggests that pre-modern cultures of transgression, such as fairs and carnivals, were not fully incorporated by the processes of commodification, rationalization and civilization (Elias, 1978, 1982) and endured as spaces marked by anti-structure, unmediation, emotional fusion and ecstatic oneness (Featherstone, 1990: 15). In the twentieth century, these sights of 'ordered disorder' became a key source of fascination, longing and nostalgia (Shields, 1990) and were displaced into art, literature, entertainment, department stores (Chaney, 1983; Williams, 1982) and theme parks (Urry, 1988). These sites of 'ordered disorder' conjured up elements of the carnivalesque in their displays, imagery and simulations. As we saw earlier, Walter Benjamin noted how the arcades and department stores were dream worlds or phantasmagoria of commodities that summoned up associations and half forgotten illusions or allegories (Benjamin, 1983). During the twentieth century, the blurring of art and commerce and the development of the design, marketing and advertising industries have intensified the tendencies outlined by Benjamin to produce the aestheticization of the urban landscape or indeed the 'aestheticization of everyday life' (Featherstone, 1992) to produce the cultural facets of postmodern culture. These include an emphasis on immediacy, intensity, sensory overload and disorientation, the mêlée or juxtaposition of signs and the mixing of symbolic codes, the unchained or floating signifiers of postmodern culture and the aesthetic hallucination of the real (Featherstone, 1990: 16). These aspects of postmodern culture have been used to highlight its transgressive and playful potential (Hebdige, 1988) and the ways in which contemporary flâneurs play with and celebrate the artificiality, randomness and superficiality of the mélange of dreams, fantasies and values to be found in the postmodern city (Calefato, 1988).

Featherstone (1990: 16) paints a positive and optimistic picture of post-modern consumption. Postmodern culture represents a move beyond individualism, a heightened emphasis on the affective and the empathetic and a new aesthetic paradigm in which people come together in fluid postmodern tribes (Maffesoli, 1996). This requires a 'controlled decontrol' of the emotions and a blasé outlook. The 'aestheticization of everyday life' dissolves the distinction between 'high' and 'low' cultures, coherent styles are fragmented, and there is an increasing focus on playing with and expanding the range of styles. Postmodernism involves a preoccupation with 'retro', pastiche, the collapse of symbolic hierarchies and the playback of cultures (Featherstone, 1990: 18). In the postmodern world, consumption constitutes an important source of agency and empowerment. According to Featherstone, as the domination of the sign system increases then our *literacy* in interpreting these signs also increases. Consumption becomes like *choosing* a path through a forest of signs in which we choose to consume what is meaningful to us and thereby construct actively our own identity. Lash and Urry (1994: 5) highlight the importance of 'aesthetic reflexivity', which entails 'self-*interpretation* and the interpretation of social background practices'. However, this exists alongside a parallel tendency for subjectivity to become 'emptied out' as manufactured cultural variety becomes 'flat' and 'deficient in affect' as symbolized in the meaningless consumption of the 'three-minute culture' produced by electronic media (Lash & Urry, *ibid*: 15).

The work of Bauman (2000, 2001, 2003) has been influential in exploring the meaning of individual choice in an uncertain future marked by 'a fluid world of globalisation, deregulation and individualization' (Bauman, 2002: 19). Bauman argues that the fluidity of modernity is not a new phenomenon and indeed, the 'ambivalence' of modernity is generated by the myth of its solidity. The institutional solidity of modernity has always been qualified by the resistance, contradictions and the softening effects of charisma (Weber, 1948), reflexivity (Giddens, 1990) and power (Foucault, 1980). The ambivalence of the modern condition was explored by Simmel in *the Metropolis and Mental Life*. The largely objectified culture of the metropolis encouraged the growth of an individualism that disembedded individuals from traditional communities and re-embedded them in fragmentary and transitory milieux emerging from the ever more sophisticated social and cultural division of labour within the metropolis. In this context, face-to-face interaction loses its social meaning and there is an increasing tension between spatial proximity and social distance. This process leads to objectification owing to the de-emotionalization of the relationship between the self and others. In the context of these contradictory tensions, ambiguous displays of 'urban cool' and 'blasé' indifference develop along-side a process of individualization premised on the assertion of individual distinctiveness. While Simmel argued that this resulted in an increase in cosmopolitanism or sociality, new forms of postmodern consumption seem to have initiated new forms on non-sociality or even loneliness.

Despite these continuities, Bauman (2000) finds it useful to differ-entiate between 'solid' and 'liquid' modernity. Liquid modernity is an era of disembedding without reembedding (Bauman & Tester, 2001: 89): the dissolution of the bonds that interlock individual choices and collective projects and actions (Bauman, *op cit*: 6). The inherent riskiness of liquid capital has resulted in an intensification of individual vulner-ability rather than collective political projects premised on the protec-tion of citizenship (Bauman, 2001). These developments have resulted in the emergence of new cultural forms that celebrate 'transience' and 'novelty' as part of a new ethic of 'desultory consumerism'. Hence, the freedom of perpetual transience is translated into the 'plenitude of consumer choice' (Bauman, 2000: 89). In liquid modernity, consump-tion is freed of sold obstacles and implicated in new levels of pleasure. Solid modernity harnessed the 'desire' of a fickle 'inner self' to a fluid and expanding consumerism. In liquid modernity, 'wish' completes the liberation of the 'pleasure principle', purging and disposing of the last residues of 'reality principle' impediments (Bauman, *ibid*: 75–76). Wish intermeshes with the 'aestheticization of everyday life' (Featherstone, *op cit*) and the compulsion to consume runs into the dead end of 'never wilting excitation' (Bauman, 2000: 83). In liquid modernity, consump-tion increasingly constitutes a form of irrationality as consumers become so fixated on the objects of consumption that they forget their own predicaments and thus the rise of the consumer equals the death of the citizen (Bauman & Tester, *op cit*: 114). Hence, the intense loneliness that marks liquid modernity. Consumption is a lonely activity even when conducted in the company of others (Bauman, 2000: 165). The heart of neo-modern darkness is located in the sphere of consumption. The estrangement of human labour through the money form in the sphere of production is replicated in the sphere of consumption as 'wish fulfil-ment' achieved in isolation from the intimate involvement of others. In a world where pleasure is derived from anonymous social relations, commitment is impossible and individuals are alienated by this sense of anonymity and the emptiness that is disguised by revolutionary high-tech forms of communication. In this context, alienation is aestheticized and reconstituted as 'cool'. This aestheticized alienation is emblematic of the ambiguous and complex nature of consumption in contemporary society.

Summary and Conclusion

In this chapter, we have argued that contemporary consumption marks out an important 'hotspot of transition' in the context of globalization and reflexive modernization. We highlighted the complex and ambiguous nature of contemporary consumption and suggested that this was a product of how the contradictions of modern money have been expanded and intensified by ICT-led globalization and the development of reflexive capitalism. We developed the work of Marx and Simmel to suggest that money is a contradictory embodiment of the concrete and the abstract and that this is manifested in the contradictory dynamics of compulsion and desire that underpin modern forms of consumption. These contradictions have resulted in the ability of money to generate magical and phantasmagorical spectacles and simulations and the objectification of individual personality into a reified culture that has resulted in the domination and alienation of individuals.

In the context of heightened levels of individual and institutional reflexivity, ambiguity has intensified as the new 'cathedrals of consumption' have simultaneously intensified the enchantment and romanticism of consumption through the generation of simulation, spectacle and implosion and intensified alienation, control and manipulation through the hyper-rationalization of large-scale and increasingly homogeneous patterns of consumption. We highlighted these patterns empirically in the context of an examination of the 'new means of consumption. We also traced the spatial manifestations of these ambiguities through an examination of the restructuring of postmodern space. Using the example of downtown LA as an emblematic example of postmodern space, we noted the wider phenomenon of postmodern consumption generating heightened levels of inequality and increasing social differentiation based on consumption status. We also noted the argument of Bauman, which suggests that the development of the postmodern consumer marks the death of the modern citizen. We will now turn to an exploration of the political identities and forms of political action that have developed in the context of globalization and the development of reflexive modernity.

6

Politics Beyond the State: New Individualities and Solidarities

The masses drift somewhere between passivity and wild spontaneity, but always as a potential energy, a reservoir of the social and of social energy.... Now, in fact, the masses have no history to write, neither past nor future, they have no vital energies to release, nor desire to fulfil; their strength is actual in the present.... And consists in their silence.

(Jean Baudrillard, 1983c: 2–3)

December 1995: two hundred thousand people take to the streets of Paris, France and engage in mass strikes in opposition to welfare cuts and employment reform. January 2003: a hundred thousand anti-globalization protestors converge on Porto Alegre, Brazil in order to discuss alternatives to global neo-liberalism. September 2001: two million peace protestors mobilize across the world in opposition to the US-led invasion and occupation of Iraq. These events provide compelling evidence that Francis Fukuyama's declaration of the 'end of history' and the ideological victory of liberal democracy was ill judged and misconceived (Fukuyama, 1992). Moreover, the masses mobilized are not the 'silent majorities' alluded to by Baudrillard in his depiction of the 'end of the social'. This is not to argue that nothing has changed and indeed, we will argue in this chapter that the arena of political mobilization and identity is an intense hotspot of social change.

Increasing global interconnectedness and the collapse of the Soviet bloc have unleashed powerful dynamics that have deconstructed key aspects of political modernity. The trajectory of the social change unleashed by the crisis and deconstruction of political modernity is complex and the consequences are ambiguous. This trajectory is not a straightforward shift from political modernity to a postmodern political paradigm marked by the end of 'movement with a direction' (Bauman, 1992: 188) or a regression into pre-modern neo-medievalism (Baudrillard, 1994b, Bauman, 1997). This post-structuralist perspective suggests that as the crisis of political modernity has deepened, the nation state has become marginalized by processes and developments at the supranational and sub-national level and that this has resulted in the undermining and decom-position of nationally defined forms of citizenship and social welfare. This has precipitated a crisis of modern political ideology and collective forms of political engagement have increasingly given way to individu-alized forms of identity politics. Central to these developments is the de-centring of the labour movement as the dynamic subject of social development and the increasing centrality of new social subjectivities and social movements that aspire to autonomy in civil society rather than a material engagement with capital and the state. In other words, polit-ical trajectories have become increasingly open, fluid and non-linear and political identities have consequently become increasingly complex and ambiguous.

In previous chapters, we highlighted the powerful processes of disembed-ding that underpin the process of globalization along with new forms of sociation that have resulted from complex processes of glocalized re-embedding. While we agree with Bauman that contemporary patterns of hyperconsumption are premised on a process of 'disembedding without reembedding' (Bauman & Tester, 2001: 89), it would be something of a linear and deterministic argument to suggest that this tendency can be generalized across the institutions and processes of 'second' or 'radicalized' modernity. Indeed, in the context of the intense processes of reflexivity generated by the parallel processes of globalization and individualization, we would expect to see collective and group identities being increasingly chosen on the basis of (re)invented hybrid tradition (Beck, 1999). In this chapter, we focus on the complex processes of reflexive re-embedding that are taking place around the new forms of sub-national and supra-national politics beyond the nation state. Following our approach in previous chapters, we focus on the new political identities that are being generated by complex and shifting patterns of inclusion and exclusion. We argue that it is possible to differentiate between parochial patterns of political realignment premised on local opportunity structures and networks of obligation and cosmopolitan patterns of political realignment premised on transnational opportunity structures and networks of obligation. The aim of this chapter is to trace the new individualities and solidarities that are being generated by these complex processes and assess the extent to which this provides the basis for effective forms of globalized cosmopolitan democracy. This is important if we are to assess the extent to which the latter is capable of civilizing the increasingly apparent negative tendencies of neo-liberal globalism associated with unsustainable capitalist growth, environmental devastation and extreme forms of religious fundament-alism and state-sponsored global terrorism.

The defining feature of political modernity was the centrality of the nation state and the embedding of the nation state into a relatively stable international system of nation states based on mutual self-recognition and fixed and stable national boundaries. Within nation states, political identities were 'fixed' by totalizing meta-ideologies or *weltanschauungen* (Mannheim, 1936) that provided a stable and consistent picture of heroic pasts and glorious utopian futures and which underpinned the 'solidity' of social and political boundaries, hierarchies and networks. The history of modernity has been marked by intense ideological struggles between these competing meta-ideologies. During the twentieth century, the obvious manifestation of this was the struggle between the totalitarian ideologies of state socialism and fascism and the pluralistic ideologies of liberalism and social democracy. In the context of reflexive modernity, these totalizing ideologies have become increasingly relativized, fragmented and decentred. Increasingly, these ideologies fail to provide either a coherent and consistent picture of past, present and future or a solid basis for either social boundaries and hierarchies or political mobilization and identity. The result of this process is a series of ideological positions that are no longer organized along the established terrain of left and right (Giddens, 1994).

In the post-war period, the dominant or 'hegemonic' ideology in the developed 'West' was the ideology of social democracy: an institutionalized form of class compromise that balanced the dynamism and individualism of liberal capitalism with the social justice and collectivism of reformist socialism. The institutional expression of this hegemony was in various varieties of 'welfare capitalism' that recognized and incorporated the power of organized labour within both the economy and polity in a complex network of corporatist institutions that regulated the welfare of individual workers in both the workplace and the community. The ideological and institutional hegemony of social democracy at the international level was maintained and reproduced by a range of transnational institutions that maintained a balance between a humanitarian discourse on human rights and an international monetary system that maintained liquidity and growth on an international scale. These arrangements were underpinned by the political power of the United States and the economic power of the US dollar. This political configuration has become increasingly relativized, fragmented and decomposed by the dynamics of globalization and reflexive modernity.

The purpose of this chapter is to explore the decomposition and fragmentation of political modernity. We begin with a discussion of the crisis and decomposition of social democracy and explore the extent to which the recent emergence of 'Third Way' politics is manifestation of a new form of individualized and reflexive social democracy for the global age. We suggest that the 'democratic deficit' associated with this form of politics has undermined the legitimacy of institutional politics and in the resulting political vacuum new forms of individualized politics and increasingly fluid forms of political identity have developed. We highlight an increasing tension between the reactionary and violent forms of nationalism, fundamentalism and political terrorism that have developed in opposition to individualization and progressive forms of radicalized democracy and new social movement politics that form a progressive accommodation with individualization. We then explore the ways in which the globalization of the latter tendency has resulted in the emergence of a global network premised on the civilizing of neo-liberal globalism and highlight the importance of the Zapatistas guerrilla movement in Mexico, the Global Justice Movement (GJM) and the World Social Forum (WSF). We then explore how the development of reflexive modernity and the tendency towards individualization are influencing the 'old' social movement politics associated with the labour movement. We highlight the development of both defensive coalitions between the labour movement and national and global neo-liberalism and positive alliances and coalitions between the labour movement and global civic networks around a strategy of 'social movement unionism' (SMU) (Waterman, 1984). We conclude the chapter with an analysis of global civil society and, based on the political mobilizations and identities explored in this chapter, analyse the limits and possibilities for cosmopolitan democracy to develop as a civilizing force against neo-liberal globalism. The overall aim of the chapter is thus to explore the new forms of political sociation that are developing alongside the globalized political opportunity structures and networks of obligation associated with reflexive modernity.

Neo-Liberal Globalism and the Crisis of Social Democracy

In the previous two chapters, we highlighted the way in which the development of the global economy has created new networks and configurations of financial and productive capital and the ways in which this is related to a global ideology of consumerism. At this point, it is useful to differentiate between globality, globalism and globalization. The condition of globality has been generated by an amalgam of forces, many technological and irreversible, that are breaking down barriers of time, space and nation and fashioning the planet into a coherent global community (Beck, 2000a: 10). This is distinct from 'globalism' which constitutes a contestable political discourse that promotes a transnational world view, a philosophy of governance and a particular set of institutional structures (Beck, *ibid*: 9). Globalization comprises the processes through which sovereign nation states are criss-crossed and undermined by transnational actors with varying prospects of power, orientations, identities and networks (Beck, *ibid*: 11). We will begin by highlighting where this power is concentrated and where the dominant networks and identities are located.

There has developed alongside globality an array of powerful individuals, groups and organizations committed to the ideology of neo-liberal globalism. The project is underpinned by a new economic orthodoxy known as the 'Washington Consensus': a policy agenda embracing fiscal discipline, tax reform, the control of public expenditure, financial liberalization, direct foreign investment, privatization, deregulation and property rights (Williamson, 2000). The dynamic of neo-liberal globalism is underpinned by what Leslie Sklair has called 'transnational political practices' or the actions of a transnational capitalist class which includes the executives of TNCs, state bureaucrats with global outlooks and bureaucrats within global institutions, capitalist inspired politicians and consumerist elites (Sklair, 1995: 70–72). These political actors organize national/local conditions in ways that are favourable to the interests of neo-liberal globalism and encourage the adoption of a 'comprador mentality' within nation states whereby local practices are downgraded in favour of global practices. While this provides important insights into the types of social actors associated with neo-liberal globalism, the problem with the approach developed by Sklair is that he presents political globalization as a part of a process that involves the linear progression from 'national' elites to 'transnational' elites. This ignores the way in which the disembedding of political power at the national level transforms in a fundamental way the very nature of power itself.

In previous chapters, we highlighted the networked form of contemporary society. In our discussion of new forms of urbanism, we highlighted the way in which the global city constitutes a nodal point in a global network of flows that constitute the global cultural economy. In our discussion of the informational workplace, we highlighted the way in which power has become embedded in the management and information systems supported by the global diffusion of ICT. In our discussion of globalized consumption, we highlighted the way in which hyperconsumption has become premised on disembedded forms of symbolic power within the networks of the global media system. The new global elites are not placeless and they tend to agglomerate around the cultural nodes and financial hubs of the global city. The power of these elites is, however, placeless and it tends to be embedded in and flow around the networks and systems of the global cultural economy. Lash and Urry (1994: 23) refer to the continued importance of hierarchies. While hierarchies have become less important in the 'microsociology of work relations', they have become more significant 'in the macro-relations of political power'. In Chapter 4, we examined examples 'post-panoptical' power in the call centre workplace and now we can observe the wider diffusion of this type of power. Post-panoptical power is no longer premised on the imagined co-presence of others, but is defined by 'escape, slippage, elision and avoidance' and 'the end of the era of mutual engagement' (Bauman, 2000: 11). The new global elite rules 'without burdening itself with the chores of administration, management [and] welfare' (Bauman, *ibid*: 13). This does not result in the marginalization of the nation state but a transformation in its form and function. As John Urry has argued:

> The fluid and turbulent nature of global complexity means that states have to adapt and co-evolve in relation to enormously different sets of global networks and fluids that transform the space beyond each state. States thus co-evolve as the legal, economic and social regulators, or gamekeepers, of systems of networks generated through the often-unpredictable consequences of many other systems. (Urry, 2005: 248)

In the context of globalization, therefore, the role of the nation state in maintaining the productive power of a particular territory is increasing in importance. The administrative apparatus of the nation state is expanding to cope with the complex demands of global systems. The power of the nation state has thus been recomposed into a polycentric and coordinated form of networked global governance. While state regulation involved the nation state mediating between the competing interest groups of civil society on issues of resource allocation, governance is premised on the multi-level coordination of networks of institutional actors, including nation states, on issues of broad value and goal consensus (Rosenau, 1999). The resulting transnational spaces are populated by the autonomous actions of a range of transnational actors including a range of intergovernmental organizations (IGOs) and international non-governmental organizations (INGOs). The main IGOs include the United Nations and subordinate agencies such as UNESCO, UNICEF, WHO, the IMF, the World Bank, WTO and NATO. IGOs have become more important at the regional level as evidenced by the development of the European Union, the North American Free Trade Agreement (NAFTA) and the Association of Southeast Asian Nations (ASIEN). The number of INGOs has proliferated since the 1960s and includes environmental pressure groups such as Greenpeace and Friends of the Earth, religious forums, sports organizations such as FIFA and welfare organizations such as the Red Cross. Global governance networks include IGOs, INGOs and MNCs and BINGOs (Business INGOs) such as international trade and employers' organizations. The notion of neo-liberal globalism highlights the extent to which the global elite have been able to dominate these transnational public spheres. This is reflected in the liberalizing agenda of organizations such as the World Trade Organization (WTO) and the International Monetary Fund (IMF) and a policy emphasis on the liberalization of trade in goods and services and the reform of social welfare and social protection systems.

The emergence of an increasingly focused opposition to this process highlights the existence of a serious 'democratic deficit' within global institutions (Held, 1995, 2000: 39). The ideology of 'Third Way' social democracy is a discursive expression of the new global elite that attempts to legitimate the inequalities associated with neo-liberal globalism. This highlights the enduring connection between social democracy and 'world events' and an important continuity between twentieth and twenty-first century politics (Shaw, 2001: 15–19). In the immediate post-war period, social democracy emerged as an ideological hegemon owing to its discursive centrality to post-war reconstruction, the post-Bretton Woods international system and the politics of the Cold War. The discursive hegemony of social democracy in the contemporary period is related to the centrality of European social democracy to the broader post-Cold War dynamic of democratization (Robinson, 1996) as manifested in eastward expansion of European integration. There remain, however, important questions with regard to the extent to which social democracy can deliver re-distributionist concessions and benefits in the global era. Indeed, the failure of Third Way social democracy is partly responsible for the emergence of complex alliances and cleavages between global elites and critics of the neo-liberal agenda on the nationalistic right, the social democratic and trade union left and the new civic networks in global civil society. Historically, the internal contradictions of social democracy led social democratic politicians to view the contradictions of capitalism as 'technical problems' that could be overcome by managerialist state planning (Taylor, 1999). This often led social democrats to, not only accept the existence of capitalism, but to initiate programmes for its improvement. The nationalization and socialization of industries and services in the post-war period, often in the face of extreme capitalist hostility, highlight the modernizing dynamic inherent to social democracy (Przeworski, 1980: 56). Significant sections of the working class nevertheless benefited materially from the modernizing dynamic associated with the Keynesian Welfare State (KWS). The KWS delivered substantive forms of social citizenship, although the *de jure* universalism of these forms of citizenship was often compromised by *de facto* exclusions around gender, race, sexuality and disability (Cook & Watt, 1992; Lister, 1993; Pateman, 1988; Williams, 1993).

The forms of citizenship associated with the KWS are undermined by three processes associated with globalization (Conway, 2004). First, intensifying transnational economic and cultural flows have expanded the reach of human rights norms and thereby eroded the administrative capacity and legitimacy of national political institutions. Second, in the context of the global institutionalization of the human rights discourse, individuals and groups are able to raise claims against states regardless of citizenship status. Third, processes of immigration have created multiple allegiances amongst diasporic communities and instantiations of dual and multiple citizenship. Furthermore, in the context of neo-liberal globalism, social democracy has faced the dilemma that a continuing support for the dynamism of capitalism is seriously compromised by forms of intervention at the national level and 'modernization' has involved various reconfigurations of community, identity and democracy at the sub-national and supra-national level. This has included support for deepening European integration or the reform of global institutions such as the IMF, WTO and the World Bank and a shift in policy priorities from Keynesian demand side policies to supply side policies designed to enhance individual and institutional dynamism and competitiveness (Clift, 2002; Stammers, 2001: 35–38). The Third Way is based on transforming the welfare state into a 'social investment state' that empowers individuals to become responsible for their own welfare or become 'entrepreneurs of the self' (Giddens, 1994, 1998).

In essence, the ideology of the Third Way, as articulated by global institutions such as the European Union, attempts to paint a cosmopolitan gloss over a process of neo-liberal restructuring that involves the imposition of 'new right' social and employment policies at the national level. The more the 'democratic deficit' has become visible within these new forms of institutional subsidiary, the greater has been the resistance and opposition to neo-liberal reform. We suggest there are three main manifestations of this resistance and opposition that are defining the terrain of the global public sphere. First, expressions of nihilistic individualism and militant and aggressive forms of nationalism and terrorism. Second, claims for post-national citizenship premised on cultural autonomy in global civil society. Third, the re-emergence of the social democratic and trade union left alongside claims for substantive material concessions at national, regional and global level. We will explore each of these tendencies in turn before considering the way in which they interact within the global public sphere.

Globalization and Individualism: Beyond Identity Politics?

The crisis of social democracy is linked to a wider crisis of modernity and the way in which this has generated a dynamic process of individualization. Individualization is a product of hyper-differentiation and the increasing impossibility of integrating fragmented individuals within functional systems with competing logics of action. The nation state played a central role in this process owing to the ways in which the regulation of welfare encouraged self-reliance and self-organization. The intensification of modernity has involved the transformation of modern biographies into 'elective' or 'risk' biographies and, in the context of increasing uncertainty, the constant threat of biographical slippage (Beck & Beck-Gernsheim, 2001 24). In this context, failure becomes personal failure and social crises, such as structural unemployment, poverty and the increasing precariousness of middle class living, are 'collectively individualized' and transformed into the risk burdens of individuals (Sennett, 1998). This is particularly evident in the discourse of the 'underclass' that has developed in the context of de-industrialization and the crisis of the social democratic state (Lash & Urry, *op cit*: 165–170). Within this discourse, the underclass has come to represent a dangerous internalized 'other' (Bauman, 1998a,: 67). The political project of neo-liberalism is of course committed deeply to a process of 'atomization' in which risk is intensified by the dismantling of those institutional resources, such as welfare systems, education and human rights that are vital to the maintenance of risk biographies. This is resulting in the sub-politicization of society and the de-politicization of national politics (Beck & Beck-Gernsheim, *op cit*: 27–28). Hence, there is an increasing crisis of representative democracy owing to a lack of trust in collective actors and the hollowing out and reconstitution of collective actors owing to the processes of globalization and individualization. The consequences of radicalized or 'second' modernity are characterized by two contradictory phenomena. On the one hand, the (re)emergence of new forms of nationalism, fundamentalism and terrorism based on ethnic and religious tribalism. On the other hand, demands for radicalized democracy premised on a reflexive recognition of the ways in which political parties, trade unions and the institutions of the welfare state negate freedom and self-realization and the way in which 'altruistic individualism' is made possible by the defence of the 'life world' from the market and communal regulation. This reflects the way in which both nationalism and globalism are essentially janus-faced phenomena: reflecting the 'dark' and 'light' sides of reflexive modernity.

The picture of postmodern politics painted by Bauman and others is thus a partial and one-sided description of a more complex and contradictory process. Postmodern politics is presented as a product of hyper-differentiation (Crook & Pakulski, 1992) and the ambivalence produced by epistemological uncertainty and ontological pluralism (Bauman, 1997). Bauman (1992) compares the modern social and political actor to a 'pilgrim' who spends a lifetime building a single, coherent and 'centred' life

project. This singular 'life project' has been replaced by a series of alternative postmodern life strategies premised on the short-term mini-projects
and the fluid and de-centred identity of the 'gambler'. Postmodern politics
involves single-issue campaigns pursued by 'imagined communities' where
the ambivalence of the postmodern condition creates a constant tendency towards irrationality and instability. The ambivalence at the heart of
the postmodern condition results in forms of identity politics in which
politics is created by individuals rather than being imposed on them.
There is a marked de-centralization of politics and the policy-making
process is increasingly localized by the actions of single-issue movements.
Postmodern politics is thus premised on liberty, diversity and tolerance,
although a liberty that is often reduced to consumer choice, a diversity
reducible to lifestyle choice and a tolerance based on a spectator curi-
osity in front of a TV screen. This is what Bauman (1991: 245) refers to
as the 'dark side' of postmodernity. Imagined communities develop tribal
conceptions of right, truth and beauty and, without the constraints of
reason, it is possible that barbarism and brutality will be applied to the
'other' on the outside of the community. In this context, privatization
and selfishness are intrinsic parts of the postmodern condition. We will
explore a range of recent developments to substantiate our argument that
the results of individualization are in fact more complex and contradictory
than suggested in the model of 'postmodern politics'.

The contemporary importance of nationalism, fundamentalism and
terrorism highlights the development of 'neo-tribal' forms of politics in
which imagined communities formed by individuals with shared values,
attitudes and beliefs draw on shared symbols to construct a common self-
identity. This has combined with a 'politics of desire' in which imagined
communities seek to acquire the 'tribal tokens' which confirm self-identity
and thereby articulate a politics of 'fear' and 'certainty' (Bauman, 1992).
The 'dark' side of this form of politics is expressed in virulent and violent
expressions of fundamentalism, nationalism and terrorism. The complex
and contradictory form of postmodern politics cannot, however, be understood solely in terms of the crisis of modern nationalism and the growth of
postmodern globalism. What we are currently witnessing is the crisis of the
modern matrix of nationalism and globalism – which was dealt a death-
blow by the global events following 9/11/2001 – and the development of
a new global matrix that overlays the old matrix in complex and contradictory ways (Nairn & James, 2005). The source of this dynamic is the
aggressive assertion of neo-liberal globalism since 1989 that has simultaneously dissolved national boundaries and reduced the power and status of
nation states. The result has been elite and mass resentment and the mobilization of often-aggressive forms of non-economic power. This reflects the
human cost of destroying national boundaries. The process of neo-liberal

restructuring and the attempt to undermine these borders has magnified the importance of 'identity politics'. Within the resulting national–global matrix, culture, language, feeling and religion have emerged in equal importance to economics and the internationalization of *homo economicus* as desired by the Washington Consensus. Hence, the relationship between ICT-led globalization, political violence and terrorism:

> Technology has fused with lowered borders, increased migratory movements, rising expectations and correspondingly inflamed resentments, to create a militant *identity-thirst*. People that despair of neo-liberal lackeys and Third Way hypocrites do not lose their wish for meaningful lives and transcendent purpose. They go elsewhere: in the West, religion, reheated xenophobia and reality TV are evident candidates.... The meaning-nexus undermined by boundary loss is reclaimed by strident affirmation of identity, or even more splendid martyrdom (Nairn, 2005: 45–46; our emphasis)

In many ways, therefore, the Islamic suicide bombers who hit the World Trade Center, New York with passenger aircraft on 9/11/2001 and its aftermath are an unintended side effect of neo-liberal globalism. The post-2001 'war on terror' or 'meta-war' (James, 2005) unleashed by the Bush regime in the United States marks an attempt to re-impose US leadership on a globalization process that has become increasingly divergent from and dysfunctional for a US-led neo-imperialist foreign policy premised on 'one market under God' (Nairn, *ibid*: 31). This is a reflection of the way in which neo-liberal globalism creates new inequalities and novel ways of both connecting places and bypassing and ignoring them (Ferguson, 2002). Hence, an engine of conflagration has developed which transforms liberal democratic capitalism into ethnic hatred (Chua, 2002). In a fluid and fragmented world, individuals fasten onto material interests and prejudice in order to satisfy their 'identity thirst'.

The events of 9/11 are the most spectacular manifestation of a form of fundamentalist politics associated with Islam that has spread throughout the developing world. This form of politics has become a state ideology in Iran and is posing a serious challenge to secular regimes in Indonesia, Egypt and Pakistan (Bruce, 2000: 40–65). In the United States, there has been a marked revival in Christian fundamentalism and the development of an important coalition between a neo-conservative 'moral majority' of Evangelical Christians and political representatives of the new right (Bruce, *ibid*: 66–93). In the context of weakening civil and national bonds, there has been the development of aggressive forms of ethnic sub-nationalism that exploit the particularities of place, religion or ethnicity (Alter, 1994: 91–119). This resurgence of nationalism has involved either the implosion of nation states or sub-national challenges to the legitimacy and integrity of nation states, often based on 'cultural' or even mystical forms of identity based on romanticism, ritual, tradition and legend. In the global South, an important legacy of colonialism was the drawing of national boundaries in ways that ignored ethnic, cultural and tribal divisions. These divisions have re-emerged recently in the form of serious sub-national conflicts in Burundi, Nigeria, Eritrea, Iran, Iraq, India, Pakistan and Indonesia (Forrest, 2003; Pfaff-Czainecka, 2005). The collapse of the Soviet bloc and the Soviet Union has revitalized ancient nationalities and ethnicities and resulted in serious ethnic conflict in Moldova, Chechnya, Georgia and Azerbaijan and civil war in the former Yugoslavia (Fowkes, 1996; Zisserman-Brodsky, 2003). There has also been the emergence of important separatist movements in North America in form of Quebec nationalism in Canada and in Europe in the form of Basques (Spain), Breton (France), Welsh and Scottish (UK) nationalisms (Keating, 1988; Reinharz & Mosse, 1992).

The re-emergence of nationalism has coincided with the resurgence in far right politics and the increasing popularity of a range of neo-fascist parties and movements. In Europe, for example, far right movements have developed a fervent nationalism in order to oppose immigration, 'big government' and European integration. Important examples include the Austrian Freedom Party, the British National Party, and the Front National in France, the German Peoples Union and the National Alliance in Italy (Eatwell, 2000; Payne, 1999). In the United States, a range of white supremacist, neo-Nazi and anti-Semitic groups, including the Ku-Klux-Klan (Castells, 1997: 84–97), constitutes the 'Patriot' movement. The re-emergence of fascism is perhaps unsurprising given the traditional focus of fascist ideology on anti-liberalism, irrationalism and the aestheticization of politics (Payne, 1995). These developments articulate the politics of risk and certainty in the context of the de-alignment of class politics associated with Third Way social democracy. Political debate and discourse has become dominated by post-material values at the same time that sections of the working class in both the developed and developing world are threatened by the neo-liberal restructuring of welfare and labour markets. In the context of the resulting disenfranchisement, support for extreme forms of right-wing populism has grown significantly (Eatwell, *op cit*: 415; Veugelers, 1999). The global challenge to social democracy has thus coalesced with the emergence of identity politics to reinvigorate the politics of 'nation' and 'place' in increasingly aggressive forms of far right nationalism and state-sponsored terrorism.

There is, however, a contrary reaction to this dark side of postmodern politics in the form of demands for radical democracy. The growth of the extreme and nationalistic right is often presented as a reaction against the post-material values of egalitarianism and cultural liberalism articulated by new social movements and the new left (Ignazi, 1992, 1997). Indeed, this is presented as an indication that values are becoming a more important determinant of political identity and alignment than class (Inglehart, 1990, Minkenberg, 1993). NSM politics pose a cultural challenge to the dominant language of an increasingly complex civil society. The actors within NSMs are presented as the transformative and prefigurative agents of post-industrial society or 'prophets of the present' who articulate alternative futures in the form of new values, identities and lifestyles (Melucci, 1989). Maffesoli (1996) has highlighted the tribal nature of new social movement politics, where 'the tribe' is not so much a fixed group as a certain ambiance or state of mind expressed through lifestyles, appearance and form. The transformative capacity of NSMs is questioned by commentators who highlight the fragmenting effects of hyper-differentiation. Touraine (1997) argues that NSM politics does not go beyond the generation of inter-subjective forms of democracy premised on social relations between subjects who confront other subjects and forms of power and struggle against domination, and for liberty, equality and tolerance (Touraine, *ibid*: 196). In essence, post-social movements express nothing but their own individuality and do not transcend identity politics. To what extent, therefore, are NSM politics simply a reflex of the tribal politics of desire, fear and certainty? There are many signs that the implosion of 'consumer' and 'citizen' associated with the process of hyper-differentiation has resulted in the politicization of articles such as food, music and clothing. The 'politics of desire' is manifested in a range of 'new age' quasi-religions or the aestheticization of politics around post-material issues such as gender, sexuality, human rights and the environment (Bagguley, 1996). NSMs attract participants through 'emotional recruitment' or through the way in which NSMs 'frame' personal experiences into individual meanings and organizational perspectives (McAllister-Groves, 1995). The liberation politics of the 1960s around black power, sexuality and gender have become increasingly focused on cultural autonomy, separatism and the positive assertion of identity. This follows the logic of 'disembedding without re-embedding' (Bauman & Tester, *op cit*: 89). There is, however, evidence of the re-embedding of identity politics in relation to glocalized opportunity structures and networks of obligation. We will illustrate this through an examination of the phenomenon of 'DIY' culture that emerged during the 1990s.

During the 1990s, radical forms of environmentalism emerged as part of a broader phenomenon of DIY culture: a youth-centred and youth-directed counter-culture premised on direct action politics and new musical sounds and experiences. The counter-culture included radical environmental groups such as *Earth First!* and *Reclaim the Streets* that were linked to alternative media such as *Indymedia* and *Squall* and new spaces of protest, pleasure and living such as Rave music and free parties (McKay, 1998).

In many ways, this was a paradigm case of postmodern politics with a number of distinctive features in comparison with earlier examples of counter-cultural politics (McKay, 1996). DIY culture resulted in forms of sub-national and localized tribal politics focused on the politics of desire, fear and certainty. This included the use of music and dress to subvert mainstream consumer culture and the refocusing of politics around 'fun', 'self-development' and affective micro-communities (Jowers et al., 1999). DIY culture tended to be vicarious, anti-intellectual and to articulate a culture of immediacy that tended towards forms of narcissistic hedonism and lifestyle anarchism associated with single issue campaigns and 'new age' spirituality. However, DIY culture also provided a reflexive challenge to 'expert systems' with regard to the environmental implications of global warming or road building and the reconstitution of trust through the development of direct and unmediated forms of media. Furthermore, DIY culture emerged as an important example of 'solidary individualism' (Berking, 1996) formed through a practical critique of the spectacular forms of mainstream politics and culture (Plant, 1992) and the demand for unmediated forms of radicalized cultural politics. In other words, DIY culture is ambiguous and lies somewhere between a reflexive 'risk community' premised on a critique of scientific rationality on the basis of counterfactual reason (Beck, 1992; Giddens, 1990) and the inter-subjective identity politics suggested by Bauman (1992) and Touraine (*op cit*). DIY culture can be understood as a form of postmodern politics within modern society (Heller & Feher, 1988): a form of politics premised on a rejection of grand narratives, the privileging of function over structure and a weakening of class politics.

The principle of postmodern politics can be witnessed in new social movements and, importantly, and can increasingly be seen as part of a labour movement reorientation around 'social movement unionism'. This form of post-ideological politics is evolving around forms of political mobilization and action based on the pursuit of 'communicative competence', 'communicative morality'(Habermas, 1987) and forms of democratic self-actualization based on post-material values. This can also be demonstrated through changes in the nature of peace politics as manifested in the global mass mobilizations in opposition to USA/UK-led campaigns in Iraq and Afghanistan. During the 1950s and 1960s, peace politics was intimately related to both the class and the nation state. Organizations such as the Campaign for Nuclear Disarmament (CND) in the United Kingdom combined mass mobilization with a lobbying role in relation to the British Labour Party. In the 1950s and 1960s, peace politics reflected a form of 'middle class radicalism' (Parkin, 1968) or the political expression of a disaffected group of workers within the welfare state (Day & Robbins, 1987). In the United Kingdom, the women peace campaigners at US airbase

Greenham Common during the 1980s presaged the emergence of a new form of postmodern peace politics. This was a politics based on symbolic direct action, a fundamental questioning of 'trust' with regard to both the US and the UK governments and the mass media and innovative forms of democratic self-organization (Blackwood, 1984; Jones, 1983; Harford & Hopkins, 1984). The contemporary anti-war mobilizations are truly a global phenomenon and combine symbolic direct action with a demand for the democratic accountability of global political actors. In relation to DIY culture and the more recent anti-war protests, we see that while political identity has been disembedded from within the nation state, the glocal implications of issues such as global warming and neo-imperialist warfare have resulted in processes of re-embedding in local and transnational opportunity structures and networks of obligation. In the last decade, this process has become even more apparent in relation to the global anti-capitalist movement, which we explore in more detail in the following section.

Anti-Globalism: Networks of Resistance and the Globalization of Politics

Neo-liberal globalism has developed in the context of oppositional social forces that have posed serious limits on its development. The emergence of a global 'networks of networks' in opposition to neo-liberal globalism raises fundamental questions with regard to the ways in social movements are analysed and understood. The analysis of modern social movements focused on the ways in which the processes of 'resource mobilization' (McCarthy & Zald, 1987: 20–25) and 'frame alignment' (Snow et al., 1986: 464) generated collective identities and movement cohesion in the context of nationally defined structures of political opportunity and representation (McAdam et al., 2001). To what extent is it possible to stretch this framework to an anti-globalization movement that has been described as a networked, non-hierarchical, leaderless and rhizomatic global fluid (Urry, *op cit*: 247)? The fluid nature of the anti-globalization movement obviously undermines that notion that it is sustained by 'collective identity' (McDonald, 2002) and the notion of a network of networks highlights the importance of 'identity work' and cross-fertilization during periods of 'latency' (Melucci, 1989, 1996a). In conditions of globality, the imposition of neo-liberal globalism 'exacerbates the divisions and fissures in the architecture of national disciplinary and control systems, and reduces their importance as sites of pressure for global social movement actors (Chesters & Welsh, 2005: 191). A complex, global planetary action system (Melucci, 1989) has developed marked by ICT-facilitated system-feedback and hypermobility (Urry, 2000). In this context, the debate on social movements has shifted from 'cyclical' patterns of social movement mobilization to iterative processes of 'becoming' associated with the antagonistic potential of forces that resist or escape the stratification, over-coding and control of neo-liberal globalism (Chesters & Welsh, *op cit*: 188; cf. Deleuze & Guattari, 1986). In this context, the anti-globalization movement has taken the form of a mode of symbolic contestation underpinned by demands for discursive democracy and manifested in antagonistic conflict that overflows borders and is iterated through various scales from the local to the global (Chesters & Welsh, *ibid*: 188). The emergence of the anti-globalization movement highlights the emergence of new democratic spaces and the 'reflexive framing' of issues in ways that contribute to 'ontological security' through the linking of personal and planetary milieux. The framing repertoires within the anti-globalization movement has been radically extended by the extensive use of ICT and the occurrence of 'events' or 'encounters' that involve processes of intense networking around nodal pints of contestation such as protest events or social forums (Chesters & Welsh, *ibid*: 192).

The Deleuzian perspective eschews the restructuration of protest and contestation, and there is a tendency to focus on the anti-globalization movement as a form of 'disorganization' that articulates an aesthetic form of reflexivity. In order to substantiate this argument, it is important to focus on both the form and content of anti-global struggles. In other words, we need to focus on the intersection between cultural innovation and experimentation and political and economic contestation in order to trace the development of new glocalized opportunity structures and networks of obligation. This becomes apparent as soon as we focus on the origins of the new oppositional movements. In the global South, these struggles originated in response to the negative impact of global institutions such as the 'IMF Riots' that have developed in response to 'structural adjustment' programmes (Walton & Seddon, 1994). In the global north, the initial resistance took the form of defensive struggles around welfare and employment rights by organized labour. More recently, however, these national forms of resistance have developed into new forms of international resistance that not only link national struggles but also create new terrains of struggle at the transnational level. This movement achieved global visibility with the insurrection of the Zapatistas in Chiapas, Mexico (Cunninghame & Ballesteros Corona, 1998; Esteva, 1999).

The Zapatistas emerged on 1 January 1994 as the Zapatistas National Liberation Army (EZLN) on the day the North American Free Trade Agreement (NAFTA) came into effect. The aim of the EZLN was to make visible the forgotten victims of neo-liberal globalism to the world through the publication of a series of communiqués on the Internet. The demands of the Zapatistas are foundational and premised on the demand for autonomy. These demands include work, land, shelter, food, health, education, independence, freedom, democracy, justice and peace in the context of municipal self-government. The distinctiveness of this guerrilla movement is that it eschews Marxism and 'vanguardism' and, in contrast to other Latin American guerrilla movements such as *Shining Path* in Peru, does not resort to random violence, fear and intimidation. The Zapatistas are anti-patriarchal, stand for the rights of self-determination and local democracy and support ecology and preservation of the environment. Manuel Castells has argued that the success of the Zapatistas was largely down to their communication strategy in which they emerged as the first 'informational guerrilla movement' (Castells, 1997). They created a media event in order to diffuse their message whilst trying to avoid a violent and bloody confrontation. Whilst the Zapatistas had arms, they did not pursue a military strategy. The use of arms was used to make a statement and force negotiations with the Mexican Government around a set of demands that found widespread support throughout Mexican society. Leading figures in the movement such as sub-commander Marcos provided an image, based on the wearing of a ski mask and the smoking of the pipe in the jungle location, which acted as a communications bridge with the media. This involved drawing on indigenous culture to provide a spectacle or display of theatrics that linked past, present and future. These images were displayed through video, telecommunications and Internet media to generate a worldwide network of solidarity that was then deployed to control and limit the repression of the Zapatistas by the Mexican state. The Zapatistas thus highlight the way in which 'weak ties' between activists can build effective 'social bridges' between diverse movements through the deliberate construction of new political spaces (Granovetter, 1973). The Zapatistas provided the first example of a 'netwar' – the worst nightmare of the architects of the new global order – a multi-organizational network arising from civil society to contest neo-liberal globalism.

The Zapatistas defined a new form of internationalism that blurred the line between global and local issues and involved the construction of alliances amongst a plurality of movements (De Angeles, 2000). In contrast to the 'socialist internationalism' of the modern era, the goals of political action are not framed outside the unification process but emerge from the unification process and generate new radical claims and social subjects. This form of internationalism grasps the multi-dimensionality of human needs and articulates a new emancipatory philosophy rooted in the universality of the human condition. The contradictions between the demands of different movements are the object of political practice and are transcended through communications and alliances in civil society (Esteva, 1999: 158–159). The Zapatistas inspired solidarity from activists around the world and unleashed an international insurrection of hope against the forces of global capitalism. The Zapatistas cry of *Ya Basta!* (enough) announced the 'the end of the end of history' and their communiqués posted on the Internet began to unite a diverse band of marginal people: vagabonds, sweatshop workers, sex workers, indigenous peoples, intellectuals, factory workers, illegal immigrants, factory workers and squatters (Notes from Nowhere, 2003: 24–25). The Zapatistas inspired the growth of electronic NGO networks: the so-called 'Zapatista effect' that has posed an increasing symbolic threat to global neo-liberalism within a media-generated public sphere (Cleaver, 1998). However, this success story highlights clearly the ambiguity between cultural innovation and symbolic contestation on the one hand, and political and economic contestation on the other. The mere existence of the Zapatistas as a potential alternative had a huge impact in the generation of a counter-power within global civil society. Yet this rhetoric of global resistance has had minimal impact on the lived poverty of the indigenous peoples of Chiapas (Chandler, 2004: 327). Ten years after the start of the Zapatistas rebellion, the Mexican Government continues to ignore their demands. This is not, however, to deny the symbolic significance of the Zapatistas uprising and the motivation the rebellion provided to protestors around the globe.

The form of politics initiated by the Zapatistas provided a language and a form of action that informed and inspired a new wave of protests towards the end of the 1990s. During this period, coordinated action spread throughout the developing world culminating in days of action against the WTO in 1998 and the G8 in 1999 with a global *Carnival against Capital*. The anti-capitalist movement only became visible to the media in the global North when protestors began to mobilize at global summits in the developed world. The Global Justice Movement (GJM) burst onto the scene during the protest at the 1999 WTO summit in Seattle, when forty thousand demonstrators drawn from a wide spectrum of movements interrupted a meeting of the WTO that had been convened to discuss the liberalization of trade in services. The protestors ranged from core sections of the American labour movement, such as the Teamsters and the Longshoremen, to a range of NGO and activist coalitions campaigning around environmental issues, fair trade and Third World debt. In the wake of Seattle, a plethora of protests targeted the global summits of institutions such as the WTO, IMF, EU, APEC, G8 and FTAA including mobilizations in Washington (2000), Millau (2000), Melbourne (2000), Seoul (2000), Nice (2000), Prague (2000), Washington (2001), Gothenburg (2001) and Genoa (2001). The emergence of Zapatistas and the GJM is part of a process through which a new transnational political space has been forged in which alternatives to neo-liberalism can be discussed by globalized political actors.

The World Social Forum (WSF) emerged from the GJM and originated from an initiative by a group of Belgian activists to develop a forum that could bring together groups and movements from around the World that shared an opposition to neo-liberalism. The first forum was held in Porto Alegre, Brazil during 2001 in opposition to the World Economic Forum that has being held in Davos, Switzerland. The WSF is a 'worldwide, movement-based, multi-scale and multi-sited cultural process' (Conway, 2004) or a space that is open, diverse and pluralistic and oriented to the generation and communication of movement-based ideas and practices. However, a key source of contention within the WSF remains whether it represents merely an 'open space' to encourage discourse and dialogue or a 'movement of movements' premised on the translation of diversity and plurality of opinion into common political will and action (Conway, 2005; Marcuse, 2005; Patomäki and Teivainen, 2004). The values of diversity, pluralism and participation are foundational and definitive and the WSFs comprise forms of coordinated self-organization that include meetings, parades, protests, music, dance and exhibitions. In 2001, 2002 and 2003, the WSF was held in Porto Alegre, Brazil and was dominated by Latin American groups concerned with issues such as the FTAA and landlessness. In 2004, the WSF was held in Mumbai, India where there was a greater focus on the historically marginal such as indigenous peoples, AIDS-sufferers and sex trade workers. At this forum, there were discussions around the issues that linked social and biological diversity such as access to water, environmental destruction and the control of nature.

The WSF is producing new forms of political participation, deliberation and popular power and a new geography of social movement organizing. The WSF is recognition that the contemporary world order is increasingly comprised of multiple and overlapping sovereignties and the lack of a recognizable or unified global sovereign constitutes the fundamental challenge to the global movement. Hence:

> global-citizens-in-the-making might also be creating a global sovereignty.... over an increasingly privatized sphere that is monopolistic in tendency, individualizing, intrusive and destructive of human sociality and creativity. (Waterman, 2000: 145)

Citizenship thus remains 'a conflictive practice related to power' (Jelin, 2000: 53). The objects of contention are the World Bank, IMF, WTO, G8, FTAA, EU and MNCs that are challenged in the name of popular sovereignty at the local, national and global levels. The new citizenship is premised on the 'right to have rights' an idea that has developed through the anti-hegemonic struggles of the excluded by social movements claiming political subjectivity. These movements demand the right to participate in order to create new forms of egalitarian sociability and reciprocal recognition in civil society (Dagnino, 1998: 50–52). The WSF embodies an emergent 'alternative, post bourgeois conception of the public sphere (Fraser, 1997: 72): the space is thus 'placed but transnational, localized but characterized by expanding globality' (Conway, 2004: 376). This space is not constituted by a public sphere of rational democratic deliberation (cf. Habermas, 1984, 1987) but a plurality of subaltern counterpublics (Fraser, *op cit*: 81) which express their exclusion from the formal universality of the liberal public sphere. The WSF is thus part of the consolidation of an emergent 'transnational civil society' (Keck & Sikkink, 1998). The new anti-globalization movements go beyond the politics of identity and difference to issues of democracy and a search for collective solutions to common problems (Gill, 2000). The WSF highlights the possibility of inclusive, egalitarian, multicultural and anti-oppressive political spaces. However, there remain significant obstacles to this process including the huge chasms across civilizational divides, regional outlooks, religions, gendered orders and worldviews. Despite these limitations, the WSF has played a central role in the convergence of the anti-globalization and anti-war movements worldwide through the promotion of pluralism. The demand for democracy, rights and participation are not being marginalized but transformed from legal and institutional claims to claims based on cultural practices (Gilbert & Philips, 2003; Isin & Turner, 2002). Citizenship is increasingly about 'being political', entering conflicts over power and recognizing the agnostic nature of citizenship (Isin, 2002). This, however, is contested terrain focused on a set of uneven, crisis ridden processes that are established by transnational practices. The liberal paradigm is in decline while the new paradigm is still under construction. The anti-globalization movement represents a form of postmodern politics within modern society (Heller & Feher, *op cit*): a form of politics premised on a rejection of grand narratives, the privileging of function over structure and a weakening of class politics. The content of the struggle, however, remains foundational and we see the liminality inherent to contemporary global politics. Hence, the WSF could be best described as a form of participatory communication and engagement 'that is *in movement*, even if it is not *a movement* of a traditional kind' (Patomäki & Teivainen, *op cit*: 152). The WSF will eventually have to face up to the insight that global democratic change will not be achievable without concrete strategies of political change and engagement with state actors and the need to engage with more traditional forms of politics (Patomäki & Teivainen, *ibid*: 151.). It is therefore appropriate that we will now turn to a consideration of the extent to which the 'old' social movement constituted by the labour movement has a future within the new paradigm.

Social Movement Unionism: The Limits and Possibilities of a Postmodern Labour Movement

In previous sections, we have highlighted the complex and non-linear patterns of social change that mark the contemporary era. It would, therefore, be problematic to accept the existence of a linear model of change in relation to the straightforward decline and marginalization of the labour movement in the shift from modernity to postmodernity. This is not to downplay the extent to which the future vitality of the labour movement is threatened by the processes and dynamics outlined in this chapter. The growth of reflexive individualism poses a threat to collective or class forms of political identity and action, and the disembedding of politics at the national level has undermined the institutional expressions of class politics. As we noted in Chapter 4, the fragmented nature of the informational labour process inhibits the development of workplace collective identity. In many ways, therefore, trade unionism has become a zombie category in the contemporary era. However, an analysis of the living-death of this category reveals a number of interesting and ambiguous trends and dynamics within global civil society. We see within the labour movement a complex realignment of opportunity structures and networks of obligation around 'place-bound' instrumentalism and 'placeless' altruism. We can illustrate the above tendencies through an analysis of the changing and ambiguous relationship between the labour movement and civil society.

The labour movement emerged during the nineteenth century as the principal oppositional movement in civil society that articulated a collective resistance to the individualizing dynamics of the capitalist market. The principal objective of the labour movement was to politicize the employment relation and social welfare. The successful expression of this was the KWS and nationally specific forms of institutional corporatism which resulted in the labour movement becoming integrated or incorporated into the institutions of the state – a process which has been presented as the 'statization of civil society' (Panitch, 1986: 189) or the 'statization of social life' (Poulantzas, 1978). The KWS represented a form of social democratic 'class compromise' in which organized labour accepted the legitimacy of the capitalist market in return for expanded welfare benefits. The resulting contradictions were responsible for both the long-term crisis of state welfare (Offe, 1984) and the erosion of the legitimacy and mobilizing capacity of the labour movement (Offe & Wiesenthal, 1985). This crisis of 'institutional politics' was the context for the emergence of the 'new right' and the 'disorganized capitalism' (Offe, 1985a) associated with globalization. The social democratic and socialist left decomposed into a series of radical new social movements concerned with rolling back the state, not in favour of the market, but in favour of advanced welfare ideals based on self-management in civil society (Offe, 1985b). In this context, the labour movement is widely perceived as representing a contracting stratum of elite workers in the developed world and becoming increasingly irrelevant as a motor for social and political change (Gorz, 1982). The crisis of trade unionism has been reflected in a marked decline in membership and representation throughout the developed world.

However, during the past decade organized labour has emerged as an active agent rather than a passive victim in the process of neo-liberal globalization (Munck, 2004). There have been examples of new inter-ventions by organized labour at the global, regional, national and local levels in which organized labour has both emerged as a key moment of resistance against neo-liberalism and as part of a progressive alliance of civil society actors. It is important to separate out the instrumental and altruistic elements of this reorientation. The instrumental elements of reorientation have been largely defensive and tend to confirm the rather pessimistic prognosis of Castells that the interests of labour are place-bound and incommunicable in the 'space of flows' (Castells, 1997). This has involved an attempt to re-embed political relations along the glocalized configurations of capital and the state. The most interesting developments are in Europe where globalization, in the form of European integration, has produced transnational labour movement actors in the form of the European Trade Union Confederation (ETUC) and a range of European Industry Federations (EIFs) at the sectoral level (Gabaglio & Hoff-mann, 1998). The ETUC is a social partner within the institutions of the EU and in that role has consultation rights with the European Commis-sion and the European Central Bank and limited negotiating rights with UNICE - the European employers confederation. These developments are part of a top-down social democratic strategy to resolve the contradictions between globalization and social democracy through international cooper-ation and coordination and the construction of a Social Europe (Clift, 2002: 495). These developments highlight the construction of a 'public sphere' by the EU and thus the undeveloped nature of European civil society and the enduring 'democratic deficit within the institutions of the EU (Rumford, 2003). This is highlighted by the limited material conces-sions achieved by both European trade unions and the alliance between European unions and the European Platform of Social NGOs: an EU forum designed to encourage the deepening of European civil society (Taylor & Mathers, 2004). The EIFs coordinate consultation and negotiation within European Works' Councils (EWCs). EWCs were introduced following an EU directive obliging TNCs that employ workers in more than one EU nation state to establish consultation machinery at the European level.

These are important examples of labour movement politics beyond the nation state that represent an important attempt by the labour move-ment to build alliances and coalitions with the interests of cosmopolitan neo-liberalism. The return to organized labour from these alliances and coalitions has been modest (Taylor, 2006). In Europe, the forums in which the ETUC participates are essentially top-down orchestrations by the EU and, while participation may constitute a symbolic victory, the ETUC has achieved few substantive concessions from the neo-liberal policies of the European Commission. The substantive agenda of EWCs has also been limited and subordinate to managerial prerogative and have tended to reproduce national rivalries and interests (Hancké, 2000; Whittall, 2000). The politics of the labour movement remain overwhelmingly negative, defensive and rooted at the national level. Throughout the 1990s, the politics of European integration resulted in coalitions between moderate trade union leaders and national political elites in the form of 'social pacts'. These arrangements involved trade unions being offered small concessions on issues of labour market restructuring in return for programmes of wage restraint and welfare reform that enabled European nation states to meet the 'convergence criteria' associated with economic and monetary union (EMU) and the introduction of the EURO currency (Pochet & Fajertag, 2000; Taylor & Mathers, 2002a,b).

There is, however, a contrary tendency to the above instrumental defens-iveness in the form of 'social movement unionism'. The development of 'second' or 'reflexive' modernity has resulted in the 'opening up' of civil society as the increasing importance of 'risk biographies' has gener-ated new forms of 'altruistic individualism' (Beck & Beck-Gernsheim, *op cit*: 24). We can see this dynamic operating within the European labour movement where opposition to European integration has resulted in both instrumental actions at the national level and new forms of transnational solidarity. The latter link the global and local struggles of activists and build bridges between the labour movement and other movements and actors in the global public sphere. The process of European integration provoked militant forms of industrial action in the form of strikes, partic-ularly amongst public sector workers, in France, Germany, Italy and Spain, and the emergence of new unions or union fractions opposed to neo-liberal restructuring such as *SUD* in France or *Sin Cobas* in Italy (Taylor & Mathers, 2002a,b). The latter development formed the basis for the devel-opment of a transnational network of resistance between oppositional trade unions and a range of campaigns involving movements representing women, black people, environmentalists, pensioners, migrants and the homeless. These became manifested in phenomena such as Euromarches, a network of movements that organized marches and demonstrations at key European summits to highlight the plight of the marginal and excluded in Europe (Mathers, 1999), ATTAC that campaigns for a tax on move-ments of capital (Patomäki, 2000) and the involvement of trade unions in the WSF and European social forums (Lee, 2004). More generally, the crisis and collapse of workplace bargaining and state-level corporatism has encouraged a 'logic of participation' between trade unions and social actors beyond the workplace (Robinson, 2000) and the emergence of 'social movement unionism' as a global phenomenon (Robinson, 2002; Munck & Waterman, 1998). We see, therefore, manifestations of altruistic indi-vidualism in the form of 'community unionism' in the United States (Gaspin & Wial, 1998; Kriesky, 1998), Canada (Cranford, 2003) and the United Kingdom (Wills, 2001; Wills & Simms, 2004) becoming aligned with more traditional forms of social movement unionism in developing societies such as South Africa, Korea. Brazil and the Philippines (Lambert, 1990, Lambert & Webster, 1988, Waterman, 1984, Webster, 1988). In the United States, trade unions organizing through local 'central labor coun-cils' have made alliances with faith groups and groups representing the low paid and the marginalized to make citizenship claims on a range of issues from minimum wages to public transport (Johnson, 2000, 2002). These developments highlight a tendency pinpointed in a report by the International Labour Organization (ILO) in 1998, that trade unions were developing innovative strategies in response to the challenges of global-ization premised on a social dynamic that made unions look more and more like genuine social movements (ILO, 1998: 2). We will conclude with an exploration of how this new manifestation of trade union politics is contributing to the politics of global civil society.

Global Civil Society: The Politics of Cosmocracy?

The process of globalization does not create automatically transnational forms of civil society. It is, therefore, important to separate normative accounts of the civilizing potential of global civil society from more empirical analyses that focus on the balance of global forces and the extent to which the global 'public sphere' has indeed been civilized. The former tendency is associated with analyses based on the notion that civil society became radicalized following the global turn and the fall of the Berlin Wall. The substantive content of global civil society is relatively unambiguous and uncontroversial comprising a 'new form of global politics' where 'the array of organizations and groups through which individuals have a voice at the global level . . . parallels and supplements formal democracy at the national level (Kaldor, 2003: 197). This is somewhat contradictory, however, as the non-governmental institutions that have a global presence in the promotion of civility contribute to an inherent pluralism that generates potential conflict (Keane, 2003: 8–14). The origins of the global turn are, moreover, unclear and contested. Kaldor highlights the collapse of the Soviet Bloc and the way in which global civil society was constructed 'from below' as networks of activists from 'East' and 'West' exploited the spaces opened up by ICT and internationalizing markets to construct new institutions beyond the nation state and forms of contestation beyond class politics. There is a normative element to this type of account which presents the emergence of global civil society as benign and irreversible. This is combined with a tendency to play down the importance of the labour movement in the struggle for democracy; particularly in places such as Latin America, Korea and South Africa (Colás, 2005: 181). Hence, it is important to recognize the extent to which 'turbo capitalism' acts as a disruptive force within global civil society through the way it creates and maintains socio-economic and political inequalities (Keane, *op cit*: 88). Global civil society is not, therefore, a unified 'third subject' but an exploitative and antagonistic domain. In this sphere, competing forces compete for power through transnational mobilization (Meiksins Wood, 2003: 11) and the nation state system is transformed into a 'puriverse' of nation states authored by the world's most powerful – the United States (Meiksins Wood, *ibid*: 141).

Global civil society is best understood as a distinctive space of transnational activism that has been fostered, however contradictorily, by the development of capitalist imperialism (Keane, *op cit*: 35) and which illuminates the enduring connections between capitalism, nationalism and imperialism. Keane (*op cit*, 125) highlights the tension between universalism and pluralism in the cosmopolitan vision of global civil society and the implausibility of the argument that the world is in the grip of a 'teleology of normative progress'. The institutions of global governance lack both the resources and the legitimacy to enforce stability and cooperation: a situation that is compounded by the enduring dominance of the United States (Keane, ibid: 98). Indeed, in the context of 9/11 and the war in Iraq, we seemingly face a war without aims and end (Meiksins Wood, *op cit*: 149). The latter has taken the form of an Anglo-American alliance that has trampled on global civil society in order to exercise global supremacy. The experience of the UK/US invasion of Iraq, however, highlights the limits of 'Empire' (cf. Hardt & Negri, 2001) and the control of territory and people in the post-colonial period. Despite the contradictions of global civil society, therefore, it represents a new transnational space to resist and contest the neo-imperialism of Empire. However, the reverse is also worth pondering. There are increasingly critical voices that doubt the transformative power of a 'global civil society' owing to the fact that it lacks an institutional counterpart in form of a global state. This is crucial, as civil society has always relied on the legal and institutional framework guaranteed by the state, even when bundling forces against state politics (Etzioni, 2004; Olesen, 2005). Moreover, there is also merit in the admittedly provocative thesis that the tendency to become the voice of the oppressed in the global arena is also a potential exit option from the more formal and daunting struggles in national political spheres – an escape to symbolic politics 'with less accountability and little pressure for representative legitimacy' (Chandler, *op cit*: 331).

Thus, the claim that global civil society is both a product of globalization and a sphere that can be civilized is a disputed one and raises questions towards its capabilities and limits. Lipschutz (1996) asserts that global civil society can form a de-centralized, democratic form of global governance, whilst Kaldor (2000) argues that it is a sphere in which alternatives models of globalization from below can be developed and mobilized. A more sceptical perspective is offered by Colas (1997) who argues that global civil society contains reactionary as well as progressive elements and Scholte (2000) who argues that the NGOs that form its mainstay are not necessarily democratic organizations. The 'Charter of Principles' of the WSF, for example, excludes right wing religious fundamentalists from participation (Patomäki & Teivainen, *op cit*: 149). In this sense, it is best to think of global civil society as a contested arena, the form of which is dependant on the changing coalitions and cleavages of its constituent organizations and movements. According to Kaldor (*op cit*: 109–111), these cleavages and coalitions are forming between organizations and movements that emphasize parochialism and cosmopolitanism and between those with neo-liberal and re-distributionist objectives. The 'old left' and the 'new right' are fragmenting into 'parochial' and 'cosmopolitan' elements and this is resulting in an increasingly complex pattern of political cleavages, coalitions and identities (see Table 1). The future shape of global civil society and the extent to which it is able to civilize globalization is likely to be dependent on the forms of coalitions that develop between the constituent elements of global civil society. These elements are outlined in Table 6.1.

The analysis in this chapter, suggests that the dominant coalition is currently between MNCs and national representatives of the New Right. This coalition provides the principal dynamic for the atomizing politics of neo-liberal globalism. This coalition has undermined the re-distributionist old left which has been either excluded from workplace, state-level and global-level corporatism or reincorporated based on a negative and defensive neo-liberal agenda with few re-distributionist concessions. In this context, there is an emerging coalition between the global civil networks and sections of the labour movement committed to developing 'social movement unionism' or 'community unionism'. This coalition has

Table 6.1 Global political cleavages. Adapted from Kaldor (2000: 109)

	Parochial	**Cosmopolitan**
Neo-liberal	New right. Religious identities and traditional values. Opposition to globalization through various forms of Nationalism and fundamentalism	MNCs, International liberalism. Supported by corporate executives, centrist politicians and economic experts. Globalization is a positive development and benefits developing nations
Re-distributionist	Old Left. Belief in strong nation state, welfare and full employment. Support de-globalization	Global civic networks i.e. NGOs, Aid Agencies, etc. Aspire to a global civilizing process. Globalization is uneven in nature and skewed to interests if rich nations

successfully mobilized against neo-liberal globalism and in the process constructed new political spaces and a nascent political subject at the global level. There is an undeveloped coalition between cosmopolitan neo-liberals and the global civic networks currently dominated by Third Way social democrats and their attempts to build new forms of social dialogue at the global, regional (particularly European) and local levels. The emerging cleavage between the parochial and the cosmopolitan is encouraging the growth of nationalism and fundamentalism. The political configuration of contemporary global politics is thus a product of this complex of competing forces in global civil society and the changing multi-level cleavages and coalitions between these interests.

Summary and Conclusion

In this chapter, we have explored the crisis of modern political institutions that has emerged in the context of globalization, reflexive modernization and individualization. We began with of discussion of the ways in which these processes have resulted in a crisis of modern political ideology with a particular focus on the crisis and decomposition of social democracy. We highlighted the hegemonic nature of this ideology both within advanced Western societies and at the international level during the post-war period and the ways in which neo-liberal elites have attempted to recompose social democracy into forms of 'Third Way'

politics that articulate the logic of neo-liberal globalism, reflexive modernization and individualization. The political impact of global neo-liberalism
and 'Third Way' politics has been to undermine the legitimacy of institutional politics still further and encourage increasingly individualized forms
of identity politics. We argued that the tendency for neo-liberalism to
break down national borders was resulting in a loss of social meaning and
identity across the developed and developing world. This was resulting in
an 'identity thirst' that was being satiated by a reinvigorated politics of
nationalism that overlaid the politics of desire, fear and certainty. We highlighted the janus-faced nature of the new matrix of globalism–nationalism:
a 'dark' side manifested in increasingly aggressive forms of nationalism,
fascism, political violence and terrorism and a 'light' side manifested in
the demands for cultural freedom and autonomy from the universalizing
tendencies of neo-liberal globalism by increasingly globalized networks of
social movement actors

An overriding objective of the chapter has been to counter the argument
that the development of postmodern politics marks the 'end of history'
or the 'end of the social'. We approached this through an analysis of
the main patterns of mobilization and demobilization, inclusion and
exclusion that can be isolated in the emerging configuration of global
civil society. We argued that this configuration can be represented most
accurately as a global public sphere constituted by fluid and shifting alliances and contestation around the axes of 'parochialism'—'universalism'
and 'neo-liberal'—'re-distributionist'. These fluid and shifting alliances
and cleavages reflect the politics of inclusion, exclusion and transclusion that have developed in response to the individualizing and fragmenting dynamics of neo-liberal globalism. The process of globalization
and the associated processes of reflexive modernization and individualization have produced new opportunity structures and networks of obligation
that have marginalized, fragmented and de-centred the political institutions and identities that dominated the modern era. We highlighted
how the decline and demobilization of the labour movement is associated with the fragmentation of trade union discourse and action across
these axes. The dominant alliance is currently between neo-liberal elites
and neo-liberal parochials, but we also noted less significant but note-
worthy alliances between re-distributionist cosmopolitans and parochials
(or between the old and new 'social movement' left) and between cosmopolitan neo-liberals and cosmopolitan re-distributionists (or between neo-
liberal elites and the social movement left). In the following chapter, it will
become increasingly evident that the further development of the latter
cleavage is likely to become centrally important if the individual and
collective environmental risks of reflexive modernity are to be managed
and lived in a sustainable and non-alienating fashion.

7

Nature, Environment and Milieu: Life in Risk Society

The discourse of nature that by now invades every aspect of our daily lives both emphasizes and conceals the dilemmas of complexity.

(Alberto Melucci, 1996b: 126)

The level of public anxiety and concern around environmental issues is perceived by many commentators to have plateaued some time during the last decade, after having peaked around the time of the Earth Summit in Rio during 1992. Nevertheless, it remains indisputable that the discourse of global environmental change has become engrained deeply in both public (sub)consciousness and public policy. The vulnerability of 'spaceship earth' to ecological meltdown has impacted powerfully on the human imagination. This concern over the environment is more than a passing fashion and is qualitatively different from the conventional 'moral panics' that have been a constant feature of modern society. Indeed, the argument of Melucci (*ibid*) suggests that 'environmental' concern can be viewed as a discursive frame for a series of more general apprehensions about the new planetary complexities that have been generated by modern technological development. The relationship between nature and society is a defining feature for all epochs of human development, but has become particularly acute during the modern era. Modern attempts to emancipate society from nature by conquering and controlling it have created unintended consequences so serious that the sustainability of human society on the planet is becoming an increasingly problematic issue. For the first time in human history, society is faced with the prospects of its own planetary-wide and irreversible impact on the environment; the full consequences of which are unknown and unforeseeable. The global environmental changes that follow in the wake of modern development are thus a major hot spot of both social and ecological transition (Macnaghten, 2003; Ungar, 2001; York et al., 2003).

The environment could indeed be *the* decisive marker of epochal change. Modernity relied on the appropriation of nature in a way that involved the externalization of nature. Nature was transformed into an 'environment' that could be controlled by technology and kept at service of society. In the ever-expanding phase of industrial modernity, the environment was used as an inexhaustible source of energy and as the playing field of science and technology. This continued until the finitude of the planetary 'environment' signalled the limits to abundance and externalizability and, in this context, 'globality has retrieved nature from the environment and rediscovered its links with humanity' (Albrow, 1996: 134). Moreover, globality, understood here as the finitude of the globe, has set an end-point to modernity as we know it and forced it to reposition itself. Thus, what we perceive as an environmental crisis is also an opportunity for alternative social development. In this context, two policy options have crystallized. First, 'ecological modernization' is a position premised on the idea that environmental challenges can be incorporated fully into the institutional framework of modern capitalism. Second, the 'radical ecologist' position is premised on the idea that environmental challenges require a fundamental change in the direction of social development including the development of new institutions and value systems. These two positions provide divergent understandings of the processes of social and ecological change that are necessary in the face of environmental challenges. While the former presents these changes as part of a process of *transition* based on clear and predictable coordinates, the latter position presents these changes as part of a *transformation* that has a direction and outcome that are far from certain (cf. Blowers, 1997: 846). Notwithstanding the divergent policy implications of these macro-perspectives, it is clear that changes are not being imposed on society by an externalized nature, but are intrinsic to developments in the modern social 'environment' and are transforming both the institutional cluster of modern society and the social fabric of everyday life. Environmental challenges thus articulate significant symbolic meaning alongside their 'real' consequences.

In this chapter, we explore the relationship between 'nature', 'environment' and 'milieu' in order to illustrate the changing experience of life in 'risk society'. We begin by highlighting the way in which the symbolic vision of 'spaceship earth' provides an Archimedean point from which we are able to view the fragmented civilizational and ecological realities generated by the 'technological fix'. We then use the recent phenomenon of avian flu to highlight the nature of 'risk' and the main contours of the 'world risk society' that has been developed by Ulrich Beck. We highlight the ways in which an understanding of risk society highlights the relationship between individual ontological insecurity and the temporal reordering underpinning contemporary patterns of social change. We then explore the relationship between risk society and reflexive modernity with a particular emphasis on the complex and ambiguous relationship between institutional and individual reflexivity. We conclude with an exploration of the ways that environmental concerns are 'embodied' within the non-rational and affective dynamics of everyday milieux. In the context of increasing patterns of organic food consumption, we highlight the intimate and ambiguous relationship between global risk society, ontological security and individual identity formation.

Archimedean Points: Globe and Body

Anthropological research suggests that throughout human civilization concern for the environment and the fear of its pollution have served as the symbolic expression of a more complex set of anxieties concerning the maintenance of precarious social order (Douglas, 1991). Thus, the contemporary manifestations of global environmental concern and the fear of global disaster should not be taken at face value. Rather, the rediscovered care for nature and increasing concerns about the environment are indicators of a far more profound set of changes underpinning the emergence of a 'complex planetary society' (Melucci, *op cit*). The growing awareness of complex planetary interdependency has raised our awareness of our own position within this social and ecological complexity. We increasingly question the power of technology, linear modes of thinking and mono-causal explanations. We perceive the unresolved tensions between omnipotence and responsibility and between possibility and limit. In this context, the debate on the environment can be seen as a 'symptom' of the increasing unease experienced by individuals in the face of the far-reaching challenges to the (industrial) economic order, (mechanistic) world views and (consumption-oriented) lifestyles (Melucci, *ibid*: 126). Indeed, Capra (1983), writing with remarkable anticipation during the early-1980s and thus prior the apocalyptic events at Chernobyl and elsewhere, sensed a deep crisis emerging within the complex institutions and processes interlinking environment, science, technology and everyday life in modern societies. Capra sensed a fast approaching 'turning point' determined by the convergence of a range of social and ecological dynamics and tendencies in the same global process. These included the deterioration of the natural environment, an over-dependency on finite resources, a decline in patriarchy, an increase of civilizational illnesses and a depletion of social relationships. Thus, for Capra: as 'individuals, as a society, as a civilization and as a planetary ecosystem, we are reaching the turning point' (Capra, *ibid*: 15).

In order to understand further the symbolic importance of environmental concern in the context of complex transition, we need to revisit the underlying dynamics of modern society. This will enable us to uncover the resonance between the increasing affinity people feel towards 'nature' and a deepening sense of their own 'existential uncertainty' (Spretnak, 1997: 221). Modern life is characterized by restless mobility, fragmented perceptions of reality and precarious constructions of identity. In this world, modern individuals have increasingly become 'nomads of the present' (Melucci, *op cit*: 43). The classic study of Berger et al. (1973) referred to the haunted existence of a 'homeless mind'. Modern science and technology had established 'componentiality' as the dominant cognitive style of ordering modern life. We controlled nature, but only by chopping it up in discrete units and losing track of their connectivity. Moreover, this componentiality extended towards social life and identity. We had become 'componential selves' that moved effortlessly between a plurality of disenchanted social worlds and technical settings. In this context, it had become difficult to manage the emotional economy induced by this fragmented and functionalized life, and Berger et al. (*ibid*: 184) argued that this all-embracing 'componentiality' induced 'a nostalgia for wholeness, unity and comprehensibility'. This urge for wholeness and meaningful totality finds resonance today in the notion of the 'global environment' and the image of 'spaceship earth'.

The affinity with a fragile 'spaceship earth' highlights the deeply ambivalent nature of contemporary environmental concerns. The image of the globe is a symbolic re-appropriation of the world as a whole. Looking at the globe from the perspective of an astronaut might indeed allow us to recover our bearings amidst the contradictory discourses and narratives on global environmental change. This could be compared to climbing a church tower when we lose our way in a large city. The image of the globe provides a powerful sensory bridge towards an understanding of a shared 'global environment' that is otherwise limited to scientific formula and predictive models on scenarios such as global warming and depletion of the ozone layer. The experience of being lifted from everyday routines and their environmental implications could indeed trigger feelings of emotional embeddedness and possibly temporary feelings of a global imagined community. However, the 'comprehensible' world that we view from a distance is a world that has lost all traces of human involvement. In its bio-spherical purification, it has become abstracted from human society. The price we pay for the pleasure of comprehensibility is simplification. Ultimately, looking at the world from a distance produces a world upon which we can reflect but not act, and this position takes the juxtaposition of society and nature to its extreme (Macnaghten, *op cit;* Urry, 2000: 200). Nevertheless, this affinity does provide the basis for an 'Archimedean point' from which we can re-assess the disconnected fragments that have resulted from the 'technological fix' (Bauman, 1993: 197). This non-human abstraction needs, however, to be counterbalanced by another Archimedean point that is more human-centred and embedded in the routines of everyday life. This counterpoint, where environmental concerns are linked to personal experience, is provided by the human body (Macnaghten, *op cit*: 68) and in the wake of rising environmental concerns there is indeed a renewed interest in the body (Melucci, *op cit*: 71). The body, like nature, has been transformed from a taken-for-granted biological resource or vehicle into something that provides meaning and self-recognition when other forms of identification are dissolving. It is our bodies we retreat to in order to 'recharge our batteries' and it is our bodies we nurture with healthy diets and fitness regimes in order to anchor our self-respect in times of fleeting relationships and precarious work arrangements. The result of this increasing attention on food and biological rhythms confirms the intrinsic link between nature 'out there' and nature 'in here' (Macnaghten, *op cit*: 73) or between the 'inner planet' and the 'external planet' (Melucci, *op cit*: 57).

Thus, the image and reality of both the planet and the body have become associated with sublime and almost sacred connotations of the 'natural'. This is a consequence of the 'technological fix' and the loss of meaning that follows its application. The 'concealment of the systemic nature of the human habitat' and the 'disassembly of the moral self' are linked inextricably as two sides of the same process (Bauman, *op cit*: 259). The increasing success of technological development has intensified the strength of unintended and unintentional rebounds, which has in turn resulted in an increasingly desperate search for a meaningful orientation within the systemic imbalances created by these rebounds. Following Bauman, we agree that it is this constellation that is at the heart of Ulrich Beck's (1992) theory of 'risk society'; a theory in which 'risk' is defined as 'a systematic way of dealing with the hazards and insecurities induced and introduced by the process of modernization itself'. In this context, 'risk' has become a magic word that describes all the mysterious, mostly hidden and invisible, but also largely unfathomable, side-effects of modern technology-induced development and as such it seems to embody a quasi-religious explanatory power (Alexander & Smith, 1996: 259). However, as Beck would be quick to point out, this is exactly what distinguishes 'risk' from 'natural hazard', for risk is not the result of some mysterious fate brought on by external powers such as gods, demons or Mother Nature, but is a perfectly explainable 'manufactured uncertainty'.

The Advance of the 'Risk Society': Exploring the Genesis and Consequences of Avian Flu

As we write this book, Europe is gripped by the fear of avian flu or H5N1 to quote the genetic code of the virus. Swans and other wild birds suffered mysterious deaths and are recovered on a daily basis, farmers have to keep their poultry indoors and the talk shows have yet another issue to focus on. The spread of the disease seems mysterious, and there is a growing fear that the virus might not just infect people in close contact with animals carrying the disease, but that H5N1 might combine with other strains of flu within the human body and bring about a new global pandemic. It would be easy to define bird flu as a new 'moral panic' in the form of a periodic media-generated amplification of concern for phenomena that seem to threaten societal values and interests (cf. Ungar, 2001). On closer inspection, however, the phenomenon reveals clearly the ecological complexity of a planetary society in which the difference between nature and society is collapsing along with the cultural categories with which we order the world. Bird flu is not *supposed* to affect humans and is not *supposed* to jump the species barrier. The anthropologist Mary Douglas reminds us of the simple fact that a social order is maintained through its imagined distance from organic processes and that whenever the barrier is ruptured 'the organic erupts into the social, (and) there is impurity' that tends to irritate us (Douglas, 1991: 210). The fear of avian flu is not an absolute fear premised on the possibility of infection and death, but symbolic fear – a break of the 'purity rule' that gives coherence to human society.

With the phenomenon of H5N1 we are not, therefore, confronted with nature flying into the face of society and its constructs; 'the monster at our door' (Davis, 2005) is a product of our own making and a creation of industrial and technological development. Hence, Davis *(ibid*: 8) argues that the origins of the phenomenon can be located at the interplay of several 'human-induced environmental shocks' in South East Asia: namely, the 'livestock revolution'; the growth of mega slums; and the development and increasingly global reach of ICT. The rapid industrialization of South East Asia has resulted in a rapid increase of population density. Many of the labourers that are drawn to the new, expanding industrial cities are rural 'circular' migrants that are housed in overcrowded dormitories. This has been accompanied by important dietary changes in the region marked by a shift from a traditional diet based on vegetables and fish towards the increasing consumption of poultry. Indeed, the consumption of poultry in some regions of China has more than doubled since 1980. These processes of industrialization and urbanization have encouraged the production of poultry on an industrial scale and this has disembedded the birds from their agricultural habitat and exposed them to the virus-promoting conditions of high-intensity and high-density factory farming methods. Meanwhile, the reduction in the diversity of breeds has facilitated short-term efficiency but has reduced 'immunological memory' (Davis, *ibid*: 57, 81). These developments are concentrated locally in regions such as Guangdong, China. However, in the context of an emergent world market for poultry and the increasing exposure to the toxins produced by extensive industrialization, the conditions have emerged for 'intensified rather than decreased microbial traffic between humans and animals' (Davis, *ibid*: 59). Poultry production has become a global business with transport technologies connecting potential seedbeds of the virus with other parts of the world with far more efficiency than could be achieved by migrating birds. This was illustrated in the outbreak of H5N1 at the Bernard Mathews turkey processing plant in Suffolk, UK during early 2007. While the initial prognosis pointed the finger of blame towards wild or migrating birds, the infection was later linked to importation of unprocessed turkey meat from Hungary (The Guardian, 14-02-07). Moreover, if the virus should infect humans and go undetected, global city airports in the vicinity of the breeding grounds of the virus, such as Hong Kong, could be transformed into 'super spreaders' (Davis, *ibid*: 70; Keil & Ali, 2006). Thus, while it may be going too far to suggest that the industrialization of poultry production in the developing world and the revolution in global transport and travel technologies have *generated* avian flu, it is nonetheless true to say that the interplay of these human-induced developments are 'exponentially expanding the surface area of contact between avian and non-avian influenzas' and thereby increasing the likelihood of a new global pandemic (Davis, *op cit*: 63).

Avian flu is the most recent version of a 'manufactured uncertainty' that is typical of 'risk society' (Beck, 2000b: 216). Manufactured uncertainties are induced by the unwanted side-effects of technological development that alter the relationship between the social and the biological world and draw 'environmental' dangers into the heart of civilization. Avian flu conforms to the model of a non-calculable global risk in the same way as nuclear disaster and global warming (Beck, 1995: 109). First, an avian flu pandemic would be devastating in its impact: Davis (*op cit*: 33) refers metaphorically to the phenomenon as a 'viral atomic bomb'. Second, an avian flu pandemic would re-map the geography of risk in both its spatial and temporal dimensions. Since its emergence in 1997, avian flu has flared up in various countries and, owing to its ability to hybridize with techno-logically sustained networks, has spread in a rather unpredictable manner. In the minor outbreak in 2003, the virus spread from a single hotel room in Hong Kong via airline connections to Singapore, Vietnam, Canada, Ireland and the USA. Moreover, owing to its genome-altering tendencies, the virus reinvents itself and is thus a 'constantly emerging disease' (Davis, *ibid*: 11; Keil & Ali, *op cit*: 108). The effects of the virus go far beyond the illnesses of those individuals that are infected. The effects of the virus protrude into the spheres of farming, food consumption and tourism and the virus thus fits perfectly Beck's (*op cit*: 109) description of manufactured risk as an ' "event" that is forever beginning, an "open ended festival" of creeping, galloping and overlapping despoliation'. Consequently, a H5N1-related global pandemic would be an incalculable and uninsurable risk. The example of avian flu provides an important insight into the cosmopolitan nature of risk society. For Beck (1996: 1), a 'risk society fully thought through means *world* risk society' and the cosmopolitan form of risk society is derived from the way in which the nation state container can no longer contain (*sic*) the fabricated risks of late modernity and, therefore, people in distant localities are interconnected through the feedback loops of ecological problems. The example of avian flu highlights the way in which nature itself has become cosmopolitan: a techno-biological hybrid that networks its way around the globe and across nation states with the technical assistance of human technology and social networks. This could be described as a form of 'unsettling environmental cosmopolitanism' (Clark, 2002), unsettling because it highlights the way that nature is not static and outside, but mobile and participating in the transnational networks of world society. To put it bluntly: 'the geography of globalization is [also] one of disease' (Keil & Ali, *op cit*: 108). This would indeed amount to the ultimate form of 'latent', 'real existing' or 'banal cosmopolitanism' (Beck, 2004), for it is a vitalist form of cosmopolitanism unconnected to the normative outlook of a transnational elite. The proposition that 'ecological hazards share the same networks' (Clark, *op cit*: 19) demonstrates that 'we are entangled for good' and that there is no outside nature anymore (Latour, 2003: 37).

According to Beck, ecological risks such as nuclear and chemical disasters, global warming and BSE/CJD, and now we can add H5N1 to this sequence, are new types of ecological challenge. These ecological risks are not products of 'nature' or the 'environment' but are 'manufactured uncertainties', 'man-made hybrids' between the physical and the social world that undermine the clear-cut distinction between nature and society (Beck, 2000b: 216–221) and part of an 'industrially transformed *inner* environment' (Beck, 1992: 81). These new risks are the symbolic markers of epochal change. Industrial society is transformed into 'risk society' or a society in which 'risk' and 'risk avoidance' become the main organizing principle. This is a transformation of truly revolutionary dimensions:

> It [the risk society perspective] maintains what until recently seemed unthinkable: that in its mere continuity the industrial society exits the stage of world history on the tip-toes of normality, via the back stairs of side-effects, and not

in the manner predicted in the picture books of social history: with a political explosion (Beck, *ibid*: 11).

This transformation towards 'risk society' affects crucial dimensions of societal organization. First, it alters significantly the 'logic of distribution' for while industrial society was characterized by the conflicts of 'wealth-distribution', risk society is dominated by forms of 'risk-distribution'. Industrial society emancipated itself from scarcity, but only to become enmeshed in the insecurity-generating side-effects of its efforts to overcome poverty (Beck, *ibid*: 19). Second, risk affects the social stratification of contemporary society, for while industrial society was a class society, risk society generates 'risk positions' that are simultaneously more global and more individualized. Risk distribution produces new regional differences in the wake of transnational and global feedback loops, even though the 'boomerang effect' of ecological risks means that they eventually will catch up with those who initially set them into gear (Beck, *ibid*: 23). The affliction of risk shows a certain disregard for class and status and yet the effects of class are not absent from risk society as sufficient wealth and access to knowledge might help individuals to navigate the shifting landscape of 'risk positions' (Beck, *ibid*: 35). Third, as risks impinge on all aspects of daily life, from place of residence to diet and lifestyle or hobby, there is a tendency towards individualization. This is a reflection of the way that class-based norms or generational knowledge is of little help when positioning one's lifestyle in relation to global hazards (Beck, *ibid*: 54). In this context, individual access to knowledge and reflexive strategies of 'self-actualization' become increasingly important (Giddens, 1991: 214) and this results in a reversal of the Marxist formula – as increasingly *consciousness* determines *being*. Thus, in order to identify 'risk position' one has to depend on expert knowledge (Beck, *op cit*: 53). Fourth, science loses its monopoly of truth and expertise and rationality is challenged by the experience of expert contradictions and cover-ups. This results in the 'demystification of science' (Beck, *ibid*: 71) as scientists find themselves in the unique and yet awkward position of being 'originators, diagnosticians and agents of salvation' (Beck, 1995: 113). This trinity is part of what Beck (2000b: 224) calls the 'relations of definition': that is, a 'legal, epistemological and cultural power matrix' in which risks are assessed and risk policies designed. Fifth, in order to escape the 'organized irresponsibility' of technocratic experts, the well-informed citizen must organize counter-expertise that brings ethical and social considerations back into play. This amounts to a process of 'sub-politicization' (1997: 151) outside the political institutions of industrial society. Finally, the integrating narrative of 'risk society' is no longer one of 'progress' associated with industrial society, but the storyline of the 'unlimited NOT' relating to the continuous avoidance of unimaginable, unlimited, unthinkable, uninsurable . . . . . global hazards' (Beck, 1992: 52).

Moreover, the model of 'risk society' developed by Beck expands our understanding of society in transition by highlighting the intimate relationship between ontological insecurity and temporal reordering. Risk is a way of dealing with global hazards, not the hazard itself, and involves the constant attempt to avoid possible hazards for the time being, pushing the consequences of action taken now further into the future. Thus, 'the essence of risk is not that it *is* happening but that it *might* be happening' (Adam & van Loon, 2000: 2). This, according to Beck (2000b: 214) 'reverses the relationship of past, present and future' as society struggles continuously in the 'here and now' with something that 'is *not* the case, but *could* happen if we were not to change course'. Drawing on Melucci (*op cit*: 20), we could argue that by being absorbed in what might happen in the future, risk society is effectively disowning the present. On a more metaphysical level, Beck (2002: 27) argues that this reversal of inner-directedness also influences the collective memory. Industrial society could rely on 'the nation-state memory of the past'. Risk society faces the prospect of a risk-induced consciousness of a globally shared future – yet no globally shared collective memory to go with it: 'that which is expected is becoming more and more different from that which has been experienced and this excites both hope and anxiety' (Beck et al., 2003: 11). In this context, the question as to whether 'risk' is '*real*' or culturally '*constructed*' is rather uninteresting as the 'risk society' will not become more real once we have final proof that global warming actually exists and is the product of human conduct. It is precisely the 'might be' status of side-effects that defines the agenda of risk society. We are uncertain of the risks of a global ecological disaster occurring but are unable to return to the status quo that existed before scientists informed us about global warming and before we experienced Chernobyl. This life in 'real virtuality' (Beck, 2000b: 213) defines the cultural logic of risk society: a 'peculiar reality status of "no-longer-but-not-yet – no longer trust/security, not yet destruction/disaster' (Beck, *ibid*: 213) that keeps contemporary society in an ongoing state of liminality.

Risk Society as 'Second' or 'Reflexive' Modernity

In the previous section, we highlighted the societal implications of risk society and it became clear that the model of risk society developed by Beck provides the basis for a powerful model of social change. However, nation state-based industrial society is not the same as modernity and the model of risk society has opened up the agenda of modernization anew. The isolation of risk as an alternative organizing principle of society, beyond and in conflict with the principle of nation-state territoriality, has opened up a completely new agenda (Elliott, 2002: 296; Rustin, 1994: 7). Ecological risks, deriving from the changed relationship of modernity with nature, are only the most (publicly) obvious aspect of a much wider process of transformation. Initially this seems obvious, as ecological questions highlight important social 'side effects'. For example, issues of social inequality, particularly between the global North and global South, are linked to disputes such as the felling of tropical rainforest, civil wars over scarce resources such as water – as the lingering conflict in Sudan suggests – and the destruction of ecosystems resulting in famine and mass migration. Thus, 'global ecological flashpoints' indicate other 'world flash points' (Beck, 1996: 12). However, in his later writings, Beck indicates clearly that ecological issues are only one of the 'touchstones' by which industrial modernity reveals the limited problem-solving capacity of its core institutions (Beck et al., 2003: 8). This is also manifested in the institutional limitations of task-oriented technology in the face of ecological risk; the welfare state in the face of mass unemployment; the mass party system in the face of declining legitimization and an upsurge in 'sub-politics'; the nuclear family in the face of growing flexibility in career and lifestyle; and science in the face of its own demystification. This is reflected in a crisis in the core operating principles of industrial modernity including the binary distinctions between nature/society, expertise/lay knowledge and insiders/outsiders that are in flux and transition (Beck et al., *ibid*: 1).

In the context of a transformation that challenges the institutional core as well as the coordinate system of society, Beck et al. (*ibid*: 2, 13) speak of a 'meta-change', a 'structural break' within modernity. The process of 'reflexive modernization' ushers in a new epoch of 'reflexive modernity'. In his early attempts to map risk society, Beck has a clear preference for the term 'reflexive modernity', in his later accounts he introduces the term 'second modernity' owing to the misunderstandings triggered by the notion of 'reflexive modernization' (Beck, 2000c: 81). 'Reflexive modernization' describes the overall transformation from 'first industrial modernity' to 'second reflexive modernity' (2000b: 211). Indeed, the term 'reflexive modernization' lends itself to being misunderstood as an increase in awareness, mastery and consciousness. For Beck (1992: 19), however, 'reflexive modernization' is nothing but the flip side of 'risk society'. Reflexive modernization occurs in a context in which industrial society faces its own side-effects and is transformed into risk society: 'modernization becomes reflexive; it is becoming its own theme'. Thus 'reflexive' is closer to 'reflex' in terms of a 'self-confrontation' of unwanted side-effects than it is to 'reflection' in terms of self-awareness and critical consciousness. 'Reflexive modernization' highlights primarily the 'self-dissolution' and 'self-endangerment' of industrial modernity (Beck, 1994a: 174). The notion that 'world risk society becomes self-critical' in the face of ecological self-endangerment and other culminating side-effects is only of secondary importance (Beck, 1996: 24). The potential for 'reflexive modernization' to steer society towards a 'responsible modernity' inheres only in the latter and secondary definition of the term (Beck, 2000b: 222).

Beck (1992: 9) is aware that to base an epochal distinction between 'first' and 'second modernity' on the process of reflexive modernization is something of a 'delicate balancing' act between continuity and rupture. Modernization becoming its own theme implies that modernization is not predominantly about the mastery of nature and development beyond pre-modern or traditional social structures, but rather about the reworking of its own institutional framework. Consequently, a society is taking shape that is radically different to industrial modernity. Hence:

> Reflexive Modernization seems to be producing a new kind of capitalism, a new kind of global order economy, a new kind of society, a new kind of nature, a new kind of subjectivity, a new kind of everyday life and a new kind of state. (Beck et al., *op cit*: 3)

While the concrete forms of reflexive modernity are undeveloped, a new type of society is emerging marked by political communities beyond the nation state; forms of social solidarity beyond the welfare state; forms of politics beyond the democracy of mass parties; and in the form of a patch-work of familial relations beyond the nuclear family. It is important to note that this 'structural break is not the result of exogenous factors but a consequence of modernization itself' (Beck et al., *ibid*: 43). Consequently, the theoretical construct of 'reflexive modernization' can be differenti-ated from both linear conceptualizations of modernization and theories of postmodernity. With regard to the former, reflexive modernization is marked by a decidedly non-linear telos and an openness with regard to the outcomes of societal development. Reflexive modernization is more than the further sophistication of modernity through the continuous differentiation of subsystems, but rather a process that simultaneously undermines and revamps modern society. In contrast to the ideas of post-modernity, reflexive modernization is presented as a process induced by modernity and within modernity (Beck, 2000c: 81; Beck et al., 2003: 2). Thus, it is marked by science and technology dealing with the ecolo-gical consequences of industrial science and technology; the democratic political system dealing with the consequences of its own legitimiza-tion deficit; and the nation state attempting to cope with the transna-tional consequences of a system of economic development induced by the international nation state system. In sum, 'it means not less but more modernity, a modernity radicalized against the paths and categories of the classical industrial setting' (Beck, *op cit*: 14). Reflexive modernity does not mark the end of modernity or the destruction of modernity through its own destructive side-effects, but rather a process of re-modernization based on the new social forms that have emerged from the unwanted challenge to modernity (Beck et al., *op cit*: 3; cf. Latour, 2003). Thus, the risk society perspective might trigger an 'owl of Minerva effect' as the focus on the deep entanglement of nature and society through techno- logy highlights the way in which the boundaries between the social and the natural were always imagined, socially constructed and never realized fully in practice within the modern project. Thus, if reflexive moderniza- tion in hindsight realizes this 'discrepancy between self-presentation and practice', it contributes to the insight that within the modern age in fact 'we have never been modern' (Latour, *ibid*: 38; cf. Rustin 1994: 7).

There are, however, a number of problems with the concept of 'reflexive modernization' particularly in relation to the underlying dynamics of this re-modernization process. The major problem concerns the relationship between the self and social institutions. In the context of the ecolo- gical side-effects of modernization, the differentiation between 'reflex' and 'reflection', self-dissolution' and 'self-criticism' and 'self-reflexive' and 'self-critical society' appear rather convincing. However, the issue becomes more problematic when we begin to examine the linkages between the two (Smith, 2005: 547). Following Elliott (*op cit*: 302), one might indeed be sceptical as to 'in what sense ... can one claim that reflection-free forms of societal self-dissolution exist independently of the reflective capacities of human agents? For what, exactly, is being dissolved if not the forms of life and social practices through which institutions are structured'? It is not easy to argue convincingly for a third trajectory towards a second modernity located between ecological doomsday and a hyper-enlightened society of well-informed citizens. On the one hand, there is the 'un- reflected, quasi-autonomous mechanisms of transition' that arise from the abstraction of the complex side-effects of task-oriented science and techno- logy (Beck, 1994b: 6). On the other, there is 'anyone who no longer wishes to accept the "fate" determined by the production of side effects' and the construction of alternative forms of public consensus, such as that found in a 'round table' between technocrats and well-informed citizens (Beck, *ibid*: 28; cf. Beck, 1997: 121). These two dynamics are not easily brought together. The tensions between reflex and reflection in Beck's argument raise further questions around the issues of risk perception and the rela- tionship between expert- and lay-knowledge. The work of Beck (cf. 1992: 30, 1994b, 1995: 11, 1997: 132) on the 'round table model' of decision- making is based on developments within the realm of sub-politics and premised on the existence of a shifting alliances of experts, counter-experts and well-informed citizens negotiating on present and future issues in front of an interested public (Mythen, 2004: 150). This model is predicated on the demystification of science, the democratization of expertise and the opening up of decision-making procedures. This idealized picture was, however, influenced heavily by the one-off developments associated with the disposal of the Brent Spar oil platform (Beck, 1996: 18; Dickson & McCulloch, 1996). There have been serious criticisms concerning the disembedded and disembodied nature of this perspective and the utilitarian and objectivist conceptualizations of risk underpinning this model (Alexander, 1996: 135; Lash, 2000; Wynne, 1996: 56; cf. Elliott, *op cit*: 300; Lupton & Tulloch, 2002: 319).

These criticisms imply the need for a more phenomenological perspective premised on the lived reality of risk society. With regard to the expert–lay knowledge divide, for example, Wynne (*op cit*) has argued that the response of lay people to expert knowledge is holistic and context-dependent. Important, in this context, is not only the content of advice but the extent to which the advice is underpinned by respect for indigenous knowledge and local ways of life. Thus, reaction to expert advice is a 'cultural response to a cultural form of intervention' (Wynne, *ibid*: 56–67f). Moreover, Wynne challenges the distinction between simple and reflexive modernity on the basis that the relationship between expert and lay knowledge throughout modernity has always been more complex than that suggested by the shift from 'automatic' to 'active trust' (Giddens, 1994: 92). Rather, dependency on expert knowledge always generates a spectrum of often intermingling responses that range from 'unreflexive trust' to 'reflexive dependency' and 'private ambivalence'. The uncontested status of expert knowledge does not, therefore, imply public trust and vice versa (Wynne, *op cit*: 48). Moreover, in times of reflexive modernization it would seem that 'risk from social dependency on institutions' is *the* essential, but largely unrecognized, aspect of 'risk awareness' (Wynne, *ibid*: 59). There is also the problem that we learn rather little from the risk society perspective on how and why certain 'risks' are placed on the public agenda, and why there is often a significant time-lag between scientific discovery of a hazard and public expressions of concern (Alexander & Smith, *op cit*: 254). The media play a role of obvious importance in the agenda-setting process of directing public attention to particular issues. Thus, while 'the news media are not successful in telling us what to think, they do succeed in telling us what to think about' (Mazur, 1998: 458). Whether or not certain ecological problems come to prominence is based on 'externals': newsworthy issues that are related but not intrinsic to the environmental problem. This is illustrated by the example of (former) US President Reagan, whose accidental brush with skin cancer was a crucial factor in pushing ozone layer depletion onto the policy agenda and into

(US) public awareness (cf. Mazur, *ibid*: 461). This highlights the importance of the demystification of science in a context of reflexive modernity.

The transfer of knowledge and the forms of communication between different forms of (counter)-expertise and (informed) lay-knowledge is thus more complex and mediated than assumed by the risk society perspective. Public awareness is embedded in the various meaning-making practices of everyday culture(s) and awareness of ecological hazards tends to be rather selective, inconsistent and of variable quality. An empirical study of lay perspectives on global climate change in the USA, following the publication of the *Global Climate Change Report*, indicated clearly how the lay public filter (scientific) information into their everyday milieux (Kempton, 1991). Kempton reported a general awareness of the 'greenhouse effect', but among the lay public conceptualizations of climate change deviated from scientific information and explanations. The lay perspective was often based on the experience of phenomena such as changes in local weather conditions and often reflected the ambiguity of individuals expressing a generalized support for environmental values alongside a neglect for the consequences of their individual lifestyle. The latter point is supported by a UK study of a Government campaign called *Helping the Earth Begins at Home* (Hinchliffe, 1996). The campaign was 'largely ineffective' as respondents saw little scope for changes in their individual lifestyle and, consequently, the responsibility for 'distant' environmental change was offloaded to government and corporate bodies. The general tendency to assimilate environmental concern into the practical outlook of everyday life and/or to blank them out is reflected in the 'issue-attention-cycle' hypothesis (Franzen & Meyer, 2004: 122). With regard to environmental issues, the hypothesis suggests that after an initial phase of enthusiasm, issues fade from public attention owing to the complexity of the issues and as the costs of problem-solving alternatives become more widely known. Obviously, this is bound to have an effect on public support for alternative policy options. The responses of lay publics are, moreover, country and culture specific. A cross-cultural comparative study on pro-environmental behaviour in the UK and the Netherlands, for example, found a greater acceptance of personal responsibility and a higher level of pro-environmental behaviour in the Netherlands (Harrison et al., 1996). These differences are related to the long-established discursive frames and mentalities of the respective national cultures. In this context, Hajer (1999: 274) contrasts an 'apocalyptic format' that is rooted deeply in the Dutch struggle against water and the 'ideology of empiricism' that shapes policy discourses in the UK.

The perception and evaluation of risk by lay publics are embedded in the overlapping structures of meaning and meaning-making practices that reflect both cognitive and emotional responses to risk. The dynamic of risk in the context of reflexive modernization can, therefore, be grasped more adequately if we consider non-rational dimensions of meaning and motivation and consider the affective structuring of behaviour by expectations, hopes and anxieties. The positioning of the self towards risk society is premised on both objective facts and rational assessment and the emotional and bodily responses associated with symbolic needs (Alexander & Smith, *op cit*: 255). Lash (1994: 135) has introduced this 'cultural-hermeneutic' dimension into the debate on reflexive modernization through the concept of 'aesthetic reflexivity': a form of self-positioning that is inscribed deeply in everyday forms of life. In this context, Lash (2000) has suggested that the notion of 'risk culture(s)' is preferable to risk society. This shift has epistemological as well as structural implications as 'risk cultures' are based on 'aesthetic reflexivity' rather than cognitive rationality. Risk cultures represent 'non-institutional sociations' in which people assemble temporarily according to their elective affinity to risks. In this process, bodily feelings of the 'sublime' are central and these result not in pure perceptions but estimations based on feelings of pleasure and displeasure or feelings like shock or being overwhelmed or feelings of fear, loathing or joyfulness. These feelings constitute the 'reflexive aesthetic judgement' that is required in order to assess risk in a holistic fashion (Lash, *ibid*: 52). The notion of 'risk culture' is thus an attempt to grasp the re-structuring process implied in the model of reflexive modernization. The 'quasi-fluid memberships' in the aesthetic reflexive sociations called 'risk cultures' imply a 'horizontal disordering' of society that deconstructs the hierarchies of simple modernity. Risk cultures inhabit the institutional void generated by de-legitimized expert systems and governmental bodies (Lash, *ibid*: 47.). Hence, we capture the sibling relationship between 'reflection' and 'reflex' in 'reflexive modernization': people (involuntarily) set free from the structures and institutions of simple modernity are increasingly involved in the making of their own constitutive rules. In so doing, they become perpetual inter-subjective rule-finders rather than people adhering to prescriptive rules. But, reflection on available resources and conditions of existence will be not a purely rational one, and so we have a non-linear search for rules based on both 'reflex' (non-rational responding) and 'reflection' (pondering over available options) (Lash, 2003).

Symbolic Reconciliation with 'Nature': Milieu and Body

The empirical studies in the previous section suggest that in the context of environmental problems individuals search for 'actionable responsibility'

(Eden cited in Harrison et al., *op cit*: 217). Individuals are faced with notions of 'global' environmental change but the complexities of processes such as global warming remain unconnected to everyday concerns and, in this context, individuals react through feelings of guilt, apathy and alienation. The difficulty of (re)connecting the global environment with the immediate environment of everyday life leads to 'reflexive strategies of non-engagement with "the big picture"' (Macnaghten, *op cit*: 78). This constellation is partly reflected in 'the changing structure of environmental concern' (Macnaghten, *ibid*: 69) where the emphasis of concern has shifted from 'nature out there' (i.e. global warming) to 'nature in here' (i.e. genetically modified [GM] food). According to Macnaghten (*ibid*: 64), the environmental concerns that impinge directly on the body allow this dominant 'value-action gap' to be bridged. This tendency towards the *'embodiment* of environmental concern' (Macnaghten, *ibid*: 81, our emphasis) is central to the issue of reflexivity. As Giddens (1991) suggests, the 'reflexive project of the self' is tied intrinsically to 'life politics', a form of lifestyle politics in which 'political issues . . . flow from processes of self-actualization in post-traditional contexts, where globalizing influences intrude deeply into the reflexive project of the self, and conversely where processes of self-actualization influence global strategies' (Giddens, *ibid*: 214). Beck (1994b: 45) has referred similarly to 'life-and-death-politics' in the realm of risk society, stating that 'in ecological culture the most general and the most intimate things are directly and inescapably interconnected in the depth of private life'. However, as Giddens (1994: 223) admits elsewhere, 'to switch from global risk to the situation of the individual may seem as an odd transition . . .'. This problem can be overcome by inserting the body as an intermediate sphere between global risk and the individual, for it is around the body that personal moral concerns and responsibilities evolve. Hence, we recall the argument of Melucci (*op cit*: 48) regarding the double meaning inherent within 'responsibility' as the 'capacity to respond': 'responding to' (recognizing ourselves in a relational field of experience and action) and 'responding for' (answering for the action we have taken). Against this analytical background, the observation that 'environmental concerns are likely to be felt most acutely when they impinge on the body' (Macnaghten, *op cit*: 68), appears rather plausible.

The personalization of environmental concern via the individual body highlights the usefulness of a sociological concept that has been largely neglected in the ecological discourse – the concept of *milieu*. This concept allows us to focus on how global ecological issues are tied up with the daily lives of individual people. Returning to the work of Scheler (1973), Schütz (1970) and Goffman (1972), we can define 'milieu' as a body-related, relatively stable configuration of action and experience in which the individual maintains in an active way a distinctive degree of familiarity and practical competence (Grathoff, 1989: *passim*). It is this familiar frame of daily conduct that filters our experience of the wider environment. The concept also reveals that while risks may not impinge directly on the body as a physical entity they still nevertheless punctuate the 'protective cocoon' provided by bodily ease. This can be illustrated through the consumption of food. Food is a crucial mechanism through which milieu and wider environment are connected intrinsically and thus food provides an 'access point' (Goffman, *op cit*: 351) between risk society and individual milieux. Following the concepts developed by Goffman, 'normalcy' and the continuity of the 'self' are threatened when the individual loses the practical competence to undertake conduct based on taken-for-granted routines (Goffman, *ibid*: *passim*). In this sense, 'food' has until recently been a safe part of everyday milieu – at least in the global North. The succession of food scares, from the salmonella in egg crisis, to listeria in soft cheese, botulisms in hazelnut yoghurt, BST in milk, Alar in apples and, more recently, BSE and avian flu (James, 1993: 214), has undermined this security in a profound and immediate way. 'Food' has turned into a source of potential practical incompetence or a source of disruption that changes familiar features of everyday life. In the terms of Goffman (*op cit*: 299, 351), it is no longer 'something that can be dis-attended safely' and becomes instead a continuous source of 'alarm'. This phenomenological perspective highlights the ways in which 'risk society' has become very personal and very real. In the context of these food scares, the individual experiences a 'double shock' (Beck, 1992: 54): first, the sudden realization of the risk deriving from formerly familiar and appreciated food items; second, the loss of sovereignty over dealing with the disruption of one's own milieu. Owing to the 'scientization' of risks, which devalues the practical stock of knowledge on which we normally rely in our daily routines, we are unable to regain competence *within* the milieu without having to rely on *external* expertise. The sudden revelation of chemicals in foodstuff confronts people in their milieu with problems that are neither detectable nor solvable within the context of everyday routine, knowledge and practice. Two typical reactions may follow this loss of familiarity and competence in everyday life. The first is the tendency to accept or even deny the newly revealed risks and to engage in what Beck terms the 'death-reflex of normality':

> There is a virtually instinctive avoidance, in the face of the greatest possible danger, of living in intolerable contradiction; the scattered constructs of normality are upheld, or even elevated, as if they remained intact. (Beck, 1995: 49)

The second is the possibility for 'empowering engagement' (Dürrschmidt, 1999: 139). Examples of this are to be found in the social and cultural networks that have evolved around the production and consumption of 'organic food'. Here people regain, at least partly, a routine of eating and cuisine around 'alternative dietetic knowledge' (Eder, 1996: 155). There is an element of 'aesthetic reflexivity' involved here as people experiment and broaden their horizons in the world of food and cooking and the generation of endogenous creativity is encouraged within an externally enforced process of self-actualization.

However, it is important to stress that while organic food networks help individuals to regain some ontological security with regard to food and diet, they do not re-establish the status quo prior to the intrusion of risk society into the milieu via food scares. Rather, they force the individual to face up to the problems of risk society. While polluted food threatens the bodily self, it also has a wider significance for, as James (*op cit*: 214) argues, the threatening pollution of the individual's body by contaminated food is at the same time experienced as a 'symbol of the environmental pollution in which human beings contemporarily dwell'. The problem of 'ecotoxicity' (Giddens, *op cit*: 226), or the circulation of chemicals through soil, air and water, is so complex that it escapes simple patterns of cause and effect. However, this implies that attempts at purification can only ever be partial and of rather marginal value. Hence, risky food raises not just a series of one-off problems that can be resolved through practical intervention, but causes lasting 'global alarm' in the *umwelt* of the individual (Goffman, 1972: 351). The individual senses the open horizon of risk society. People experience in their dealing with contaminated food what Melucci refers to as the 'ecological issue as a systemic problem':

> That is to say, it reveals behind its surface the phenomenon of planetary interdependence and creates new frontiers of human consciousness and action. We have come to an end of linear causality, of monocausal explanations. (Melucci, *op cit*: 58)

The consumption of (organic) food in context of 'ecotoxicity' highlights the way in which the contradictory complexity of global risk society enters irrevocably the milieu of the individual. The issues of care for the body and the self are thus tied inextricably to questions of moral responsibility and concern for wider global issues. The question of 'what shall I eat' turns into the question of 'how do I want to live'? In other words, organic food networks encourage people 'to view the world through food' (Moore-Lappé cited in Eder, 1996: 156). The individual is encouraged into a symbolic self-actualization towards wider world risk society.

What, for instance, about organically grown beans from Kenya? Is it OK to buy these in the context of the environmental side-effects of 'food mileage'? If we decline to consume on these grounds, what about the life-chances of the people who hope to earn a living by growing them? What about organically grown food that is not also part of a fair trade agreement (Raynolds, 2000)? Moreover, the basic principles of simple or first modernity are challenged as many organic food schemes encourage their customers to visit the organic farm and perhaps even establish a 'personal' relationship with the turkey they have ordered for Christmas (James, *op cit*: 209). Hence, the 'sequestration of experience' (Giddens, 1991: 164) is partly undermined as customers are encouraged to enter contracts that follow the cycles of (local) organic farming thus (re)establishing long(er) term bonds between grower and consumer. These illustrations indicate a dimension of moral responsibility for individual acts of consumption. 'Going organic' is more than simply a choice over what type of food to consume and extends to a wider concern with a whole range of social and ecological issues. The symbolic dimension of organic food or 'natural' food takes us to the core of modern society and the relationship between human and natural world. At the deepest level, 'going organic' can be regarded as a symbolic rejection of an industrial relationship with nature and an attempt to rekindle non-instrumental and non-economic interaction with nature. This confirms Eder's (*op cit*: 152) observation that 'natural food movements' such as the 'natural reform movement' and the 'vegetarian movement' have been accompanying modern industrialism since its beginnings and have been growing in parallel with industrial food production. Contemporary risk society, with its unending succession of food scares, has generated a higher level of public resonance with regard to these sub-currents of modern development and there has been a considerable expansion of both organic farming and the consumption of organic food following BSE and concerns over GM-food (Wehling et al., 2005: 143).

The 'return to the natural' (Giddens, 1994: 225) that can be observed in such diverse areas as food, farming, medicine and sports is centred on feelings of an elective affinity between nature and the body or between 'external planet' and 'inner planet' (Melucci, *op cit*: 71). Modern industrialism has not just appropriated outside nature but also regimented the natural rhythms of the body. Modern technologies have not just deeply intruded into nature but, in the form of reproductive technologies, have invaded deeply into bodily nature. New technologies such as GM-food that have been developed with insufficient trials and testing effectively transform both the 'external planet' and the 'internal planet' into a laboratory of science (Adam, 2000: 127). Thus, the search for 'true nature' is paralleled by the rediscovering of the body as site of integrity. The re-enchanting of the 'external planet' through, for example, invocations of the goddess Gaia is paralleled by the body becoming 'the new sacred' in late modernity (Varga, 2005). 'Clean', non-industrial food becomes the symbolic execution of this elective affinity. It is symbolic, not just because of the comparatively tiny proportion of organically produced (and consumed) food, but because the mobility of the already released genetically modified organisms amounts to a situation where 'the clear boundary between conventional, GM-based and organic farming can be no longer guaranteed and maintained' (Adam, *op cit*: 128; cf. Mythen, 2004: 163). Participating in an organic food network is also a symbolic reconnection to a pre-industrial past in the form of a way of life that was supposedly more 'natural' and in which humans, animals and plants lived in harmony (James, *op cit*: 212). The consumption of organic food does not necessarily amount to a reflexive change or challenge to modern lifestyles. For many consumers, organic food provides a postmodern touch to their lifestyle and in this context, the symbolic significance of the product is the primary object of consumption. Eating 'green' is a lifestyle choice, but not a choice of lifestyle, at least in most cases (Dürrschmidt, *op cit*: 142). Rephrasing Eder (*op cit*: 160), one could state provocatively that a sentimental relationship to nature and the body has become possible precisely because of the distance generated between them by modern science and industrial technology. 'Risk cultures' (Lash, 2000) challenge the dominant cultural codes of industrial modernity (Melucci, *op cit*) but not the dominant institutional structures of risk society. The challenge '(occurs) outside rather than within present social structures' (James, *op cit*: 212).

Organic food networks could thus be described as a seedbed of a 'self-creative society' (Hegedus, 1989), a society in which empowered citizens generate alternative problem-solving capacities beyond the market. However, a serious structural problem has become apparent in the relationship between the quasi-tribal and fluid identity commitments of such non-institutional associations and their claims to manifest alternative forms of life applicable to wider society (Purdue et al., 1997: 663). Moreover, during the last decade large food companies have transformed the concern for healthy and organic food into a global industry. In this context, both small farmers and producers and consumers have become increasingly dependent on the market mechanisms for the distribution and sale of these products (Lockie et al., 2000; Raynolds, 2000). The risk culture present in the organic food networks is an inevitable expression of a 'symbolic "greening" in risk society' (Lockie et al., *op cit*: 316). This provides a reflexive way of finding symbolic reconciliation with nature by incorporating the 'organic' into individual milieu. Hence, the environmental sinner can continue his/her 'bad good life' (Beck, 2000b: 215) by confessing some of his/her sins while continuing to have his/her cake (ecological balance) and eat it (participate in the benefits of technological development and economic growth).

Summary and Conclusion

In this chapter, we have explored the complex and ambiguous relationship between nature, environment and milieu in global risk society. We began with the observation that throughout the history of human civilization the fear of environmental pollution has been linked intimately with concerns about societal order. We argued that contemporary concerns about the environment are symptomatic of a deeper social crisis in which the fractured nature of social reality and the resulting ontological insecurity are connected intimately with the 'componentiality' produced by scientific and technological development. We suggested that just as the perception of the 'globe' provides an Archimedean point to reconnect the fragments generated by the 'technological fix', the human body has become an Archimedean point that links internal and external nature. We then used the example of avian flu to highlight the way in which the boundaries between nature and society are collapsing and the way in which this is captured by Ulrich Beck's conceptualization of risk as 'manufactured uncertainty'.

In the context of looking at contemporary society as a society in transition, Beck's account of risk society has to be credited with bringing the socioecological dimension of contemporary change back into consideration. In contrast to one-dimensional accounts of enthusiastic social engineering or scaremongering environmentalism, we get a clear picture of a social nature that is both discursively mediated (mainly by science) and real (in its potential consequences). The central concept of 'global risk' highlights the existence of a human-generated global 'environment' that escapes the modernist logic of control. Moreover, it highlights the perpetual state of liminality in which we now exist and how any attempt to deal with unfamiliar global hazards carries a residual risk of generating further complexities associated with unforeseen side-effects. Furthermore, Beck is effective in outlining the 'this-as-well-as-that-realities' where clear-cut borders between the natural and the social become increasingly blurred, as could be illustrated with the 'unsettling environmental cosmopolitanism' of avian flu. However, the attempt by Beck to encase his theory of risk society in the wider framework of 'reflexive modernization' and 'second modernity' is somewhat problematic. Beck is correct to argue that contemporary society is characterized by 'ambivalence', 'ambiguity', perplexity' and 'contradiction' and that this implies an end to the developmental logic of modernity. However, it is difficult to extend this argument to the proposition that this new configuration of society is necessarily constituted as 're-modernization' and 'second modernity' (Beck & Lau, 2005; Beck et al., 2003).

While it is clear that contemporary society is experiencing an epochal break, it is less clear why an understanding of this break needs to be derived from an understanding of the inconsistencies of institutional modernity rather than the altered relationship between modernity and its socioecological environment (Benton, 2000). Indeed, if contemporary society is characterized by multiple transformations that affect both the basic institutions of modernity (such as science and rationality) and its basic guiding principles (such as the distinction between nature/society) (Beck & Lau, *op cit*; Beck et al., 2003), what then is rationale for attempting to grasp novelty and change within the foregone conclusions provided by the narrative of modernity? One possible answer to this question could be the perceptible fear of drifting into the muddy waters of a postmodernism that lacks a matrix of orientation (Beck et al., *ibid*: 3; Münch, 2002: 424). Yet what is left of modernity if its basic institutions and basic principles are undermined by processes of non-linear change? Here, the 'reflexive modernization' approach becomes less convincing. The notion that there is continuity between first and second modernity is hinged on a 'peculiar normative and cognitive infrastructure' that includes principles such as validity claims in communication, the political mouldability of society and an egalitarian approach to social inclusion (Beck & Lau, 2003: 9; Beck et al., 2005: 115f.). However, there is another line of argument that is much more in tune with Beck's initial risk society thesis. Beck is correct to stress the uncontrollable externalities of industrial development as markers of an epochal break. However, his model underestimates the role of globality in establishing the limits to externalizability. It is globality – the materiality and finitude of Planet Earth – that generates the non-linear feedback loops of industrial modernity and sets the new frame of reference for acting and thinking and this includes the practice and discourse of re-modernization. In other words, globality sets the very real reference points that impose a new agenda on contemporary society – beyond the inherent logic of modern institutions and principles (Albrow, 1996: 133ff.).

There are, moreover, a number of more specific problems and tensions with the concept of reflexive modernization. These includes the ambiguous relationship between individual and institutional risk and the relationship between 'reflex' and 'reflection' within the concept of 'reflexivity'. We argued that these tensions could be addressed through a phenomenological approach that explored the context-dependent and often non-rational ways in which individual risk positions and wider risk cultures are generated and maintained in everyday milieux. However, as we illustrated with the case of the increasing popularity of organic food consumption, everyday culture tends towards a symbolic recon-ciliation with risk society rather than pushing towards the built-in 'utopia of a responsible modernity' or a 'self-critical society' (Beck, 2000: 218–222).

8
Reconstructing the Social

We started our journey through the hotspots of contemporary social transition by highlighting the liminality or in-betweenness that marks contemporary society. We highlighted the analytical ambiguity and cultural dissonance that is generated by the condition of liminality. We argued that the dominant sociological analyses of social change tend to obscure this liminality, either by postulating the transcendence of modernity or by over-stretching the categories and concepts of modern society in order to take account of the radicalization or reflexivity of modernity. In contrast, we argued against the delineation of an overall definition for society in transition in favour of a process of 'complexification' based on a sociological approach that hovers between 'the known and the unknown' (Esping-Andersen, 2000: 60). We are sympathetic to the argument that contemporary patterns of social change are non-linear and underpinned by a process of societal complexification (Urry, 2005). However, rather than simply accepting yet another theory premised on binary opposites – this time between simple modernity and complex (post)modernity and/or globality – we have proceeded on the basis of 'an intentional and purposeful empiricism' (Esping-Andersen , *op cit*: 72) to chart this complexity and ambiguity. This is not a recipe for a narrow positivism but the basis for a contextualized analysis of social relationships in a changing world. We will conclude this book with a discussion of the main forms of sociation that have been uncovered by our investigation. Thus while we accept the corrosive impact of disembedding mechanisms, we remain critical of analyses of contemporary society that postulate the death of the 'social'.

The 'hotspots' of social change in this book highlight the need for theoretical and conceptual complexification in order to grasp the non-linear and processual character of new and reconstituted forms of sociality. Whilst accepting the non-linear direction of complex social change as propounded by the emerging complexity paradigm (Urry, 2003, 2005), we would agree with McLennan (2003: 458) that 'there are many unresolved issues in the complexity debate which counsel against seeing 'complexity theory' as a ready made tool for sociological upgrading. The problem with the complexity paradigm is that it leads to a form of reductionism where phenomena such as 'system equilibrium' and 'feedback loops' obscure on-going patterns of social continuity and change. While the process of disembedding associated with globalization has contributed to the generation of 'postmodern' cultural forms, this has not occurred in a linear way and there remain a plethora of gaps, disjunctures and 'path dependent' continuities with industrial or 'first' modernity. It makes little sense to speak of the global city, the global workplace, global culture or the global environment in the context of these disjuncture and continuities. Each of these concepts as defined by the 'global' prefix would need further qualification and this highlights the enduring and lasting impact of the modern epoch.

The global city is also defined as the post-metropolis, the global workplace can have substantial Fordist segments, global culture carries post-imperial regional patterns and the global environment is based on the continuing realities of industrial society. Alongside the 'space of flows' there exists an enduringly important 'space of place'. The inhabitants of the marginalized and depressed border regions, the cyber-coolies working the night shifts in the Indian call centres or the ecologically concerned citizen must 'live' and maintain ontological security in the context of these corrosive processes of disembedding. The hotpots of social change explored in this book highlight the difficulties individuals face in the generation of meaningful new communities. However, we have also highlighted processes of re-embedding made possible by people 'jumping' scales within the new landscape of the global cultural economy. In the globalizing contemporary world of today, opportunity structures and networks of obligation stretch beyond face-to-face forms of social interaction. These have their own patterns of territoriality even if detached somewhat from the constraints of geographic space. Intense patterns of hypermobility can have the obverse and often ambiguous result of strengthening the 'symbolism of belonging' within the immediate milieu of the life world. This can also include a reflexive revitalization of face-to-face quasi-intimacy along the lines of what Simmel (1971: 127–140) described as 'sociability', the non-consequential and playful encounter of the moment that has no other purpose than to generate a joyful moment for the parties involved. In this context, it makes equally little sense to describe contemporary social institutions as 'postmodern'. The intense processes of fragmentation, relativization and implosion associated with disembedding are only one side of a more complex process of societal restructuring that simultaneously involves de-fragmentation, re-signification, re-differentiation and active re-appropriation. This is not the end of the social but the emergence of new forms of complex and ambiguous sociality made possible by the disembedding dynamics of globalizing modernity

Throughout this book, we have highlighted the corrosive effects of powerful disembeddding mechanisms and the ways in which these are responsible for processes of de-traditionalization and individualization and an intensification of alienation and anomie. While Bauman's description of social change as 'disembedding without re-embedding' is a tempting position to adopt (Bauman & Tester, 2001), a close analysis of contemporary hotspots of transition shows that disembedding is always accompanied by at least partial re-embedding – albeit in a fragmented and ephemeral way. Even spaces of intense liminality require social attachment and forms of social presence somewhere. The development and application of ICT provides the basis for increasingly ambiguous forms of social engagement. As Urry (2004: 121) points out, in order to sustain and realize fully the social capital in global networks, there is a new 'tyranny of proximity'. This is based on the need for frequent face-to-face encounters and highlights the importance of global cities, universities, airport facilities and other non-places as the infrastructure on which global networks rely. We will now explore the new forms of sociality that are developing in the context of complex patterns of presence, absence and co-presence. In the context of time–space distanciation, the concept of 'community' is ineluctably 'place-bound' and we explore the analytical potential of the alternative conceptualizations of 'neo-communities' (Lash & Urry, 1994) and 'sociospheres' (Albrow, 1997). We argue that in a 'network society' (Castells, 2000a) 'abstract systems' (Giddens, 1990) do not lead unproblematically to the 'colonisation of the life-world' (Habermas, 1987) but have an enabling and empowering function with regard to the maintenance of life-worlds across time and space.

Whither Community?

While the process of de-traditionalization is often analysed in terms of the shift from *gemeinschaft* to *gesellschaft* type community, social reality was always, in fact, more complex and modernity was constituted by forms of social cohesion and solidarity premised on both 'community' and 'civil society' (Tönnies, 2001). Clearly, both these types of solidarity are undermined by the processes of social change outlined in this book. Industrial and urban restructuring have increasingly challenged kinship and neighbourhood communities. Nationally determined forms of civil society were essentially 'imagined' communities created and maintained by the nation state (Anderson, 1983) which have been de-centred and marginalized by the process of globalization. In this context, the 'social networks' that nourish communities are perceived widely to be in decline and this is resulting in a diminution of 'social capital' and ultimately a threat to democratic order (Putnam, 2000). In the sphere of consumption, this tendency can be seen in the increasing importance of online and TV shopping or the tendency towards 'self-service' within the new means of consumption. In the informational workplace, workers are fragmented by the informational labour process and interact with the disembedded and disembodied voices of clients in distant cities and continents. The global city is a hub in which the face-to-face interaction of elite 'networkers' plays a vital role in the maintenance of the global cultural economy. The elite are, however, functionally and spatially separated from those that service the global city, whose spatial and temporal displacement, in terms of housing and un-sociable shift patterns, attenuates face-to-face interaction within the dispersed localities of the global city. In the 'borderlands', the face-to-face interaction between individuals within and across political borders is undermined by path dependent and nationally framed opportunity structures and networks of obligation. The development of politics beyond the nation state has resulted in power becoming increasingly 'faceless', placeless and abstract and this has resulted in the individualization of politics around notions of 'risk biography'. Living in a society dominated by human-generated environmental risks tends to generate reflexive strategies of non-engagement with the daunting picture of planetary society and yet at the same time a hyper-engagement with lifestyle politics. These examples highlight the importance of the continuous interplay between disembedding *and* re-embedding in the current phase of societal transformation. These processes of reconstitution are occurring mainly at the intersection of the life world and the abstract systems generated by the process of time–space distanciation.

In the context of abstract systems, trust in impersonal principles and anonymous others becomes indispensable to social existence. Abstract systems include 'symbolic tokens' such as money and 'expert systems' such as institutional science that have disembedded trust relations from the local context. Giddens is critical of sociological approaches that counterpoise abstract systems with the intimacies of personal life and argues that personal life and the social ties that it entails are deeply intertwined with the most far-reaching abstract systems (Giddens, 1990: 120). Indeed, place has become increasingly 'phantasmagorical' and a site for locally situated expressions of distanciated relations (Giddens, *ibid*: 108–109). This is especially the case in respect of the global city, as the transnationally re-routed post-metropolis can be seen as one big 'phantasmagoria'. The supermarket and the shopping mall are more mundane examples of phantasmagoria, in contrast to the more spectacular examples in the form of theme parks and the casino hotels in Las Vegas. In both cases, 'place' is the location for the grounding of temporally and spatially disembedded images and relations. In this context, the dialectical relationship between 'face work commitments' and 'faceless commitments' becomes increasingly important in the generation and maintenance of trust; particularly in relation to the 'access points' where these intersect (Giddens, *ibid*: 80–88). The performance of 'emotional labour', observable in the smile of the airline attendant or the pleasing demeanour of the checkout assistant at the local supermarket, has become increasingly important to the generation of 'trust' that individuals must have for the complex 'expert systems' which underpin the airline industry and the logistics of retail sourcing and distribution networks. However, the increasing sophistication of ICT has enabled the emergence of phenomenon such as call centres in which the relationship between abstract systems and individuals is totally 'face-less' and call centre agents perform 'emotional labour at a distance'. The customer of HSBC, who interacts with the bank primarily through the Internet and telephone agents in India, nonetheless maintains a level of trust commensurate to the customer of a high street bank with human tellers and a high visibility manager. Thus, while trust is a central determinant of ontological security or the continuity of self-identity, trust in nonhuman technological systems is based on a more primitive faith in the reliability and nurturance of human individuals (Giddens, *ibid*: 97). However, in the context of reflexive modernity, trust in abstract systems is typically ambivalent and contingent and marked by a mixture of deference and scepticism; comfort and fear; and ontological security and existential angst. This ambivalence is, indeed, a persistent feature of the 'homeless mind' (Berger et al., 1973) that travels the landscape of technologized (post)modernity.

On the other hand, there is also a tendency towards the appropriation of abstract systems into the very privacy of the home environment. The development of phenomena such as online banking, TV home shopping, online dating and Internet pornography highlights the ambiguity that develops where abstract systems become an integral part of the home environment. This can have empowering and liberating effects as physical appearance and temporal constraints, such as the opening hours of banks and shops, are increasingly reduced or overcome. Thus, the search for self-fulfilment through abstract systems can lead to a transformation of the life world and the very meaning of the 'personal' and the 'private'. The private is thus accentuated and undermined by these developments and the price of the appropriation of abstract systems is increased surveillance and traceability. In other words, globalization does not intensify the shift from 'communal' to 'impersonal' forms of community or the colonization of the life world by instrumental system imperatives (cf. Habermas, 1987), but transforms the nature of community and life world. This transformation has occurred in a context in which the risks and dangers of late modernity have become increasingly intensive, expansive, remote, visible and ultimately uncontrollable. In the context of high-intensity and life-threatening risks, individuals react in a number of ways including pragmatic acceptance, sustained optimism, cynical pessimism and radical engagement (Giddens, 1990: 134–137). These are simultaneously reactions against disembedding and moments of re-embedding. As Giddens (*ibid*: 140–148) argues, modernity transforms the tissue of spatial experience. Through the conjoining of proximity and distance, the familiar is increasingly mediated by time–space distanciation or distant events are 'placed into' the locality. Individuals are inserted into globalized cultural and informational settings and thereby integrated into globalized communities of 'shared experience'. The world beyond the neighbourhood is not an impersonal one. Intimate relations are increasingly sustained at a distance and indeed, abstract systems in the form of advanced ICT allows a potential expansion in personal ties and acquaintances. Indeed, technical expertise is simultaneously sequestrated and expropriated in the interaction between individuals and abstract systems. Thus while we need to maintain a focus on the centrality of social relationships, we need to re-think the centrality of 'primary', that is, face-to-face relations over 'secondary' or 'mediated' relations.

The global shift has thus created an increasing tensions between the concepts of locality, community and citizenship. The locality is increasingly constituted by a range of social realities that coexist without creating a local culture or community. Within a locality, there exist individuals whose lives are marked by different time horizons and social networks with varying spatial extent. The result, however is not the fragmented and dislocated reality of postmodern theory, but highlights the existence of new form of sociality marked by networks of social relations with varying intensity and different territorial extents that barely touch on one another in the locality. The concept of 'sociospheres' highlights this sense of varying but overlapping spatial scope, discrete movement and separateness (Albrow, 1997: 51). Hence, new forms of spatial and temporal segregation have developed within localities and this forms the basis for new forms of spatial and temporal stratification.

> The new conflicts are not between established and outsiders in the globalized localities but between locals, cosmopolitans, and all gradations between, where the local may be the newcomers and the cosmopolitans may be long-term residents. The stratification layers are vividly represented by the different modes of transport available, the use of telecommunications and the use made of space. Very frequently, the greatest living space is available to those who occupy it least. (Albrow, *ibid*: 54)

In the global city, we have neighbourhoods where local neighbours are strangers and engage in worlds with different horizons and extensions. In the borderlands, people are compelled into 'communities of fate' but inhabit different frames of life and opportunity structures and engage with different 'communities of relevance' (Held, 2000). In the informational workplace, workers spend the day in real proximity with colleagues, but engage with different aspects of global systems and networks. In these extreme cases of co-presence and divergent life worlds, does the concept of 'community' retain an analytical usefulness in describing contemporary social relationships? Lash and Urry (*op cit*: 315–318) highlight the emergence of two potential forms of neo-community based on divergent understandings of the global. On the one hand, we have universalistic forms of global community premised on the increasing domination of the particular by the universal and the abstract. These are the evolutionary universalisms associated with Marxist world systems theory (Wallerstein, 1990) and Parsonian functionalism (Robertson, 1990) and the worldview of global elites and counter-elites. These abstract and mediated communities approximate to 'imagined communities' (Anderson, 1983) located in abstract time, abstract space and an abstract 'social' in which people and social relations are located. On the other hand, globalization opens up the possibility for 'invented communities' that are 'rooted' and 'worlded' rather than global. This is a community premised on Heidegger's notion of 'being-in-the-world' or Hegel's notion of *Sitten* or non-rule regulated customs in which meaning is generated in the immediacy of day-to-day routines (Lash & Urry, *op cit*: 315).

Indeed, in the context of reflexive modernity, the invention of community becomes the exception rather than the rule. According to Lash and Urry (*ibid*: 316–317), invented communities are generated through aesthetic or hermeneutic reflexivity that involves making choices about background assumptions and shared practices as the basis for cognitive and normative reflection. Invented communities thus tend to be 'taste communities' premised on the pre-judgements and predispositions of 'habitus' (Bourdieu, 1986). In the cultural geography of the global era, racist 'neo-tribes' tend to emerge in the 'wild zones', such as Eastern Germany, that are disconnected from the dense communication and information networks and where there is a lack of aesthetic and other resources. In contrast, cosmopolitan NSMs tend to be concentrated in the 'tame zones' marked by densely concentrated information and communication structures. Hence, neo-community building is not necessarily a normatively progressive process (Bauman, 1987).

In 'wild zones' and 'tame zones' of the global cultural economy we have manifestations of intense forms of racially motivated ethnic hatreds and nationalisms and new forms of cosmopolitan new social movement activity associated with the global justice movement. Anti-capitalist resistance has become re-embedded in alternative 'post-bourgeois' conceptions of the public sphere (Fraser, 1997: 72) that is 'placed but transnational, localized but characterized by expanding globality' (Conway, 2004: 376). A specific manifestation of this is the invented neo-communities that emerge through the immediate dangers of risk society. This includes elements of DIY culture, which have evolved around issues such as food to link the personal and the global milieu. These types of community are, however, fragmented and ephemeral and are linked to particular issues rather than the reproduction of class or status. However, these communities can also develop both an individual and global focus. Groups such as *Reclaim the Streets* challenge the implosion of the urban environment into an amorphous arena of auto-mobilization and anti-capitalist networks challenge the institutional manifestations of neo-liberal globalism at the core of their urban hubs – London, New York, Seattle and Brussels.

The dynamic process of re-affiliation and re-attachment is also increasingly apparent with regard to the reorientation of the labour movement. In the context of hostile social and technical relations within the state and workplace, the labour movement has been institutionally disembedded and is becoming re-embedded in a range of new alliances and networks in civil society including the development of new forms of 'community unionism'. These developments are reaction against the new configurations of power that have developed through the concentration of 'informational power' amongst a 'knowledge elite' within corporations and the parallel process of automation that has increasingly eliminated low-skilled jobs – particularly amongst blue-collar, unionized workers in manufacturing. Castells (2000a) argues that the restructuring of the global economy has combined with the informational mode of development to transform all areas of social and personal life according to the social logic of the network. This logic is premised on the decline of place-bound power as 'flows of power' are superseded the 'power of flows' between nodes in the network and the elites that control the networks. This creates an increasing disjuncture between the meaning and experience of everyday life and work in local places and the constitution of power and knowledge in the 'space of flows' through a culture of 'real virtuality'. However, commentators such as Castells overestimate the degree of disembedding from national and local configurations of economic and political power and underestimate the extent of re-embedding, re-appropriation and re-engagement in, against and through the space of flows.

Sociology for a Changing World

In this book we have explored the shifting contours of a society undergoing a process of rapid change. The process of globalization has produced a heightened sense of ambiguity and liminality as the institutions and practices that defined the modern era are reflected back on themselves and lose their solidity. The social relationships and identities that underpinned the institutions of modernity appear equally to have become dissolved by this process of intense social change. Where does this leave sociology – a discipline whose task is to investigate and explain social relationships? While we agree with Albrow (2004: 48), that in a context of rapid social change the principal focus of sociology is likely to be on the 'robustness and durability of structures of social relations', we are less confident in his claim that, following the decline of nation-state sociology, a new dominant paradigm will soon establish itself as dominant. We have only just started to grapple with the complex and contradictory realities of an in-between society beyond modernity, and this surely demands that we resist the temptation of replacing nation-state sociology with yet another simplifying framework. Rather we need to return to the analytical toolbox we inherited from modern sociology and ensure that we acquire the necessary skills to enable the effective application of these tools to an analysis of the complex forms of social relationships and social identities that mark the contemporary era. However, while most of the toolkit is indeed inherited from modern sociology, society and the social are persistent ideas throughout human history far beyond modernity. Thus a sociology for a changing world also needs to be sensitive to the varying responses of different historical worlds to the persistent problems of human existence; particularly the problem of dealing with presence and absence in the maintenance of social relationships. Consequently, we need to provide a conscious contextualization of research that states clearly where and when our arguments are embedded before we parade these as a universally relevant theory (cf. Robinson, 2004: 571f.). In this context, a sociology for a changing world needs also to be sympathetic towards a 'pragmatic universalism' (Albrow, 1996: 5) that facilitates the communication of human experience across epochs rather than naively claiming unprecedented novelty for contemporary forms of the social.

The contemporary world is complex but this does not justify rushing headlong into yet another sociological 'turn', this time the 'complexity turn' (cf. McLennan, 2003; Urry, 2005), and in so doing jettison the tools and techniques we have inherited from modern sociology in order adopt in a quick and convenient way the tools and techniques of other disciplines. As Rojek & Turner (2000) have argued, the tendency for sociology to adopt the conceptual and methodological tools of other disciplines is a form of intellectual laziness and an attempt to 'short cut' the difficult sociological task of applying our conceptual tools and methods to a rapidly changing and increasingly complex world. Thus, we need to differentiate between the 'rhetoric' of complexity and 'real' complexity. The latter position is not premised on clinging naïvely to a realist ontology of the social world that downplays its social construction, but rather the focus on how contemporary social complexity involves the intermingling of presence and absence, past and presence and here and there in the lived experience of the contemporary individual.

This is both an exiting and a somewhat daunting time to be a sociologist. It is of course daunting to be faced with a complex social reality which lacks the theoretical and conceptual reference points that were prominent in the modern era. It is also exiting as we are in a position where we can make new sociological discoveries outside a dominant or over-arching paradigm. We are not arguing against cross-disciplinary or trans-disciplinary study. Indeed, we have highlighted the important synergies that can be developed through inter-disciplinary work in this book. Sociology has always drawn strength from the insights of anthropology, political science, economics, geography, history and indeed, the natural sciences. However, the key contribution of sociology has emerged from the 'core' enterprise of uncovering how social relations and social relationships generate and sustain more complex social entities. Ultimately, these disciplines look at the world from a different perspective than sociology – the central focus is not the structure of social relations. In the current era, effective trans-disciplinary work requires sociology to become once again a disciple that is confident with its own conceptual toolkit. The origins of professional insecurity and intellectual laziness can be located in the same dynamics that underpin the other hotspots explored in this book – the increasingly ambiguous role of academia in the context of globalization and reflexive modernity and the way in which this imposes temporal and spatial challenges to doing effective social research. In the end, however, what is at stake is the future of sociology as a viable intellectual discipline. As Karl Marx, one of the founders of the modern discipline argued, 'there is no royal road to science, and only those who do not dread the fatiguing climb of its steep paths have a chance of gaining its luminous summits' (Marx, 1845/1972: 5). This may require that we all once again recognize our intellectual humility and, for a short-time at least, become apprentices that undertake the painstaking and rigorous work that is required to understand a complex and liminal society in transition.

Bibliography

Abu-Lughod, J.L. (1995) 'Comparing Chicago, New York and Los Angeles: Testing some world city hypotheses', in P.T. Knox & P.J. Taylor (eds) *World Cities in a World System*. Cambridge: Cambridge University Press.

Abu-Lughod, J.L. (1999) *New York, Chicago, Los Angeles: America's Global Cities*. Minneapolis, MN: University of Minnesota Press.

Adam, B. (2000) 'The temporal gaze: The challenge for social theory in the context of GM food', *British Journal of Sociology* Vol. 51, No. 1, pp. 125–142.

Adam, B. (2002) 'The gendered time politics of globalisation: Of shadow lands and elusive justice', *Feminist Review* Vol. 70, No. 1, pp. 2–29.

Adam, B. & van Loon, J. (2000) 'Introduction: repositioning risk: The challenge for social theory', in B. Adam, U. Beck & J. van Loon (eds) *The Risk Society and Beyond: Critical Issues for Social Theory*. London: Sage.

Adkins, L. (1995) *Gendered Work*. Milton Keynes: Open University Press.

Adorno, T. (1991) *The Culture Industry: Selected Essays on Mass Culture*. London: Routledge.

Agnew, J. (2001) 'How many Europes? The European Union, eastwards enlargement and uneven development', *European Urban and Regional Studies* Vol. 8, No. 1, pp. 29–38.

Albrow, M. (1996) *The Global Age: State and Society Beyond Modernity*. Cambridge: Polity.

Albrow, M. (1997) 'Travelling beyond local cultures: Socioscapes in a global city', in J. Eade (ed.) *Living the Global City: Globalization as Local Process*. London: Routledge.

Albrow, M. (2004) 'The global shift and its consequences for Sociology', in N. Genov (ed.) *Advances in Sociological Knowledge: Over Half a Century*. Wiesbaden: VS Verlag.

Albrow, M. & O'Byrne, D. (2000) 'Rethinking citizenship under globalized conditions', in H. Goverde (ed.) *Global and European Polity: Organizations, Policies, Contexts*. Aldershot: Ashgate.

Alderson, A.S. & Beckfield, J. (2005) 'Power and position in the world city system', *American Journal of Sociology* Vol. 109, No. 4, pp. 811–851.

Alexander, J. (1996) 'Critical reflections on "reflexive modernization"', *Theory, Culture & Society* Vol. 13, No. 4, pp. 133–138.

Alexander, J.C. & Smith, P. (1996) 'Social science and salvation: Risk society as mythical discourse', *Zeitschrift für Soziologie* Vol. 25, No. 4, pp. 251–262.

Alleyne-Dettmers, P. (1997) ' "Tribal Arts": A case study of global compression in the Notting Hill Carnival', in J. Eade (ed.) *Living the Global City: Globalization as Local Process*. London: Routledge.

Alter, P. (1994) *Nationalism*, Second Edition. London: Edward Arnold.

Alvarez Jr, R.R. (1995) 'The Mexican–US border: The making of an anthropology of border-lands', *Annual Review of Anthropology* Vol. 24, pp. 447–470.

Alvarez Jr, R.R. (1999) 'Towards an anthropology of the borderlands: The Mexican–U.S. border and the crossing of the 21st century', in T. Wendl & M. Rösler (eds) *Frontiers and Borderlands: Anthropological Perspectives*. New York: Peter Lang.

Amin, A. & Thrift, N. (1997) 'Globalisation, socio-economics, territoriality', in J. Wills & R. Lee (eds) *Geographies of Economies*. London: Arnold.

Amin, A. & Thrift, N. (2004) *Cities: Reimagining the Urban*. Cambridge: Polity.

Amoore, L. (2006) 'Biometric borders: Governing mobilities in the war on terror', *Political Geography* Vol. 25, pp. 336–351.

Anderson, P. (1983) *Imagined Communities: Reflections on the Origins and Spread of Nationalism*. London: Verso.

169

Anderson, J. & O'Dowd, L. (1999) 'Borders, border regions and territoriality: Contradictory meanings, changing significance', *Regional Studies* Vol. 33, No. 7, pp. 593–604.

Appadurai, A. (1990) 'Disjuncture and difference in the global economy', *Political Culture* Vol. 2, No. 3, pp. 1–24.

Appadurai, A. (1992) 'Disjuncture and difference in the global cultural economy' in M. Featherstone (ed.) *Global Culture: Nationalism, Globalization and Modernity*. London: Sage.

Appadurai, A. (1998) *Modernity at Large: Cultural Dimensions of Globalization*. Minneapolis, MN: University of Minnesota Press.

Arreola, D.D. (1996) 'Border City: Idee Fixe', *Geographical Review* Vol. 86, No. 3, pp. 356–369.

Ashton, D. & Green, F. (1996) *Education, Training and the Gobal Economy*. Cheltenham: Edward Elgar.

Axford, B. (2000) 'Globalization', in G. Browning, A. Halcli & F. Webster (eds) *Understanding Contemporary Society: Theories of the present*. London: Sage.

Bagguley, P. (1996) 'Protest, poverty and power: A case study of the anti-poll tax movement', *Sociological Review* Vol. 44, No. 4, pp. 693–719.

Bain, P. & Taylor, P. (2002) 'Ringing the changes? Union recognition and organisation in call centres in the UK finance sector', *Industrial Relations Journal* Vol. 33, No. 3, pp. 246–61.

Balcerowicz, L. (2000) 'Understanding post-communist transitions', in W. Kostecki, K. Murkowski & B. Góralczyk (eds) *Transformations of Post-Communist States*. London: Macmillan.

Barber, B.R. (1996) *Jihad vs. McWorld: How Globalism and Tribalism Are Reshaping the World*. New York: Ballantine Books.

Baudrillard, J. (1973) *The Mirror of Production*. St Louis, MO: Telos Press.

Baudrillard, J. (1983a) *Fatal Strategies*. New York: Semiotext (e).

Baudrillard, J. (1983b) *Simulations*. New York: Semiotext (e).

Baudrillard, J. (1983c) *In the Shadow of Silent Majorities*. New York: Semiotext (e)

Baudrillard, J. (1994a) *Simulacra and Simulation*. Ann Arbor, MI: University of Michigan Press.

Baudrillard, J. (1994b) *The Transparency of Evil: Essays on Extreme Phenomena*. London: Verso.

Baudrillard, J. (1998) *The Consumer Society: Myths and Structures*. London: Sage.

Bauman, Z. (1987) *Legislators and Interpreters*. Cambridge: Polity Press.

Bauman, Z. (1989) *Modernity and the Holocaust*. Cambridge: Polity Press.

Bauman, Z. (1991) *Modernity and Ambivalence*. Cambridge: Polity.

Bauman, Z. (1992) *Intimations of Postmodernity*. London: Routledge.

Bauman, Z. (1993) *Postmodern Ethics*. Oxford: Basil Blackwell.

Bauman, Z. (1994) 'After the patronage state: A model in search of a class interest', in C. Bryant & E. Mokrzycki (eds) *The New Great Transformation? Change and Continuity in East-Central Europe*. London: Routledge.

Bauman, Z. (1997) *Postmodernity and Its Discontents*. Cambridge: Polity.

Bauman, Z. (1998a) *Work, Consumption and the New Poor*. Cambridge: Polity.

Bauman, Z. (1998b) *Globalization: The Human Consequences*. Cambridge: Polity.

Bauman, Z. (2000) *Liquid Modernity*. Cambridge: Polity.

Bauman, Z. (2001) *The Individualized Society*. Cambridge: Polity.

Bauman, Z. (2002) 'The 20th century: End or beginning', *Thesis Eleven* No. 70, pp. 15–25.

Bauman, Z. (2003) *Liquid Love*. Cambridge: Polity.

Bauman, Z. (2004) *Wasted Lives: Modernity and Its Outcasts*. Cambridge: Polity.

Bauman, Z. & Tester, K. (2001) *Conversations with Zygmunt Bauman*. Cambridge: Polity.

Beauregard, R.A. (2006) 'The radical break in late twentieth-century urbanization', *Arena* Vol. 38, No. 2, pp. 218–220.

Beaverstock, J.V., Hoyler, M., Pain, K. & Taylor, P.J. (2005) 'Demystifying the Euro in European financial centre relations: London and Frankfurt, 2000–2001', *Journal of Contemporary European Studies* Vol. 13, No. 2, pp. 143–157.

Beck, U. (1992) *Risk Society: Towards a New Modernity*. London: Sage.

Beck, U. (1994a) 'Self-dissolution and self-endangerment of industrial society: What does this mean?', in U. Beck, A. Giddens & S. Lash (eds) *Reflexive Modernization: Politics, Tradition and Aesthetics in the Modern Social Order*. Cambridge: Polity.

Beck, U. (1994b) 'The reinvention of politics: Towards a theory of reflexive modernization', in U. Beck, A. Giddens & S. Lash (eds) *Reflexive Modernization: Politics, Tradition and Aesthetics in the Modern Social Order.* Cambridge: Polity.

Beck, U. (1995) *Ecological Politics in an Age of Risk.* Cambridge: Polity.

Beck, U. (1996) 'World risk society as a cosmopolitan society? Ecological questions in a framework of manufactured uncertainties', *Theory, Culture & Society* Vol. 14, No. 4, pp. 1–32.

Beck, U. (1997) *The Reinvention of Politics: Rethinking Modernity in the Global Social Order.* Cambridge: Polity.

Beck, U. (1999) *World Risk Society.* Cambridge: Polity.

Beck, U. (2000a) *What is Globalization?* Cambridge: Polity

Beck, U. (2000b) 'Risk society revisited: Theory, politics and research programmes', in B. Adam, U. Beck, & J. van Loon (eds) *The Risk Society and Beyond: Critical Issues for Social Theory.* London: Sage.

Beck, U. (2000c) 'The cosmopolitan perspective: Sociology of the second age of modernity', *British Journal of Sociology* Vol. 51, No. 1, pp. 79–105.

Beck, U. (2002) 'The cosmopolitan society and its enemies', *Theory, Culture & Society* Vol. 19, No. 1–2, pp. 17–44.

Beck, U. (2004) 'Cosmopolitan realism: On the distinction between cosmopolitanism in philosophy and the social sciences', *Global Networks* Vol. 4, No. 2, pp. 131–156.

Beck, U. & Beck-Gernsheim, E. (2001) *Individualization.* London: Sage.

Beck, U. & Lau, C. (2003) 'The theory of reflexive modernization: Problematic hypotheses and research programme', *Theory, Culture & Society* Vol. 20, No. 2, pp. 1–33.

Beck, U. & Lau, C.H. (2005) 'Theorie und Empirie reflexiver Modernisierung: von der Notwendigkeit und den Schwierigkeiten, einen historischen Gesellschaftswandel innerhalb der Moderne zu beobachten und zu begreifen', *Soziale Welt* Vol. 56, No. 2/3, pp. 107–135.

Beck, U. & Willms, J. (2003) *Conversations with Ulrich Beck.* Cambridge: Polity.

Beck, U., Giddens, A. & Lash, S. (1994) *Reflexive Modernization: Politics, Tradition and Aesthetics in the Modern Social Order.* Cambridge: Polity.

Beck, U., Bonss, W., & Lau, C. (2003) 'The theory of reflexive modernization: Problematic, hypotheses and research programme', *Theory, Culture & Society* Vol. 20, No. 2, pp. 1–33.

Bell, D. (1973) *The Coming of Post-Industrial Society: A Venture in Social Forecasting.* New York: Basic Books.

Bell, D. (1976) *The Cultural Contradictions of Capitalism.* New York: Basic Books.

Belt, V., Richardson, R. & Webster, J. (2000) 'Women's work in the information economy: The case of telephone call centres'. *Information, Communication and Society* Vol. 3, No. 3, pp. 366–385.

Benjamin, W. (1983) *Das Passagen-Werk.* Frankfurt, Suhkamp.

Benton, T. (2000) 'Reflexive modernization', in G. Browning, A. Halcli & F. Webster (eds) *Understanding Contemporary Society: Theories of the Present.* London: Sage.

Berezin, M. & Schain, M. (eds) (2004) *Europe without Borders: Remapping Territory, Citizenship, and Identity in a Transnational Age.* Baltimore, MD: John Hopkins University Press.

Berger, J. (2004) 'Tethering the butterfly: Revisiting Jameson's "Postmodernism and Consumer Society" and the paradox of resistance', *Cultural Logic: An Electronic Journal of Marxist Theory and Practice* Vol. 7, http://eserver.org/clogic/2004/berger.html.

Berger, P.L., Berger, B. & Kellner, H. (1973) *The Homeless Mind: Modernization and Consciousness.* Harmondsworth: Penguin.

Berger, P.L., Berger, B. & Kellner, H. (1994) *The Homeless Mind: Modernization and Consciousness.* Harmondsworth: Penguin.

Bergeron, S. (2001) 'Political economy discourses of globalisation and feminist politics', *Signs: Journal of Women, Culture and Society* Vol. 26, No. 4, pp. 983–1006.

Berggren, C. (1987) 'New production concepts in final assembly – The Swedish experience', in S. Wood (ed.) *The Transformation of Work.* London: Unwin Hyman.

Berking, H. (1996) 'Solidary individualism: The moral impact of cultural modernisation in late modernity', in S. Lash, B. Szerszynski & B. Wynne (eds) *Risk, Environment and Modernity.* London: Sage.

Bhabha, H.K. (1994) *The Location of Culture.* London: Routledge.

Bitner, M., Booms, B. & Mohr, L. (1994) 'Critical service encounters: The employees view', *Journal of Marketing* Vol. 58, pp. 95–106.

Blackwood, C. (1984) *On the Perimeter*. London: Heinmann.

Blowers, A. (1997) 'Environmental policy: Ecological modernization or risk society?' *Urban Studies* Vol. 34, No. 5/6, pp. 845–871.

Bourdieu, P. (1986) *Distinction: A Social Critique of the Judgement of Taste*. London: Routledge.

Boxhorn, B. (1996) 'European identity and the process of European unification: Compatible notions?', in M. Wintle (ed.) *Culture and Identity in Europe: Perceptions of Divergence and Unity in Past and Present*. Aldershot: Avebury.

Bradley, H., Erickson, M., Stephenson, C. & Williams, S. (2000) *Myths at Work*. Cambridge: Polity.

Braverman, H. (1974) *Labor and Monopoly Capital: The Degradation of Work in the Twentieth Century*. New York: Monthly Review Press.

Breman, J. (2006) 'Slumlands', *New Left Review* Vol. 39, pp. 141–148.

Brenner, N. (2001) 'World city theory, globalization and the comparative-historical method: Reflections on Janet Abu-Lughod's interpretation of contemporary urban restructuring', *Urban Affairs Review* Vol. 37, No. 1, pp. 24–147.

Bromley, S. (1999) 'The space of flows and timeless time: Manuel Castells's The Information Age', *Radical Philosophy* September/October, pp. 6–17.

Bruce, S. (2000) *Fundamentalism*. Cambridge: Polity.

Bryant, C.G.A. (1994) 'Economic utopianism and sociological realism: Strategies for transformation in East-Central Europe', in C. Bryant & E. Mokrzycki (eds) *The New Great Transformation? Change and Continuity in East-Central Europe*. London: Routledge.

Bryant, C.G.A. & Mokrzycki, E. (1994) 'Introduction', in C. Bryant & E. Mokrzycki (eds) *The New Great Transformation? Change and Continuity in East-Central Europe*. London: Routledge.

Budd, L. & Whimster, S. (1992) *Global Finance and Urban Living: A Study of Metropolitan Change*. London: Routledge.

Bürkner, H.-J. & Matthiesen, U. (2001) 'Antagonistic structures in border areas: Local milieux and local politics in the Polish–German twin city Guben/Gubin', *GeoJournal* Vol. 54, pp. 43–50.

Calefato, P. (1988) 'Fashion, the passage, the body', *Cultural Studies* Vol. 2, No. 2, pp. 223–228.

Callaghan, G. & Thompson, P. (2001) 'Edwards revisited: Technical control and call centres', *Economic and Industrial Democracy* Vol. 22, No. 1, pp. 13–37.

Campbell, C. (1989) *The Romantic Ethic and the Spirit of Modern Consumerism*. Oxford: Basil Blackwell.

Capra, F. (1983) *The Turning Point: Science, Society and the Rising Culture*. London: Flamingo.

Casey, C. (1995) *Work, Self and Society: After Industrialism*. London: Routledge.

Castells, M. (1997) *The Information Age: Economy, Society and Culture. Volume Two: The Power of Identity*. Oxford: Blackwell.

Castells, M. (2000a) *The Information Age: Economy, Society and Culture. Volume One: The Rise of the Network Society*, Second Edition. Oxford: Blackwell.

Castells, M. (2000b) *The Information Age: Economy, Society and Culture. Volume Three: The End of Millennium*, Second Edition. Oxford: Blackwell.

Chandler, D. (2004) 'Building global civil society "from below"?' *Millennium* Vol. 33, No. 2, pp. 313–339.

Chaney, D. (1983) 'The department store as cultural form', *Theory, Culture & Society* Vol. 3, No. 1, pp. 22–31.

Chessa, C. (2004) 'State subsidies, international diffusion, and transnational civil society: The case of Frankfurt-Oder and Słubice', *Eastern European Politics and Societies* Vol. 18, pp. 70–109.

Chesters, G. & Welsh, I. (2005) 'Complexity and social movements: Process and emergence in planetary action systems', *Theory, Culture and Society* Vol. 22, No. 5, pp. 187–211.

Chua, A. (2002) 'A world on the edge', *The Wilson Quarterly* Vol. 26, No. 4, p. 62.

Clammer, J. (1997) *Contemporary Urban Japan: A Sociology of Consumption*. Oxford: Basil Blackwell.

Clark, D. (1996) *Urban World/Global City*. London: Routledge.

Clark, N. (2002) 'The demon seeds: Bio invasion as the unsettling of environmental cosmo-politanism', *Theory, Culture & Society* Vol. 19, No. 1–2, pp. 101–125.

Cleaver, H.M. (1998) 'The Zapatistas effect: The Internet and the rise of an alternative political fabric', *Journal of International Affairs* Vol. 51, No. 2, pp. 621–640.

Clift, B. (2002) 'Social democracy and globalization: The cases of Britain and France', *Government and Opposition* Vol. 37, No. 4, pp. 466–500.

Closa, C. (2001) 'Requirements of a European public sphere: Civil society, self and the institutionalization of citizenship', in K. Eder & B. Gieson (eds) *European Citizenship Between National Legacies and Postnational Projects*. Oxford: Oxford University Press.

Colas, A. (1997) 'The promise of an international civil society', *Global Society* No. 3, pp. 261–277.

Colás, A. (2005) 'Imperious civility: Violence and the dilemmas of global civil society', *Contemporary Politics* Vol. 11, No. 2/3, pp. 179–188.

Collinson, D. & Hearn, J. (1994) 'Naming men as men: Implications for work organisation and management', *Gender, Work and Organisation* Vol. 1, No. 1, pp. 2–22.

Collinson, D. & Hearn, J. (eds) (1996) *Men as Managers, Managers as Men*. London: Sage.

Conway, J. (2004) 'Citizenship in a time of empire: The World Social Forum as a new public space', *Citizenship Studies* Vol. 8, No. 4, pp. 367–381.

Conway, J. (2005) 'Social forums, social movements and social change: A response to Peter Marcuse on the subject of the World Social Forum', *International Journal of Urban and Regional Research* Vol. 29, No. 2, pp. 425–428.

Cook, J. & Watt, S. (1992) 'Racism, women and poverty', in C. Glendinning & J. Millar (eds) *Women and Poverty in Britain: The 1990s*. London: Harvester Wheatsheaf.

Cooper, C., Dewe, P. & O'Driscoll, M. (2001) *Organisational Stress*. London: Sage.

Cornelius, W.A. (2001) 'Death at the border: Efficacy and unintended consequences of US immigration control policy', *Population and Development Review* Vol. 27, No. 4, pp. 661–685.

Cranford, C.J. (2003) 'Community unionism: Organizing for fair employment in Canada', *Just Labour* Vol. 3, Fall.

Crook, S. & Pakulski, J. (1992) *Postmodernization: Change in Advanced Society*. London: Sage.

Crow, C. & Hardey, M. (1999) 'Diversity and ambiguity among lone-parent households in modern Britain', in G. Allen (ed.) *The Sociology of the Family*. Oxford: Blackwell.

Cunninghame, P. & Ballesteros Corona, C. (1998) 'A rainbow at midnight: Zapatistas and autonomy', *Capital & Class* No. 66, pp. 12–22.

Dagnino, E. (1998) 'Culture, citizenship and democracy: Changing discourses and practices of the Latin American left', in S.E. Alvarez et al. (eds) *Cultures of Politics, Politics of Culture: Re-Visioning Latin American Social Movements*. Boulder, CO: Westview.

Dahrendorf, R. (1990) *Reflections on the Revolution in Europe*. London: Chatto & Windus.

Davis, M. (1998) *City of Quartz: Excavating the Future in Los Angeles*. London: Pimlico.

Davis, M. (2000) *Ecology of Fear: Los Angeles and the Imagination of Disaster*. London: Picador.

Davis, M. (2004) 'Planet of slums: Urban involution and the informal proletariat', *New Left Review* No. 26, pp. 5–34.

Davis, M. (2005) *The Monster at Our Door: The Global Threat of Avian Flu*. New York: The New Press.

Day, G. & Robbins, D. (1987) 'Activists for peace: The social basis of a local peace movement', in C. Creighton & M. Shaw (eds) *The Sociology of War and Peace*. London: Macmillan.

De Angeles, M. (2000) 'New internationalism and the Zapatistas', *Capital & Class* No. 70, pp. 9–35.

Deflem, M. (2003) 'The sociology of the sociology of money: Simmel and the contemporary battle of the classics', *Journal of Classical Sociology* Vol. 3, No. 1, pp. 67–96.

Delanty, G. (1998) 'Social theory and European transformation: Is there a European society?' *Sociological Research Online* Vol. 3, No. 1.

Delbridge, R (1998) *Life on the Line in Contemporary Manufacturing*. Oxford: Oxford University Press.

Deleuze, G. & Guattari, F. (1986) *Nomadology: The War Machine*. New York: Semiotext(e)

Deleuze, G. & Guattari, F. (2004) *Anti-Oepidipus: Capitalism and Schizophrenia*. London: Continuum.

Derrida, J. (1994) 'Spectres of Marx', *New Left Review* No. 205, pp. 75–109.

Derudder, B., Taylor, P.J., Wiltox, F. & Catalono, G. (2003) 'Hierarchical tendencies and regional patterns in the world city network: A global urban analysis of 234 cities', *Regional Studies* Vol. 37, No. 9, pp. 875–886.

Dickson, L. & McCulloch, A. (1996) 'Shell, the Brent Spar and Greenpeace: A doomed tryst?' *Environmental Politics* Vol. 5, No. 1, pp. 122–129.

Dolińska, X. & Fałkowski, M. (2001) *Polen und Deutsche vor der Osterweiterung der Europäischen Union.* Warsaw: Institute of Public Affairs.

Donnan, H. & Wilson, T.M. (1999) *Borders: Frontiers of Identity, Nation and State.* Oxford: Berg.

Douglas, M. (1991) *Implicit Meanings: Essays in Anthropology.* London: Routledge.

Douglas, M. (1996) *Purity and Danger: An Analysis of the Concepts of Pollution and Taboo.* London: Routledge.

du Gay, P. (1996) *Consumption and Identity at Work.* London: Sage.

Dürrschmidt, J. (1997) 'The delinking of locale and milieu: On the situatedness of extended milieux in a global environment', in J. Eade (ed.) *Living the Global City: Globalization as Local Process.* London: Routledge.

Dürrschmidt, J. (1999) 'The local versus the global? – Individualized milieux in a complex risk society: The case of organic food box schemes in the South West', in J. Hearn & S. Roseneil (eds) *Consuming Cultures: Power and Resistance.* Oxford: Blackwell.

Dürrschmidt, J. (2000) *Everyday Lives in the Global City: The Delinking of Locale and Milieu.* London: Routledge.

Dürrschmidt, J. (2002) ' "They're worse off than us" – The social construction of European space and boundaries in the German/Polish twin-city of Guben–Gubin', *Identities* Vol. 9, No. 2, pp. 123–150.

Dürrschmidt, J. (2006) 'So near yet so far: Blocked networks, global links and multiple exclusion in the German–Polish borderlands', *Global Networks* Vol. 6, No. 3, pp. 245–263.

Dürrschmidt, J. & U. Matthiesen (2002) 'Everyday milieux and culture of displacement: A comparative investigation into space, place, and (non) attachment within the German–Polish twin city Guben/Gubin', *Canadian Journal of Urban Research* Vol. 11, No. 1, pp. 17–45.

Eade, J. (1997) *Living the Global City: Globalization as Local Process.* London: Routledge.

Eade, J. (2000) *Placing London: From Imperial Capital to Global City.* Oxford: Berghahn Books.

Eaton, J. (2000) *Comparative Employment Relations.* Cambridge: Polity.

Eatwell, R. (2000) 'The rebirth of the "extreme right" in Western Europe', *Parliamentary Affairs* Vol. 53, pp. 407–425.

Eckardt, F. (2005) 'In search of meaning: Berlin as national capital and global city', *Journal of Contemporary European Studies* Vol. 13, No. 2, pp. 189–201.

Eder, K. (1996) *The Social Construction of Nature: A Sociology of Ecological Enlightenment.* London: Sage.

Edwards, R. (1979) *Contested Terrain: The Transformation of the Workplace in the Twentieth Century.* London: Heinmann.

Edwards, R. (1984) 'Forms of control in the labour process; An historical analysis', in F. Fischer & C. Sirriani (eds) *Organization and Bureaucracy.* Philadelphia, PA.: Temple University Press.

Edwards, T. (2000) *Contradictions of Consumption.* Buckingham: Open University Press.

Ehrenfeld, D. (1978) *The Arrogance of Humanism.* Oxford: Oxford University Press.

Elias, N. (1978) *The Civilising Process, Volume I.* Oxford: Blackwell.

Elias, N. (1982) *The Civilising Process, Volume II.* Oxford: Blackwell.

Elliott, A. (2002) 'Beck's sociology of risk: A critical assessment', *Sociology* Vol. 36, No. 2, pp. 293–315.

Entrikin, J.N. (1999) 'Political community, identity and cosmopolitan place', *International Sociology* Vol. 14, No. 3, pp. 269–282.

Eschbach, K., Hagan, J., Rodriguez, N., Hernandez-Leon, R. & Bailey, S. (1999) 'Death at the border', *International Migration Review* Vol. 33, No. 2, pp. 430–454.

Esping-Andersen, G. (1990) *The Three Worlds of Welfare Capitalism.* Cambridge: Polity.

Esping-Andersen, G. (2000) 'Two societies, one sociology and no theory'. *British Journal of Sociology* Vol. 51, No. 1, pp. 59–79.

Esteva, G. (1999) 'The Zapatistas and people's power', *Capital & Class* No. 68, pp. 153–182.

Etzioni, A. (2004) 'The capabilities and limits of the global civil society', *Millennium* Vol. 33, No. 2, pp. 341–353.

Featherstone, M. (1990) 'Perspectives on consumer culture', *Sociology* Vol. 24, No. 1, pp. 5–22.

Featherstone, M. (1991) *Consumer Culture and Postmodernism*. London: Sage.

Featherstone, M. (1992) 'Postmodernism and the aestheticization of everyday life', in S. Lash & J. Friedman (eds) *Modernity and Identity*. Oxford: Basil Blackwell.

Ferguson, J. (2002) 'Global disconnect: Abjection and the aftermath of modernism', in J.X. Inda & R. Rosado (eds) *The Anthropology of Globalization*. London: Blackwell.

Fernandez Kelly, M.P. (1981) '*Review: The U.S.-Mexico Border: Recent publications and the state of current research*', Latin American Review Vol. 16, No. 3, pp. 250–267.

Fernie, S. & Metcalf, D. (1988) *(Not) Hanging on the Telephone: Payment Systems in the New Sweatshops*. London: Centre for Economic Performance, London School of Economics.

Filby, M. (1992) 'The figures, the personality and the bums: Service work and sexuality', *Work, Employment and Society* Vol. 6, No. 1, pp. 23–42.

Flynn, D.K. (1997) ' "We are the border": Identity, exchange, and the state along the Bénin–Nigeria border', *American Ethnologist* Vol. 24, No. 2, pp. 311–330.

Forrest, J.B. (2003) (ed.) *Subnationalism in Africa: Ethnicity, Alliances and Politics*. Boulder, CO: Lynne Rienner.

Foucault, M. (1977) *Discipline and Punish: The Birth of the Prison*. Harmondsworth: Penguin.

Foucault, M. (1980) *Power/Knowledge*. London: Harvester Wheatsheaf.

Fowkes, B. (1996) *The Disintegration of the Soviet Union: A Study in the Rise and Triumph of Nationalism*. London: Palgrave.

Franzen, A. & Meyer, R. (2004) 'Klimawandel des Umweltbewusstseins? Eine Analyse des ISSP 2000', *Zeitschrift für Soziologie* Vol. 33, No. 2, pp. 119–137.

Fraser, N. (1997) *Justice Interuptus: Reflections on the Postsocialist Condition*. London: Routledge.

Frenkel, S., Korczynski, M., Donaghue, L. & Shire, K. (1995) 'Re-constituting work: trends towards knowledge work and info-normative control', *Work, Employment and Society* Vol. 9, No. 4, pp. 773–796.

Friedmann, J. (1986) 'The world city hypothesis', *Development and Change* Vol. 17, No. 1, pp. 69–83.

Friedmann, J. (1995) 'Where we stand: A decade of world city research', in P.L. Knox & P.J. Taylor (eds) *World Cities in a World System*. Cambridge: Cambridge University Press.

Fröbel, F., Heinrichs, J. & Drey, O. (1980) *The New International Division of Labour*. Cambridge: Cambridge University Press.

Fukuyama, F. (1992) *The End of History and the Last Man*. New York: The Free Press.

Gabaglio, E. & Hoffmann, R. (1998) *The ETUC in the Mirror of Industrial Relations Research*. Brussels: ETUI.

Galasiński, D. & Meinhof, U.H. (2002) 'Looking across the river: German–Polish border communities and the construction of the other', *Journal of Language and Politics* Vol. 1, No. 1, pp. 23–58.

Gallagher, J. (2004) 'Detroit suburbanization', in P. Oswalt (ed.) *Shrinking Cities: International Research*. Ostfildern-Ruit: Hatje Cantz.

Gandy, M. (2005) 'Learning from Lagos', *New Left Review* No. 33, pp. 37–52.

Garnet, T. (1996) 'Farming the city: The potential of urban agriculture', *The Ecologist* Vol. 26, No. 6, pp. 299–307.

Gaspin, F. & Wial, H. 'The role of central labor councils in union organizing in the 1990s', in K. Bronfenbrenner, S. Friedman, R. Hurd, R.A. Oswald & R.L. Seeber (eds) *Organizing to Win: Research on Union Strategies*. New York: Cornell University Press.

Gibbins, R. (1997) 'Meaning and significance of the Canadian–American border', in P. Ganster, A. Sweedler, J. Scott & W.-D. Eberwein (eds) *Borders and Border Regions in Europe and America*. San Diego, CA: San Dego University Press.

Gibbons, M., Limoges, C., Nowotny, H., Schwartzman, S., Scott, P. & Trow, M. (1994) *The New Production of Knowledge: The Dynamics of Science and Research in Contemporary Societies*. London: Sage.

Gibson-Graham, J.K. (1996) *The End of Capitalism (As We Knew It)*. Oxford: Blackwell.

Giddens, A. (1986) *The Constitution of Society: Outline of a Theory of Structuration*. Cambridge: Polity Press.

Giddens, A. (1990) *The Consequences of Modernity*. Cambridge: Polity.

Giddens, A. (1991) *Modernity and Self-Identity: Self and Society in Late Modern Age*. Cambridge: Polity.

Giddens, A. (1994) *Beyond Left and Right: The Future of Radical Politics*. Cambridge: Polity.

Giddens, A. (1998) *The Third Way: The Renewal of Social Democracy*. Cambridge: Polity.

Gilbert, L. & Philips, C. (2003) 'Practices of urban environmental citizenship: Rights to the city and rights to nature in Toronto', *Citizenship Studies* Vol. 7, No. 3, pp. 313–330.

Gill, S. (2000) 'Towards a postmodern prince? The Battle of Seattle as a moment in the new politics of globalization', *Millennium: Journal of International Studies* Vol. 29, No. 1, pp. 131–140.

Girardet, H. (2004) *Cities, People Planet: Liveable Cities for a Sustainable World*. Chister: Wiley-Academy.

Goffman, E. (1972) *Relations in Public: Microstudies of the Public Order*. Harmondsworth: Penguin.

Gornig, M. & Häussermann, H. (2002) 'Berlin: Economic and spatial change', *European Urban and Regional Studies* Vol. 9, No. 4, pp. 331–341.

Gorz, A. (1982) *Farewell to the Working Class*. London: Pluto.

Gorzelak, G. & Jałowiecki, B. (2002) 'European boundaries: Unity or division of the continent?' *Regional Studies* Vol. 36, No. 4, pp. 409–419.

Gottdiener, M. (2002) 'Urban analysis as merchandising: The "LA School" and the understanding of metropolitan development', in J. Eade & C. Mele (eds) *Understanding the City: Contemporary and Future Perspectives*. Oxford: Blackwell.

Grabher, G. & Stark, D. (1997) 'Organizing diversity: Evolutionary theory, network analysis and post-socialism', in G. Grabher & D. Stark (eds) *Restructuring Networks in Post-Socialism*. Oxford: Oxford University Press.

Granovetter, M.S. (1973) 'The strength of weak ties', *American Journal of Sociology* Vol. 78, No. 6, pp. 1360–1380.

Grathoff, R. (1989) *Milieu und Lebenswelt: Einführung in die Phänomenologische Soziologie und die Sozialphänomenologische Forschung*. Frankfurt/M.: Suhrkamp.

Grewal, I. & Kaplan, C. (1994) 'Introduction: Transnational feminist practices and questions of postmodernity', in I. Grewal & C. Caplan (eds) *Scattered Hegemonies: Postmodernity and Transnational Feminist Practices*. Minneapolis, MN: University of Minnesota Press.

Grosfoguel, R. (1995) 'Global logics in the Caribbean city system: The case of Miami', in P.L. Knox & P.J. Taylor (eds) *World Cities in a World System*. Cambridge: Cambridge University Press.

Gruchman, B. & Walk, F. (1997) 'Transboundary cooperation in the Polish–German border region', in P. Ganster, A. Sweedler, J. Scott & W.-D. Eberwein (eds) *Borders and Border Regions in Europe and America*. San Diego, CA: San Diego University Press.

Grzymała-Busse, A. & Innes, A. (2003) 'Great expectations: the EU and domestic political competition in East Central Europe', *East European Politics and Societies* Vol. 17, No. 1, pp. 64–73.

Habermas, J. (1976) *Legitimation Crisis*. London: Heinmann.

Habermas, J. (1984) *The Theory of Communicative Action, Volume 1, Reason and the Rationalization of Society*. Boston, MA: Beacon Press.

Habermas, J. (1987) *The Theory of Communicative Action, Volume 2, System and Lifeworld: A Critique of Functionalist Reason*. Boston, MA: Beacon Press.

Hajer, M.A. (1999) *The Politics of Environmental Discourse: Ecological Modernization and the Policy Process*. Oxford: Clarendon Press.

Hall, P. (1996) 'The global city', *International Social Science Journal* Vol. 147, pp. 17–23.

Hammer, M. & Champy, J. (1993) *Reengineering the Corporation: A Manifesto for Business Revolution*. London: Nicolas Brealey.

Hancké, B. (2000) 'European works councils and industrial restructuring in the European motor industry', *European Journal of Industrial Relations* Vol. 6, No. 1, pp. 35–59.

Handy, C. (1994) *The Empty Raincoat*. London: Hutchinson.

Handy, C. (1995) *The Future of Work*. Oxford: Blackwell.

Hannerz, U. (1998) *Transnational Connections: Culture, People, Places*. London: Routledge.

Hardt, M. & Negri, A. (2001) *Empire*. Cambridge, MA: Harvard University Press.

Harford, B. & Hopkins, S. (1984) *Women at the Wire*. London: Virago.

Harloe, M. (1996) 'Cities in transition', in G. Andrusz, M. Harloe & I. Szelenyi (eds) *Cities after Socialism: Urban and Regional Change and Conflict in Post-Socialist Societies*. Oxford: Blackwell.

Harrison, C.M., Burgess, J. & Filius, P. (1996) 'Rationalizing environmental responsibilities: A comparison of lay publics in the UK and the Netherlands', *Global Environmental Change* Vol. 6, No. 3, pp. 215–234.

Harvey, D. (1989) *The Condition of Postmodernity*. Blackwell: Oxford.

Harvey, D. (1996) *Justice, Nature, and the Geography of Difference*. London: Blackwell.

Haughton, G. & Hunter, C. (1994) *Sustainable Cities*. London: Kingsley.

Häußermann, H. (1997) Armut in den Großstädten: Eine neue städtische Unterklasse?' *Leviathan* Vol. 25, No. 1, pp. 12–27.

Häußermann, H. & Siebel, W. (1993) 'Die Politik der festivalisierung und die festivalisierung der politik: Grosse ereignisse in der stadtpolitik', in H. Häußermann & W. Siebel (eds) *Festivalisierung der Stadtpolitik: Stadtentwicklung durch grosse Feste*. Opladen: Westdeutscher Verlag.

Healey, P.S., Cameron, D., Davoudi, S.G. & Madani-Pour, A. (eds) (1995) 'Introduction: the city – crisis, change and invention', in *Managing Cities: The New Urban Context*. Chister: Wiley.

Hebdidge, D. (1988) *Hiding in the Light: On Images and Things*. London: Routledge.

Heidenreich, M. (2003) 'Territoriale ungleichheiten in der EU', *Kölner Zeitschrift für Soziologie und Sozialpsychologie* Vol. 55, No. 1, pp. 1–28.

Held, D. (1995) *Democracy and the Global Order*. Cambridge: Polity.

Held, D. (2000) 'Regulating globalization? The reinvention of politics', *International Sociology* Vol. 15, No. 2, pp. 394–408.

Hegedus, Z. (1989) 'Social movements and social change in self-creative society: New civil initiatives in the international arena', *International Sociology* Vol. 4, No. 1, pp. 19–36.

Heller, A. & Feher, F. (1988) *The Postmodern Political Condition*. Cambridge: Polity.

Hill, R.C. & Fujita, K. (2003) 'The nested city: Introduction', *Urban Studies* Vol. 40, No. 2, pp. 207–217.

Hinchliffe, S. (1996) 'Helping the earth begins at home: The social construction of socio-environmental responsibilities', *Global Environmental Change* Vol. 6, No. 1, pp. 53–62.

Hirst, P. & Thompson, G. (1999) *Globalization in Question*, Second Edition. Cambridge: Polity.

Hochschild, A. (1983) *The Managed Heart*. Berkeley, CA: University of California Press.

Horkheimer, M. & Adorno, T. (1972) *Dialectic of Enlightenment*. New York: Herder & Herder.

Hudson, R. (2003) 'European integration and forms of uneven development: But not the end of territorially distinctive capitalisms in Europe', *European Urban and Regional Studies* Vol. 10, pp. 49–67.

Huxtable, A. (1997) *The Unreal America: Architecture and Illusion*. New York: New Press.

Hyman, R. (1994) 'Changing trade union identities and strategies', in R. Hyman & A. Ferner (eds) *New Frontiers in European Industrial Relations*. London: Blackwell.

Hyman, R. (2001) *Understanding European Trade Unionism: Between Market, Class and Society*. London: Sage.

Hyman, J., Baldry, C., Scholarios, D. & Bunzel, D. (2003) 'Work-life imbalance in call centre and software development', *British Journal of Industrial Relations* Vol. 41, No. 2, pp. 215–239.

Ignazi, P. (1992) 'The silent counter-revolution: Hypotheses on the emergence of extreme right parties in Europe', *European Journal of Political Research* Vol. 22, No. 1, pp. 3–34.

Ignazi, P. (1997) New challenges: Postmaterialism and the extreme right', in M. Rhodes et al. (eds) *Developments in Western European Politics*. London: Macmillan.

Illouz, E. (1997) *Consuming the Romantic Utopia*. Berkeley, CA: University of California Press.

ILO (1998) *Trade Union Responses to Globalization: Outline for Case Studies*. Geneva: ILO.

Inglehart, R. (1990) *Culture Shift in Advanced Industrial Society*. Princeton, NJ: Princeton University Press.

Isin, E.F. (2002) 'Citizenship after orientalism', in E.F. Isin & B.S. Turner (eds) *Handbook of Citizenship Studies*. London: Sage.

Isin, E.F. & Turner, B. (2002) 'Citizenship studies: an introduction', in E.F. Isin & B.S. Turner (eds) *Handbook of Citizenship Studies*. London: Sage.

Jacobs, J. (1996) *Edge of Empire: Postcolonialism and the City*. London: Routledge.

Jajeśniak-Quast, D. & Stokłosa, K. (2000) *Geteilte Städte zwischen Oder und Neiße: Frankfurt (Oder)-Słubice, Guben-Gubin und Görlitz-Zgorzelec 1945–1995*. Berlin: Verlin Verlag/Arno Spitz.

James, A. (1993) 'Eating green(s): Discourses on organic food', in K. Milton (ed.) *Environmentalism: The View from Anthropology*. London: Routledge.

James, P. (2005) 'Meta-war and the insecurity of the United States', in T. Nairn & P. James (eds) *Global Matrix: Nationalism, Globalism and State-Terrorism*. London: Pluto Press.

Jameson, F. (1984) 'Postmodernism, or the cultural logic of late capitalism?' *New Left Review* No. 146, pp. 53–92.

Jameson, F. (1991) *Postmodernism? Or, The Cultural Logic of Late Capitalism*. London: Verso.

Jameson, F. (1998) *The Cultural Turn: Selected Writings on the Postmodern 1983–1998*. London: Verso.

Jelin, E. (2000) 'Towards a global environmental citizenship', *Citizenship Studies* Vol. 4, No. 1, pp. 47–63.

Jenks, M., Burton, E. & Williams, K. (eds) (2000) *The Compact City: A Sustainable Urban Form?* London: Spon.

Jenson, J., Hagen, E. & Reddy, C. (1988) *Feminisation of the Labour Force*. Cambridge: Polity.

Johnston, P. (2000) 'The resurgence of labor as a citizenship movement in the new labor relations envirnoment', *Critical Sociology* Vol. 26, No.1–2, pp. 109–138.

Johnston, P. (2002) 'Citizen Movement Unionism: For the defense of local communities in the global age', in B. Nissen (ed.) *Unions in a Globalized Environment: Changing Borders, Organizational Boundaries and Social Roles*. New York: M.E. Sharpe.

Jones, L. (1983) (ed.) *Keeping the Peace*. London: The Women's Press.

Jones, E. (1990) *Metropolis: The World's Great Cities*. Oxford: Oxford University Press.

Jowers, P., Dürrschmidt, J., O'Doherty, R. & Purdue, D. (1999) 'Affective and aesthetic dimensions of contemporary social movements in South West England', *Innovation* Vol. 12, No. 1, pp. 99–118.

Jupiter Research (2006) 'Online Retail Sales Grew in 2005', http://www.clickz.com/stats/sectors/retailing/article.php/3575456 (accessed on 08-02-06).

Kaldor, M. (2000) 'Civilising globalisation? The implications of the "Battle of Seattle"', *Millennium: Journal of International Studies* Vol. 29, No. 1, pp. 105–114.

Kaldor, M. (2003) *Global Civil Society: An Answer to War*. Cambridge: Polity.

Katz, C. (2001) 'On the grounds of globalisation: A topography for feminist political engagement', *Signs: Journal of Women, Culture and Society* Vol. 26, No. 4, pp. 1213–1234.

Keane, J. (2003) *Global Civil Society?* Cambridge: Cambridge University Press.

Keating, M. (1988) *State and Regional Nationalism: Territorial Politics and the European State*. Hemel Hempstead: Harvester Wheatsheaf.

Keck, M.E. & Sikkink, K. (1998) *Activists Beyond Borders: Advocacy Networks in International Politics*. Ithaca, NY: Cornell University Press.

Keil, R. (1995) 'The environmental problematic in world cities', in P.L. Knox & P.J. Taylor (eds) *World Cities in a World System*. Cambridge: Cambridge University Press.

Keil, R. & Ali, S.H. (2006) 'The avian flu: Some lessons learned from the 2003 SARS outbreak in Toronto', *Arena* Vol. 38, No. 1, pp. 107–109.

Keil, R. & Olds, C. (2001) 'Introduction: Review Symposium', *Urban Affairs Review* Vol. 37, No. 1, pp. 119–123.

Keim, K-D. (1997) 'Milieu und moderne: Zum gebrauch und gehalt eines nachtraditionalen milieubegriffs', *Berliner Journal für Soziologie* Vol. 7, No. 3, pp. 387–399.

Kempton, W. (1991) 'Lay perspectives on global climate change', *Global Environmental Change* Vol. 1, No. 3, pp. 183–208.

Kennedy, P. & Roudometof, V. (2002) 'Transnationalism in a global age', in P. Kennedy & V. Roudometof (eds) *Communities Across Borders: New Immigrants and Transnational Cultures*. London: Routledge.

King, A.D. (1991) *Global Cities: Post-imperialism and the Internationalization of London*. London: Routledge.

King, A.D. (1995) 'Re-presenting world cities: Cultural theory/social practice', in P.L. Knox, & P.J. Taylor (eds) *World Cities in a World System*. Cambridge: Cambridge University Press.

King, A.D. (2002) 'Global cities, local places: Cultural specificity in global representations', *Migration* Vol. 33–35, pp. 19–36.

Kiss, E. (2004) 'Spatial impacts of post socialist industrial transformation in the major Hungarian cities', *European Urban and Regional Studies* Vol. 11, No. 1, pp. 81–87.

Knight, R.V. & Gappert, G. (1989) 'Introduction: Redefining cities', in R.V. Knight & G. Gappert (eds) *Global Cities in a Global Society*. London: Sage.

Knights, D. & McCabe, D. (2001) 'A different world: Shifting masculinities in the transition to call centres', *Organization* Vol. 8, No. 4, pp. 619–645.

Knights, D. & McCabe, D. (2003) 'Governing through teamwork: Reconstituting subjectivity in a call centre', *Journal of Management Studies* Vol. 40, No. 7, pp. 1587–1618.

Knights, D. & Odih, P. (2002) ' "Big Brother is watching you": Call centre surveillance and the time disciplined subject', in G. Crow & S. Heath (eds) *Social Conceptions of Time: Structure and Process in Work and Everyday Life*. London: Palgrave.

Knights, D., Wilmott, H. & Collinson, D. (1985) (eds) *Job Redesign: Critical Perspectives on the Labour Process*. London: Gower.

Knorr-Cetina, K. (2001) 'Postsocial relations: Theorizing sociality in a postsocial environment', in G. Ritzer & B. Smart (eds) *Handbook of Social Theory*. London: Sage.

Kondo, D.K. (1990) *Crafting Selves: Power, Gender and Discourses of Identity in a Japanese Workplace*. Chicago, IL: University of Chicago Press.

Konrad, V. & Nicol, H. (2004) 'Boundaries and corridors: Rethinking the Canada–United States borderlands in the 9/11 era', *Canadian–American Public Policy* Vol. 60, pp. 767–790.

Korczynski, M. (2002) *Human Resource Management in Service Work*. London: Palgrave.

Korczynski, M. (2003) 'Communities of coping: Collective emotional labour in service work', *Organization* Vol. 10, No. 1, pp. 55–79.

Korczynski, M., Shire, K., Frenkel, S. & Tamm, M. (2000) 'Service work in consumer capitalism: Customers, control and contradictions', *Work, Employment and Society* Vol. 14, No. 4, pp. 69–87.

Kostecki, W. (2000) 'Ten years after', in W. Kostecki, K. Zukrowska & B. Góralczyk (eds) *Transformations of Post-Communist States*. London: Macmillan.

Kowinski, W.S. (1985) *The Malling of America: An Inside Look at the Great Consumer Paradise*. New York: William Morrow.

Krätke, S. (1996) 'Where east meets west: The German–Polish border region in transformation', *European Planning Studies* Vol. 4, No. 6, pp. 647–669.

Krätke, S. (1998) 'Problems of cross-border regional integration: The case of the German–Polish border area', *European Urban and Regional Studies* Vol. 5, No. 3, pp. 249–262.

Krätke, S. (1999) 'Regional integration or fragmentation? The German–Polish border region in a new Europe', *Regional Studies* Vol. 33, No. 7, pp. 631–641.

Kuisel, R.F. (1993) *Seducing the French: The Dilemmas of Americanization*. Berkeley, CA: University of California Press.

Lambert, R. (1990) 'Kilusang Mayo Uno and the rise of social movement unionism in the Philippines', *Labour and Industry* Vol. 3, No. 2/3, pp. 258–281.

Lambert, R. & Webster, E. (1988) 'The re-emergence of political unionism in contemporary South Africa', in W. Cobbbett & R. Cohen (eds) *Popular Struggles in South Africa*. Trenton NJ: Africa World Press.

Lash, S. (1994) 'Reflexivity and its doubles: Structure, aesthetics, community', in U. Beck, A. Giddens & S. Lash (eds) *Reflexive Modernization: Politics, Tradition and Aesthetics in the Modern Social Order*. Cambridge: Polity.

Lash, S. (2000) 'Risk culture', in B. Adam, U. Beck & J. van Loon (eds) *The Risk Society and Beyond: Critical Issues for Social Theory*. London: Sage.

Lash, S. (2003) 'Reflexivity as non-linearity', *Theory, Culture & Society* Vol. 20, No. 2, pp. 49–57.

Lash, S. & Urry, J. (1987) *The End of Organised Capitalism*. Cambridge: Polity.

Lash, S. & Urry, J. (1994) *Economies of Signs and Space*. London: Sage.

Latour, B. (2003) 'Is re-modernization occurring – And if so, how to prove it? A commentary on Ulrich Beck', *Theory, Culture & Society* Vol. 20, No. 2, pp. 35–48.

Lee, J. (2004) *The European Social Forum at 3: Facing Old Challenges to Go Forward.* Geneva: Centre for Applied Studies in International Negotiations (CASIN).

Lefébvre, H. (1990) *Die Revolution der Städte.* Frankfurt/M.: Anton Hain.

Leidner, R. (1993) *Fast Food, Fast Talk.* Berkerley, University of California Press.

Leidner, L. (1999) 'Emotional labour in service work', *Annals of the American Academy of Political and Social Science* Vol. 56, pp. 81–95.

Lindner, R.E. (1990) *Die Entdeckung der Stadtkultur: Soziologie aus der Erfahrung der Reportage.* Frankfurt/M.: Suhrkamp.

Linz, J.J. & Stephan, A. (1996) *Problems of Democratic Transition and Consolidation: Southern Europe, South America, and Post-Communist Europe.* Baltimore, MD: John Hopkins University Press.

Lipschutz, R.D. (1996) *Global Civil Society and Global Environmental Governance.* Albany, NY: SUNY Press.

Lipschutz, R.D. (2004) 'Constituting political community: Globalization, citizenship and human rights', in A. Brisk & G. Shafir (eds) *People Out of Place: Human Rights and the Citizenship Gap.* London: Routledge.

Lisiecki, S. (ed.) (1996) *Die Offene Grenze: Forschungsbericht polnisch-deutsche Grenzregion (1991–1993).* Potsdam: Verlag Berlin-Brandenburg.

Lister, R. (1993) 'Tracing the contours of women's citizenship', *Policy and Politics* Vol. 21, No. 1, pp. 3–16.

Lockie, S., Lyons, K. & Lawrence, G. (2000) 'Constructing "green" food: Corporate capital, risk, and organic farming in Australia and New Zealand', *Agriculture and Human Values* Vol. 17, pp. 315–322.

Lukács, G. (1971) *History and Class Consciousness.* London: Merlin.

Lukács, G. (1978) *The Ontology of Social Being: 3. Labour.* London: Merlin Press.

Lupton, D. & Tulloch, J. (2002) ' "Risk is part of your life": Risk epistemologies among a group of Australians', *Sociology* Vol. 36, No. 2, pp. 317–334.

Lyon, D. (2000) 'Post-modernity', in G. Browning, A. Halcli & F. Webster (eds) *Understanding Contemporary Society: Theories of the Present.* London: Sage.

Machin, S. & Wilkinson, D. (1995) Employee Training: Unequal Access and Economic Performance. London: Institute of Public Policy Performance.

MacLeod, G., Mike Raco, M. & Ward, K. (2003) 'Negotiating the contemporary city: Introduction', *Urban Studies* Vol. 40, No. 9, pp. 1655–1671.

Macnaghten, P. (2003) 'Embodying the environment in everyday "life practices" ', *Sociological Review* Vol. 51, No. 1, pp. 63–84.

Maffesoli, M. (1996) *The Time of the Tribes.* London: Sage.

Mannheim, K. (1936) *Ideology and Utopia: An Introduction to the Sociology of Knowledge.* London: RKP.

Marcuse, H. (1964) *One Dimensional Man.* London: Routledge.

Marcuse, P. (2005) 'Are social forums the future of social movements?' *International Journal of Urban and Regional Research* Vol. 29, No. 2, pp. 417–424.

Marcuse, P. & van Kempen, R. (2000) 'Conclusion: A changed spatial order', in P. Marcuse & R. van Kempen (eds) *Globalizing Cities: A New Spatial Order?* Oxford: Blackwell.

Marshall, J.N. & Richardson, R. (1996) 'The impact of "tele-mediated" services on corporate structures: The example of "branchless" retail banking in Britain', *Environment and Planning* Vol. 28, pp. 1843–1858.

Martinez, O.J. (1994) 'The dynamics of border interaction: New approaches to border analysis', in C.H. Schofield (ed.) *Global Boundaries: World Boundaries,* Volume 1. London: Routledge.

Martinez, O.J. (1997) 'Border cultures and their cultural roles: The case of the U.S.–Mexican borderlands', in P. Ganster, A. Sweedler, J. Scott & W.-D. Eberwein (eds) *Borders and Border Regions in Europe and America.* San Diego, CA: San Diego University Press.

Marx, K. (1845/1972) 'Thesis on Feuerbach' *Collected Works* Vol. 5, p. 5.

Marx, K. (1975) 'Economic and philosophical manuscripts', in *Early Writings.* Harmondsworth: Penguin Books.

Marx, K. (1976) *Capital: Volume One*. Harmondsworth: Penguin.
Mathers, A. (1999) 'Euromarch; The struggle for a social Europe', *Capital & Class* No. 69, pp. 15–19.
Matthiesen, U. (2002) 'Transformational pathways and institutional capacity building: The case of the German–Polish twin city Guben/Gubin, in G. Cars, P. Healey, A. Madanipour & C. de Maghalhães (eds) *Urban Governance, Institutional Capacity and Social Milieux*. Aldershot: Ashgate.
Matthiesen, U. (2005) 'Governance milieus in shrinking post-socialist city regions – and their respective forms of creativity: Case miniatures and conceptual propositions', *disP* Vol. 162, No. 3, pp. 53–61.
May, T. & Perry, B. (eds) (2005) with responses from Patrick Le Galés, Saskia Sassen and Mike Savage 'The future of urban sociology', *Sociology* Vol. 39, No. 2, pp. 343–370.
Mazur, A. (1998) 'Global environmental change in the news: 1987–90 vs. 1992–6', *International Sociology* Vol. 13, No. 4, pp. 457–472.
McAdam, D., Tarrow, S. & Tilly, C. (2001) *Dynamics of Contention*. Cambridge: Cambridge University Press.
McAllister-Groves, B. (1995) 'Learning to feel: The neglected sociology of social movements', *Sociology Review* Vol. 43, No. 3, pp. 435–461.
McCarthy, J.D. & Zald, M.N. (1987) 'Resource mobilization and social movements', in J.D. McCarthy & M.N. Zald (eds) *Social Movements in an Organizational Society*. New Brunswick, NJ: Transaction Books.
McCulloch, A. (1996) 'Shell, the Brent Spar and Greenpeace: A doomed tryst?', *Environmental Politics* Vol. 5, No. 1, pp. 122–129.
McDonald, K. (2002) 'From solidarity to fluidarity: Social movements beyond "collective identity" – The case of globalization conflicts', *Social Movement Studies* Vol. 1, No. 2, pp. 109–128.
McDowell, L. (1997) *Capital Culture*. Oxford: Blackwell.
McKay, G. (1996) *Senseless Acts of Beauty: Cultures of Resistance since the Sixties*. London: Verso.
McKay, G. (1998) *DIY Culture: Party and Protest in Nineties Britain*. London: Verso.
McLennan, G. (2003) 'Sociology's complexity', *Sociology* Vol. 37, No. 3, pp. 547–564.
Meiksins Wood, E. (2003) *Empire of Capital*. London: Verso.
Meinhof, U.H. (ed.) (2002) *Living (with) Borders: Identity Discourses on East–West Borders in Europe*. Aldershot: Ashgate.
Meinhof, U.H. (2003) 'Migrating borders: An introduction to European identity construction in progress', *Journal of Ethnic and Migration Studies* Vol. 29, No. 5, pp. 781–796.
Melucci, A. (1989) *Nomads of the Present*. London: Hutchinson.
Melucci, A. (1996a) *Challenging Codes: Collective Action in the Information Age*. Cambridge: Cambridge University Press.
Melucci, A. (1996b) *The Playing Self: Person and Meaning in the Planetary Society*. Cambridge: Cambridge University Press.
Miller, P. & Rose, N. (1990) 'Governing economic life', *Economy and Society* Vol. 19, No. 1, pp. 1–31.
Minkenberg, M. (1993) *The New Right in Comparative Perspective: The USA and Germany*. Ithaca, NY.: Cornell University Press.
Mirchandani, K. (2004) 'Practices of global capital: Gaps, cracks and ironies in transactional call centres in India', *Global Networks* Vol. 4, No. 4, pp. 355–373.
Mollenkopf, J. & Castells, M. (eds) (1991) *Dual City: Restructuring New York*. New York: Russel Sage Foundation.
Mudde, C. (2000) 'In the name of the peasantry, the proletariat and the people: Populism in Eastern Europe', *Eastern European Politics and Societies* Vol. 14, No. 2, pp. 33–53.
Mumford, L. (1991) *The City in History: Its Origins, Its Transformations and Its Prospects*. London: Penguin.
Münch, R. (2002) 'Die "Zweite Moderne": Realität oder Fiktion? Kritische Fragen an die Theorie der "reflexiven" Modernisierung', *Kölner Zeitschrift für Soziologie und Sozialpsychologie* Vol. 54, No. 3, pp. 417–443.

Munck, R. (2004) *Labour and Globalization: Results and Prospects*. Liverpool: Liverpool University Press.

Munck, R. & Waterman, P. (1998) *Labour Worldwide in the Era of Globalization: Alternative Union Models in the New World Order*. London: Macmillan.

Mythen, G. (2004) *Ulrich Beck: A Critical Introduction to the Risk Society*. London: Pluto Press.

Nairn, T. (2005) 'Global trajectories: America and the unchosen', in T. Nairn & P. James (eds) *Global Matrix: Nationalism, Globalism and State-Terrorism*. London: Pluto Press.

Nairn, T. & James, P. (2005) *Global Matrix: Nationalism, Globalism and State-Terrorism*. London: Pluto Press.

Neary, M. & Taylor, G. (1998) *Money and the Human Condition*. London: Macmillan.

Newman, D. (2006) 'The lines that continue to separate us: Borders in our "borderless" world', *Progress in Human Geography* Vol. 30, No. 2, pp. 142–161.

Noon, M. & Blyton, P. (2002) *The Realities of Work*, Second Edition. London: Palgrave.

Notes from Nowhere (2003) *We are Everywhere: The Irresistible Rise of Global Anti-Capitalism*. London: Verso.

Offe, C. (1984) *Contradictions of the Welfare State*. London: Hutchinson.

Offe, C. (1985a) *Disorganized Capitalism*. Cambridge: Polity Press.

Offe, C. (1985b) 'New social movements: Challenging the boundaries of institutional politics', *Social Research* Vol. 52, No. 4, pp. 817–868.

Offe, C. (1996) *Varieties of Transition: The East European and East German Experience*. Cambridge: Polity.

Offe, C. & Wiesenthal, H. (1985) 'Two logics of collective action', in C. Offe (ed.) *Disorganized Capitalism*. Cambridge: Polity.

Olesen, T. (2005) 'Transnational publics: New spaces of social movement activism and the problem of global long-sightedness', *Current Sociology* Vol. 53, No. 3, pp. 419–440.

Orr, D.W. (1999) 'Our urban future', *The Ecologist* Vol. 29, No. 1, pp. 2–15.

Paasi, A. (1999) 'Boundaries as social practice and discourse: the Finish-Russian border', *Regional Studies* Vol. 33, No. 7, pp. 669–680.

Paasi, A. (2001) 'Europe as a social process and discourse: Considerations of place, boundaries and identity', *European Urban and Regional Studies* Vol. 8, No. 1, pp. 7–28.

Panitch, L. (1986) *Working Class Politics in Crisis: Essays on Labour and the State*. London: Verso.

Panther, S. (1998) 'Historisches Erbe und Transformation: "Lateinische" Gewinner – "Orthodoxe" Verlierer?', in G. Wegner & J. Wieland (eds) *Formelle und informelle Institutionen: Genese, Interaktion und Wandel*. Marburg: Metropolis.

Parkin, F. (1968) *Middle Class Radicalism: The Social Bases of the British Campaign for Nuclear Disarmament*. Manchester: Manchester University Press.

Pateman, C. (1988) 'The patriarchal welfare state', in A. Guttmann (ed.) *Democracy and the Welfare State*. Princeton, NJ: Princeton University Press.

Patomäki, H. (2000) 'The Tobin Tax: A new phase in the politics of globalization', *Theory, Culture & Society* Vol. 17, No. 4, pp. 77–91.

Patomäki, H. & Teivainen, T. (2004) 'The World Social Forum: An open space or a movement of movements', *Theory, Culture and Society* Vol. 21, No. 6, pp. 145–154.

Payne, S. (1995) *A History of Fascism 1915–1945*. London: UCL Press.

Payne, S. (1999) *Fascism: Theory and Practice*. London: Pluto.

Pfaff-Czainecka, J. (2005) *Ethnic Futures: The State and Identity Politics in Asia*. London: Sage.

Pickvance, C. (1998) Inequality and conflict in the post-socialist city: Some analytical issues concerning the transition from state socialism', in O. Källtorp, I. Elander, O. Ericsson & M. Franzén (eds) *Cities in Transformation – Transformation in Cities: Social and Symbolic Change of Urban Space*. Aldershot: Ashgate.

Pickvance, C. (2002) 'State socialism, post-socialism and their urban patterns: Theorizing the Central and Eastern European experience', in J. Eade & C. Mele (eds) *Understanding the City: Contemporary and Future Perspectives*. London: Blackwell.

Plant, S. (1992) *The Most Radical Gesture: The Situationist International in a Postmodern Age*. London: Routledge.

Plato (1977) *Phaedrus & Letters VII and VIII*. Harmondsworth: Penguin.

Pochet, P. & Fajertag, G. (2000) *Social Pacts in Europe: New Dynamics*. Brussels: European Trade Union Institute.

Poulantzas, N. (1978) *State, Power, Socialism*. London: New Left Books.

Pries, L. (1998) 'Transnationale Räume: theoretisch-empirische Skizze am Beispiel der Arbeitswanderung Mexiko – USA', in U. Beck (ed.) *Perspektiven der Weltgesellschaft*. Frankfurt/M.: Suhrkamp.

Prottas, J.M. (1979) *People-Processing*. Lexington, MA: Lexington Books.

Przeworski, A. (1980) 'Social democracy as a historical phenomenon', *New Left Review* No. 122, pp. 27–49.

Purdue, D., Dürrschmidt, J., Jowers, P. & O'Doherty, R. (1997) 'DIY culture and extended milieux: LETS, veggie boxes and festivals', *Sociological Review* Vol. 45, No. 4, pp. 643–667.

Putnam, R.D. (2000) *Bowling Alone: The Collapse and Revival of American Community*. New York: Simon & Schuster.

Quinn, B. (2005) 'Arts festivals and the city', *Urban Studies* Vol. 42, No. 5/6, pp. 927–943.

Raynolds, L.T. (2000) 'Re-embedding global agriculture: The international organic and fair trade movement', *Agriculture and Human Values* Vol. 17, pp. 297–309.

Reinharz, J. & Mosse, G.L. (1992) (eds) *The Impact of Western Nationalisms*. London: Sage.

Ritzer, G. (1995) *Expressing America: A Critique of the Global Credit Card Society*. Thousand Oaks, CA: Pine Forge Press.

Ritzer, G. (2003) *The McDonaldization of Society*. Thousand Oaks, CA: Pine Forge Press.

Ritzer, G. (2004) *The Globalization of Nothing*. Thousand Oaks, CA: Pine Forge Press.

Ritzer, G. (2005) *Enchanting a Disenchanted World*. London: Pine Forge Press.

Robertson, R. (1992) *Globalization: Social Theory and Global Culture*. London: Sage.

Robertson, R. & Khondker, H.H. (1998) 'Discourses of globalization', *International Sociology* Vol. 13, No. 1, pp. 25–40.

Robinson, W.I. (1996) *Promoting Polyarchy*. Cambridge: Cambridge University Press.

Robinson, I. (2000) 'Neo-liberal restructuring and U.S. unions: Towards social movement unions', *Critical Sociology* Vol. 26, No. 1/2, pp. 109–138.

Robinson, I. (2002) 'Does neo-liberal restructuring promote social movement unionism? Developments in comparative perspective', in B. Nissen (ed.) *Unions in a Globalized Environment: Changing Borders, Organizational Boundaries and Social Roles*. New York: M.E. Sharpe.

Robinson, J. (2004) 'A world of cities', *British Journal of Sociology* Vol. 55, No. 4, pp. 569–578.

Rojek, C.H. & Turner, B. (2000) 'Decorative sociology: Towards a critique of the cultural turn', *The Sociological Review* Vol. 48, No. 4, pp. 629–648.

Rosenau, J. (1999) 'Toward an ontology for global governance', in M. Hewson & T.J. Sinclair (eds) *Approaches to Global Governance Theory*, New York: University of New York Press.

Ross, A. (1994) *The Chicago Gangster Theory of Life: Nature's Debt to Society*. London: Verso.

Rumford, C. (2003) 'European civil society or transnational social space? Conceptions of society in discourses of EU citizenship, governance and the democratic deficit: An emerging agenda', *European Journal of Social Theory* Vol. 6, No. 1, pp. 25–43.

Rustin, M. (1994) 'Incomplete modernity: Ulrich Beck's risk society', *Radical Philosophy* Vol. 67, pp. 3–11.

Sadowski-Smith, C. (ed.) (2002) *Globalization On the Line: Culture, Capital and Citizenship at U.S. Borders*. London: Palgrave.

Saito, A. & Thornley, A. (2003) 'Shifts in Tokyo's world city status and the urban planning response', *Urban Studies* Vol. 40, No. 4, pp. 665–685.

Sarker, S. & Niyogi, E. (2002) *Trans-status Subject: Gender and the Globalisation of South and South East Asia*. Durham, NC: Duke University Press.

Sassen, S. (1991) *The Global City: New York, London, Tokyo*. Princeton, NJ: Princeton University Press.

Sassen, S. (2000a) 'New frontiers facing urban sociology at the Millennium', *British Journal of Sociology* Vol. 51, No. 1, pp. 143–159.

Sassen, S. (2000b) 'Spatialities and temporalities of the global: Elements for a theorisation', *Public Culture* Vol. 12, No. 1, pp. 215–232.

Sassen, S. (2001a) 'Global cities and global city-regions: A comparison', in A.J. Scott (ed.) *Global City-Region: Trends, Theory, Policy*. Oxford: Oxford University Press.

Sassen, S. (2001b) 'Cracked casings: Notes towards an analytics for studying transnational processes', in L. Price (ed.) *Transnational Social Spaces: International Migration and Transnational Companies in the Early 21st Century.* New York: Routledge.

Sassen, S. (2002) 'Locating cities on global circuits', in S. Sassen (ed.) *Global Networks – Linked Cities.* London: Routledge.

Scase, R. (2002) *Living in the Corporate Zoo.* Oxford: Capstone.

Scheler, M. (1973) *Formalism in Ethics and Non-Formal Values: A New Attempt Towards the Foundations of Ethical Personalism.* Evanston, IL: Northwestern University Press.

Schnabel, A. & Webster, J. (1999) *Participating on Equal Terms? The Gender Dimensions of Direct Participation. The Findings of the EPOC Survey.* Dublin: European Foundation for the Improvement of Living and Working Conditions.

Schmidt, S. (1997) 'Stereotypes, culture, and cooperation in the U.S.–Mexican borderlands', in P. Ganster, A. Sweedler, J. Scott & W.-D. Eberwein (eds) *Borders and Border Regions in Europe and America* San Diego, CA: San Diego University Press.

Scholte, J.A. (2000) 'Cautionary reflections on Seattle', *Millennium: Journal of International Studies* Vol. 29, No. 1, pp. 115–121.

Scholte, J.A. (2005) *Globalization: A Critical Introduction,* Second Edition. London: Palgrave.

Schor, J.B. (1991) *The Overworked American: The Unexpected Decline of Leisure.* New York: Basic Books.

Schütz, A. (1970) *Reflections on the Problem of Relevance* (edited by R.M. Zaner). New Haven, CT: Yale University Press.

Scott, J.W. (1999) 'European and North American context for cross-border regionalism', *Regional Studies* Vol. 33, No. 7, pp. 605–617.

Scott, A.J., Agnew, J., Soja, E.W. & Storper, M. (2001) 'Global city regions', in A.J. Scott (ed.) *Global City-Region: Trends, Theory, Policy.* Oxford: Oxford University Press.

Seabrook, J. (2003) 'Progress on hold: Call centres may be creating thousands of jobs for Indians but the price they pay is a loss of culture and alienation', *The Guardian* (24/10/03).

Sennett, R. (1993) *The Fall of Public Man.* London: Faber and Faber.

Sennett, R. (1998) *The Corrosion of Character: The Personal Consequences of Work in the New Capitalism.* New York: W.W. Norton.

Sennett, R. (1999) 'Growth and failure: The new political economy and its culture', in M. Featherstone & S. Lash (eds) *Spaces of Culture: City, Nation, World.* London: Sage.

Sennett, R. (2006) *The Culture of New Capitalism.* New Haven, CT: Yale University Press.

Sewell, G. (1998) 'The discipline of teams: The control of team-based industrial work through electronic and peer surveillance', *Administrative Science Quarterly* Vol. 43, pp. 406–469.

Shaw, M. (2001) 'Social democracy in the global revolution: An historical perspective', in L. Martell (ed.) *Social Democracy: Global and National Perspectives.* London: Palgrave.

Shields, R. (1990) 'The system of pleasure: Liminality and the Carnivalesque in Brighton', *Theory, Culture & Society* Vol. 7, No. 1, pp. 39–72.

Short, J.R. & Yeoung-Hyun, K. (1999) *Globalization and the City.* Harlow: London.

Sieverts, T. (2003) *Cities without Cities: An Interpretation of the 'Zwischenstadt'.* London: Spon Press.

Simmel, G. (1969) *The Sociology of Georg Simmel* (edited by K.H. Wolff). London: Macmillan.

Simmel, G. (1971) *On Individuality and Social Forms.* Chicago, IL: Chicago University Press.

Simmel, G. (1978) *The Philosophy of Money.* London: Routledge.

Simmel, G. (1994) 'Bridge and door' (translated by M. Ritter), *Theory, Culture and Society* Vol. 11, No. 1, pp. 5–10.

Simpson, R. (2000) 'Presenteeism and the impact of long hours on managers', in D. Winstanley & J. Woodall (eds) *Ethical Issues in Contemporary Human Resource Management.* London: Macmillan.

Sinha, R.P. (1984) *Social Dimensions of Trade Unionism in India.* New Delhi: Uppal Publishing House.

Sklair, L. (1995) *A Sociology of the Global System,* Second Edition. London: Harvester Wheatsheaf.

Sklair, L. (2002) *Globalization: Capitalism and Its Alternatives.* Oxford: Oxford University Press.

Smith, A. (1983) *The Ethnic Origins of Nations.* Oxford: Blackwell.

Smith, M.P. (2001) *Transnational Urbanism: Locating Globalization*. Oxford: Blackwell.

Smith, M. (2005) 'Risk society and ethical responsibility', *Sociology* Vol. 39, No. 3, pp. 543–550.

Snow, D., Rochford, B., Worden, S. & Benford, R. (1986) 'Frame alignment processes: Micro-mobilization and movement participation', *American Sociological Review* No. 51, pp. 464–481.

Soja, E.W. (2000) *Postmetropolis: Critical Studies of Cities and Regions*. London: Blackwell.

Sparrow, G. (2001) 'San Diego–Tijuan: Not quite a binational city or region', *GeoJournal* Vol. 54, No. 1, pp. 73–83.

Spohn, W. (2000) 'Die Osterweiterung der Europäischen Union und die Bedeutung kollektiver Identitäten', *Berliner Journal für Soziologie* Vol. 10, No. 2, pp. 219–240.

Spretnak, C. (1997) *The Resurgence of the Real: Body, Nature and Place in a Hypermodern World*. London: Addison-Wesley.

Srubar, I. (1994) 'Variants of the transformation process in Central Europe: A comparative assessment', *Zeitschrift für Soziologie* Vol. 23, No. 3, pp. 198–221.

Stammers, N. (2001) 'Social democracy and global governance', in L. Martell (ed.) *Social Democracy: Global and National Perspectives*. London: Palgrave.

Stanworth, M. (2000) 'Women and work in the information age', *Gender, Work & Organization* Vol. 7, No. 1, pp. 20–32.

Stark, D. & Bruszt, L. (1998) *Postsocialist Pathways: Transforming Politics and Property in East Central Europe*. Cambridge: Cambridge University Press.

Sugrue, T.J. (2004) 'Racism and urban decline', in P. Oswalt (ed.) *Shrinking Cities: International Research*. Ostfildern-Ruit: Hatje Cantz.

Szelenyi, I. (1996) 'Cities under socialism – and after', in G. Andrusz, M. Harloe & I. Szelenyi (eds) *Cities after Socialism: Urban and Regional Change and Conflict in Post-Socialist Societies*. Oxford: Blackwell.

Sztompka, P. (1993) 'Civilizational incompetence: The trap of post-communist societies', *Zeitschrift für Soziologie* Vol. 22, No. 2, pp. 85–95.

Szymańska, D. & Matczak, A. (2002) 'Urbanization in Poland: Tendencies and transformation', *European Urban and Regional Studies* Vol. 9, No. 1, pp. 39–46.

Taylor, G. (1999) *State Regulation and the Politics of Public Service: The Case of the Water Industry*. London: Mansell.

Taylor, G. (2006) 'European employment policy: Governance as regulation', in G.P.E. Walzenbach (ed.) *European Governance: Policy Making Between Politicization and Control*. Aldershot: Ashgate.

Taylor, P.J. (2005) 'Leading world cities: Empirical evaluations of urban nodes in multiple networks', *Urban Studies* Vol. 42, No. 9, pp. 1593–1608.

Taylor, P. & Bain, P. (1999) 'An assembly line in the head: Work and employee relations in the call centre', *Industrial Relations Journal* Vol. 30, No. 2, pp. 107–117.

Taylor, P. & Bain, P. (2001) 'Trade unions, workers rights and the frontier of control in UK call centres', *Economic and Industrial Democracy* Vol. 22, No. 1, pp. 39–66.

Taylor, P. & Bain, P. (2005) 'India calling to the far away towns: The call centre labour process and globalization', *Work, Employment and Society* Vol. 19, No. 2, pp. 261–282.

Taylor, G. & Mathers, A. (2002a) 'The politics of European integration: A European labour movement in the making?' *Capital & Class* No. 77, pp. 37–78.

Taylor, G. & Mathers, A. (2002b) 'Social partner or social movement? European integration and trade union renewal in Europe', *Labor Studies Journal* Vol. 27, No. 1, pp. 93–108.

Taylor, G. & Mathers, A. (2004) 'The European Trade Union Confederation at the crossroads of change? Traversing the variable geometry of European Trade Unionism', *European Journal of Industrial Relations* Vol. 10, No. 3, pp. 267–285.

Therborn, G. (1995) 'Routes to/through modernity', in M. Featherstone, S. Lash & R. Robertson (eds) *Global Modernities*. London: Sage.

Therborn, G. (2000) 'Globalizations: Dimensions, historical waves, regional effects, normative governance', *International Sociology* Vol. 15, No. 2, pp. 151–179.

Tönnies, F. (2001) *Community and Civil Society*. Cambridge: Cambridge University Press.

Touraine, A. (1974) *The Post-Industrial Society*, New York: Wildwood Press.

Touraine, A. (1997) *What Is Democracy?* Boulder, CO: Westview Press.

Toynbee, A.J. (1957) *Civilization on Trial.* Oxford: Oxford University Press.

Turner, V. (1969) *The Ritual Process: Structure and Anti-Structure.* Ithaca, NY: Cornell University Press.

Turner, V. (1997/1969) *The Ritual Process: Structure and Anti-Structure.* New York: Aldine de Gruyter.

Ungar, S. (2001) 'Moral panic versus risk society: The implications of the changing sites of social anxiety', *British Journal of Sociology* Vol. 52, No. 2, pp. 271–291.

Urry, J. (1988) 'Cultural change and contemporary holiday-making', *Theory, Culture & Society* Vol. 5, No. 1, pp. 35–55.

Urry, J. (2000) *Sociology Beyond Societies: Mobilities for the Twenty-first Century.* London: Routledge.

Urry, J. (2003) *Global Complexity.* Cambridge: Polity.

Urry, J. (2004) 'Small worlds and the new "social physics"', *Global Networks* Vol. 4, No. 2, pp. 109–130.

Urry, J. (2005) 'The complexities of the global', *Theory, Culture and Society* Vol. 22, No. 5, pp. 235–254.

van Criekingen, M., Decroly, J.-M., Lennert, M., Cornut, P. & Vandermotten, C. (2005) 'Local geographies of global players: International law firms in Brussels', *Journal of Contemporary European Studies* Vol. 13, No. 2, pp. 173–187.

van den Broek, D., Callaghan, G. & Thompson, P. (2004) 'Teams without teamwork? Explaining the call centre paradox', *Economic and Industrial Democracy* Vol. 25, No. 2, pp. 197–218.

Varga, I. (2005) 'The body – The new sacred? The body in hypermodernity', *Current Sociology* Vol. 53, No. 2, pp. 209–235.

Veugelers, J.W.P. (1999) 'The challenge for political sociology: The rise of far-right parties in contemporary Western Europe', *Current Sociology* Vol. 47, No. 4, pp. 78–100.

Wajcman, J. (1998) *Managing Like a Man.* Cambridge: Polity.

Wallerstein, I. (1990) 'Culture as the ideological battleground of the modern world-system', *Theory, Culture & Society* Vol. 7, pp. 31–56.

Wallerstein, I. (2000) 'Globalization or the age of transition? A long term view of the trajectory of the world-system', *International Sociology* Vol. 15, No. 2, pp. 249–265.

Walton, J. & Seddon, D. (1994) *Free Markets and Food Riots: The Politics of Global Adjustment.* Oxford: Blackwell.

Wastl-Walter, D., Váradi, M.M. & Veider, F. (2003) 'Coping with marginality: To stay or to go', *Journal of Ethnic and Migration Studies* Vol. 29, No. 5, pp. 797–817.

Waterman, P. (1984) *For a New Labour Internationalism.* The Hague: International Labour Education, Research and Information Foundation.

Waterman, P. (2000) 'Social movements, local places and globalized spaces: Implications for "globalization from below"', in B. Gills (ed.) *Globalization and the Politics of Resistance.* London: Palgrave.

Watson, J.L. (ed.) (1997) *Golden Arches East: McDonalds in East Asia.* Stanford, CA: Stanford University Press.

Weber, M. (1948) *From Max Weber: Essays in Sociology* (translated and edited by H.H. Garth & C.W. Mills). Oxford: Oxford University Press.

Weber, M. (1966) *The City.* New York: The Free Press.

Webster, E. (1988) 'The rise of social movement unionism: The two faces of the black trade union movement in South Africa', in P. Frankel, N. Pines & M. Swilling (eds) *State Resistance and Change in South Africa.* London: Croom Helm.

Wehling, P., Viehöver, W. & Keller, R. (2005) 'Wo endet die Natur, wo beginnt die Gesellschaft? Doping, Genfood, Klimawandel und Lebensbeginn: die Entstehung kosmopolitaner Hybride', *Soziale Welt* Vol. 56, No. 1, pp. 137–158.

Welsh, J. (1997) 'Call centres in crisis over staff shortages', *People Management* Vol. 3, No. 20, p. 9.

Wendl, T. & Rösler, M. (1999) (eds) *Frontiers and Borderlands: Anthropological Perspectives.* New York: Peter Lang.

Whitehead, M. (2003) '(Re)analysing the sustainable city: Nature, urbanization, and the regulation of socio-environmental relations in the UK', *Urban Studies* Vol. 40, No. 7, pp. 1183–1206.

Whittall, M. (2000) 'The BMW European works council: A cause for European industrial relations optimism?' *European Journal of Industrial Relations* Vol. 6, No. 1, pp. 61–83.

Williams, R. (1982) *Dream Worlds*. Berkeley, CA: University of California Press.

Williams, F. (1993) 'Gender, race and class in British Welfare Policy', in A. Cochrane & J. Clarke (eds) *Comparing Welfare States*. Milton Keynes: Open University Press.

Williamson, J. (2000) 'What should the World Bank think about the Washington consensus?' *World Bank Research Observer* Vol. 15, No. 2, pp. 251–264.

Wills, J. (2001) 'Community unionism and trade union renewal in the UK: Moving beyond the fragments at last?' *Transactions of the Institute of British Geographers* Vol. 26, pp. 465–483.

Wills, J. & Simms, M. (2004) 'Building reciprocal community unionism in the UK'. *Capital & Class* No. 82, pp. 59–84.

Wingens, M. (1999) 'Der "gelernte DDR-Bürger": Biographischer modernisierungsrückstand als transformationsblockade?' *Soziale Welt* Vol. 50, pp. 255–280.

Wirth, L. (1969) *On Cities and Social Life*. Chicago, IL: University of Chicago Press.

Wood, A.G. (2004) *On the Border: Society and Culture between the United States and Mexico*. Lanham: SR Books.

Wynne, B. (1996) 'May the sheep safely graze? A reflexive view of the expert-lay knowledge divide', in S. Lash, B. Szerszynski & B. Wynne (eds) *Risk, Environment and Modernity: Towards a New Ecology*. London: Sage.

York, R., Rosa, E.A. & Dietz, T. (2003) 'Footprints on the Earth: The environmental consequences of modernity', *American Sociological Review* Vol. 68, No. 2, pp. 279–280.

Zisserman-Brodsky, D. (ed.) (2003) *Constructing Ethnopolitics in the Soviet Union: Samizdat, Deprivation and the Rise of Ethnic Nationalism*. London: Palgrave.

Zook, M.A. & Brunn, S.D. (2005) 'Hierarchies, regions and legacies: European cities and global commercial passenger air travel', *Journal of Contemporary European Studies* Vol. 13, No. 2, pp. 203–220.

Zukin, S. (1993) *Landscapes of Power: From Detroit to Disneyworld*. Berkeley, CA: University of California Press.

Zukin, S. (2004) *Point of Purchase: How Shopping Changed American Culture*. New York: Routledge.

Zukrowska, K. (2000) 'Poland: An effective strategy of systemic change', in W. Kostecki, K. Murkowski & B. Góralczyk (eds) *Transformations of Post-Communist States*. London: Macmillan.

Index

188

and McCabe, D., 70, 71, 74
and Odih, P., 70
Knorr-Cetina, K., 93
knowledge (expert, lay, indigenous, everyday), 3, 34, 60, 61, 64, 70, 72, 77, 142, 143, 145, 147, 148, 149, 153, 166
Kondo, D.K., 77
Konrad, V. and Nicol, H., 42
Korczynski, M., 74
et al, 70
Kostecki, W., 48, 49
Krätke, S., 43, 44, 45, 46
Kriesky, 130
Kuisel, R.F., 95

Labor and Monopoly Capital (Braverman), 66
labour movement, 127–30
labour process, 65–8
Lagos, 19, 20, 23
Lambert, R., 130
and Webster, E., 130
Lash, S., 148, 150, 155
and Urry, J., 12, 24, 25, 78, 84, 92, 104, 111, 115, 161, 165
Latour, B., 142
Lee, J., 130
Lefébvre, H., 14
Leidner, L., 76
life world, 11, 12, 26, 27, 31, 34, 46, 49, 115, 160, 161, 162, 163, 165
liminality, liminal space, 1, 2, 3, 5, 51, 78, 81, 82, 84, 88, 126, 144, 156, 159, 161, 166
Lindner, R.E., 14
Linz, J.J. and Stephan, A., 51
Lipschutz, R.D., 132
Lisiecki, S., 44
Lockie, S. *et al*, 155
London, 16, 17, 24, 29, 31, 32–3
Los Angeles, 17, 21–2, 23, 30, 31, 32, 33, 99–101, 106
Lukács, G., 88
Lupton, D. and Tulloch, J., 148
Lyon, D., 5

McAdam, D. *et al*, 121
McAllister-Groves, B., 119
McCarthy, J.D. and Zald, M.N., 121
McDonald, K., 121
McDonaldization, 96
Machin, S. and Wilkinson, D., 65
McKay, G., 119, 120
McLennan, G., 159, 167
MacLeod, G. *et al*, 21, 22, 24
Macnaghten, P., 135, 139, 151
Maffesoli, M., 104
Mannheim, K., 109
Marcuse, H., 88, 89
Marcuse, P., 125

and van Kempen, R., 31
Marshall, J.N. and Richardson, R., 73
Martinez, O.J., 40, 41
Marx, K., 85, 86–7, 106, 168
Mathers, A., 130
Matthiesen, U., 44, 45, 47, 48
May, T. and Perry, B., 35
Mazur, A., 148–9
Meiksins Wood, E., 131
Meinhof, U.H., 38, 43, 44
Melucci, A., 2, 5, 119, 121, 135, 137, 138, 139, 151, 153, 154, 155
The Metropolis and Mental Life (Simmel), 104–5
Mexico, border with USA, 40–1
Miami, 32
Milan, 31
milieu, 11, 27, 35, 136, 150, 151, 152, 153, 155, 156, 160, 160, 166
Miller, P. and Rose, N., 70
Minkenberg, M., 119
Mirchandani, K., 76, 77
modernity, ambiguity of, 104–5
crisis of, 114–15
and globalization, 4
high/low, 3
radicalized, 3–4, 5
reflexive/second, 3–4, 5, 7, 59, 60, 85–6, 108, 109–10, 115, 122, 144–50, 156–8, 165
solid/liquid distinction, 3, 7, 105
modernity (conceptual legacy), 4
Mollenkopf, J. and Castells, M., 24
money, and capital accumulation, 85
and cathedrals of consumption, 86, 91–5
and commodification/identity link, 86–91
and consumption, 106
and fetishism of consumer, 85
and globalization, 85–6
Marxian view, 85, 86–7
and reflexive modernity, 85–6
Mudde, C., 48
multinational corporations (MNCs), 62, 76, 79, 80, 112, 125, 132
Mumford, L., 15, 28
Munck, R., 128
and Waterman, P., 130
Mythen, G., 148, 155

Nairn, T., 117
and James, P., 116
nationalism, 116–18
nature, 135–56
Neary, M. and Taylor, G., 86
neo-liberalism, 134
nested urbanism, 15, 23
networked society, 60–4
new international division of labour (NIDL), 24